26-page portfolio

LIFE

50 YEARS

COLORS n.7

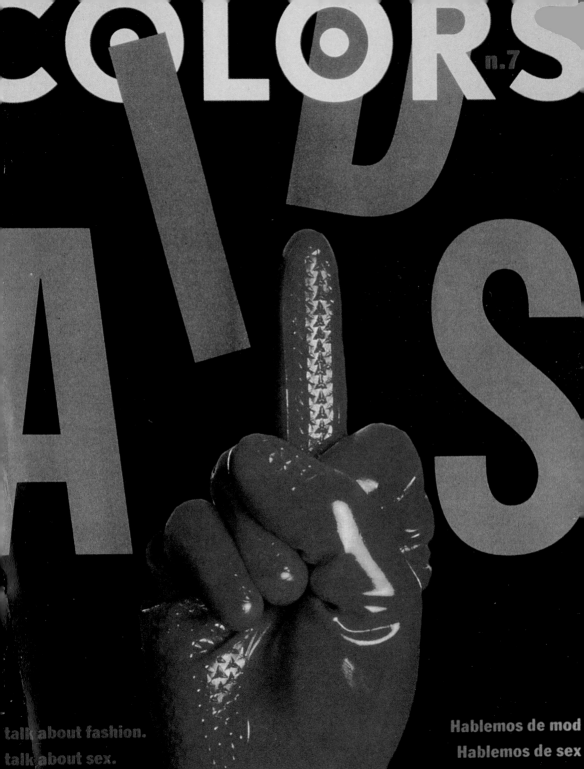

talk about fashion.
talk about sex.
talk about death.
really talk about Aids.

Hablemos de mod
Hablemos de sex
Hablemos de muert
Hablemos en serio del SID

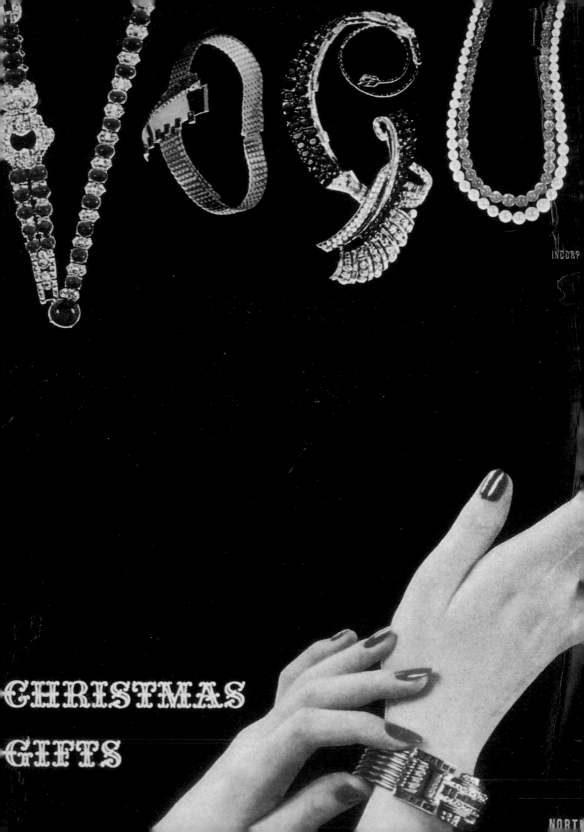

VOGUE

CHRISTMAS
GIFTS

Solid Gold: 40 Years of Award-Winning Magazine Design from the Society of Publication Designers

Copyright © 2005 by The Society of Publication Designers, Inc.

First published in the United States of America by:

Rockport Publishers, Inc.
33 Commercial Street
Gloucester, MA 01930
t: 978.282.9590
f: 978.283.2742

ISBN 1-59253-250-0

About SPD
Since 1965, The Society of Publication Designers has been promoting quality and innovation in publication design. SPD encourages artistic excellence and editorial involvement with an annual judging of thousands of entries from design professionals in the United States and abroad. Each year the winners are celebrated at the Awards Gala and the winning work is featured in the SPD Annual, the most prestigious record of the best work in our field.

In addition, the Society's activities promote the role of the art director and photo editor as visual journalists and collaborative partners in the editorial process, responsible for telescoping and shaping information, and giving visual expression to the editorial voice of a publication. Through our Speaker Series, our Student Competition & the B.W. Honeycutt Award, our Spots Competition, our newsletter, GRIDS, and other events, the Society provides opportunities for members and future members to explore the evolving nature of publication design.

SPD is a not-for-profit professional and educational organization. A Board of Directors comprised of the leading editorial art directors and allied professionals in the publishing industry guides it.

The Society of Publication Designers, Inc.
17 East 47th Street, Floor 6
New York, NY 10017-1920
t: 212.223.3332
f: 212.223.5880
mail@spd.org
www.spd.org

Contents

Editors' Letter:

SPD turned forty this year. In the spirit of our celebration, we are pleased to present you with *Solid Gold: 40 Years of Award-Winning Magazine Design from the Society of Publication Designers.*

While celebratory, our main goal was that this book would chronicle the preeminent work of SPD's forty years through its singular focus on excellence in publication design.

Never before has there been such a book! Over the past 4 decades publication designers from around the world have submitted their top work to our design competitions. Critically acclaimed judges have carefully reviewed thousands of submissions to compile annual records of the award winners. *Solid Gold* gives you the gold medal winners, magazine of the year winners and lifetime achievement honorees from these years in one volume.

We hope that you will use this book as both historic reference and a tool of inspiration. Keep it alongside all your SPD annuals for a complete record of award winning publication design. *Solid Gold* contains the best of the best.

—*Solid Gold* project coordinators

Solid Gold: 40 Years of Award-Winning Magazine Design from the Society of Publication Designers

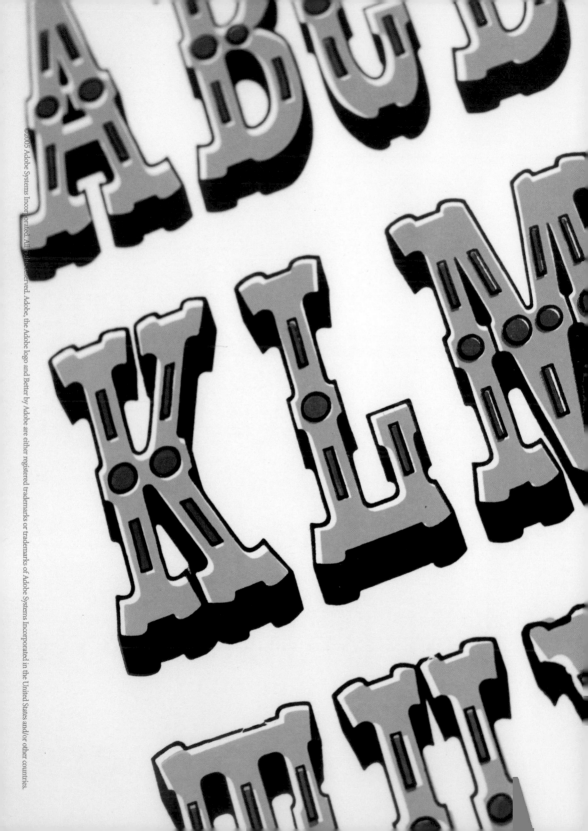

Passion + Innovation

Editorial designers help us see the world through the eyes of journalists, writers, authors and editors. Your role in the editorial process is essential; while an editor's article, essay or story may express ideas and opinions or convey information, it is editorial designers who shape the way we understand and interpret editorial content.

As a visual journalist, you help us hear the tone behind the editorial voice, providing both illumination and insight.

For more than forty years, the Society of Publication Designers has proven itself to be a driving force for passion and innovation in publication design.

By supporting SPD, we are proud to help continue this quest.

Forty years.

A lot can happen

Especially in the v

information busi

for instance, the n

books in existence

was...none.

n forty years.

ast and volatile

ness. In 1455,

umber of printed

in Europe

Forty years later, though, the number was approaching twenty mill-ion. And peo-ple found them-selves nervous-ly facing the pros-pect of having to adapt to a fright-ening new tech-nology. Print.

To function in the world of new Commerce and new Culture, they—we—would need to learn how to read. (Those twenty million books, by the way, were produced by applying ink under pressure to paper, a technology that seems to have served pretty well for the last six hundred years or so.) The world into which SPD was born, the world of 1965, can seem almost as distant and mysterious as the world of Gutenberg. And as irretrievable. In 1965, the largest-circulation magazines in America included *The Saturday Evening Post* and *Look*, *Pageant* and *Holiday* and *True*, *Photoplay* and *McCall's* and *Ingenue*. And *Life*. A postage stamp cost five cents back then, a gallon of gas could be had for a quarter, and a six-room apartment on Fifth Avenue, overlooking Central Park, rented for a thousand dollars a month. The first all-news radio station went on the air, and the first can of Spaghetti-O's appeared on supermarket shelves. Pope Paul VI became the first Pope to visit America, and the Grateful Dead played their first concert. The first indoor Major League Baseball game was played in the Astrodome, and the Buffalo Bills won the championship of the American Football League. In 1965, an Art Director's vocabulary would include words now almost lost in the mists of history: Lucigraph, Cello-Tak, Keyline, Rubylith, Chromalin, Tabouret. Back then, every Art Director's desk would have featured an aluminum can rimmed with a lumpy excrescence of dried rubber cement, and a smaller, red, cone-shaped contraption with a crooked brass spout. (The contents of these vessels were both highly flammable and dangerously toxic.) The Art Department still-life would likely have included a coffee can full of used x-acto blades, a brass-colored two-roll tape dispenser (the approximate weight of a bowling ball), several dried-up double-zero rapidographs and, very likely, an ashtray. By 1965, it was already fashionable to speculate whether magazines could survive, whether the age of print was over. That speculation continues, nagging, chronic, a permanent part of our professional consciousness. (In 1996, when SPD held its first Magazine Design

Conference in Monterey, participants wore buttons that said "Print Is Alive".) But if we look back over the history of invention, we find that rarely does a new medium condemn another to obsolescence. Rather, as Marshall McLuhan pointed out in Understanding Media, the effect is a more gradual and more benign one. It was only after the Industrial Revolution, for instance, that Man began to regard Nature as a source of aesthetic and spiritual values. Previously, Nature was simply the machine that produced sustenance and shelter. In the McLuhan-esque vision of human progress, every new technology elevates the one it replaces to the status of Art.

Or so we might hope.

It would be foolish to dare to predict the role of the magazine forty years hence. If history is a guide, some of today's best-loved and most successful titles will disappear. Knowledge and information will be transmitted, not in ways we haven't yet perfected, but in ways we haven't yet imagined. But perhaps, perhaps more than perhaps, the narrative, pictorial, three-dimensional, hand-held magazine will still be part of our cultural and intellectual experience.

Consider this:

If the designers attending the first SPD meeting in 1965 could have looked into a crystal ball, they would have been startled to see magazine readers paying five dollars for a single copy, and media conglomerates paying five hundred million dollars for a successful title. But, in the swirling mists of that crystal ball, they might also have seen this book: a celebration of the most beautiful, the most dramatic, the most intelligent expression of the affairs and ideas of our own time. And they would see that we still bring those ideas to life by pressing ink onto sheets of paper.

—Tom Bentkowski

Herb Lubalin

Award

The Herb Lubalin A-ward hon-ors life-time a-chieve-ment. It is giv-en by SPD to indi-viduals whose out-standing profes-sional contri-butions to our com-munity dem-onstrate their commit-ment to excel-

lence in
publication
design.

Named in
honor of
legendary
typographer
and art di-
rector Herb
Lubalin,
it is the
higest honor
the Society
presents.

Martin Pedersen

Herb Lubalin Award
1983

Cipe Pineles
Burtin

Herb Lubalin Award
1985

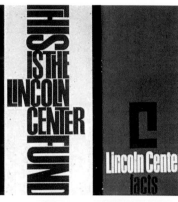

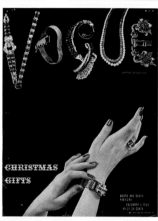

Bradbury
Thompson

Herb Lubalin Award
1986

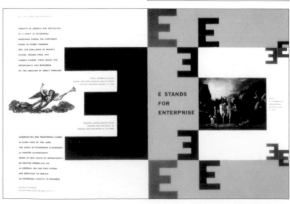

Will Hopkins

Herb Lubalin Award
1987

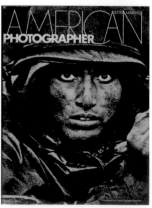

Frank Zachary

Herb Lubalin Award
1988

Henry Wolf

Herb Lubalin Award
1989

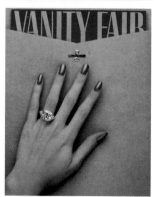

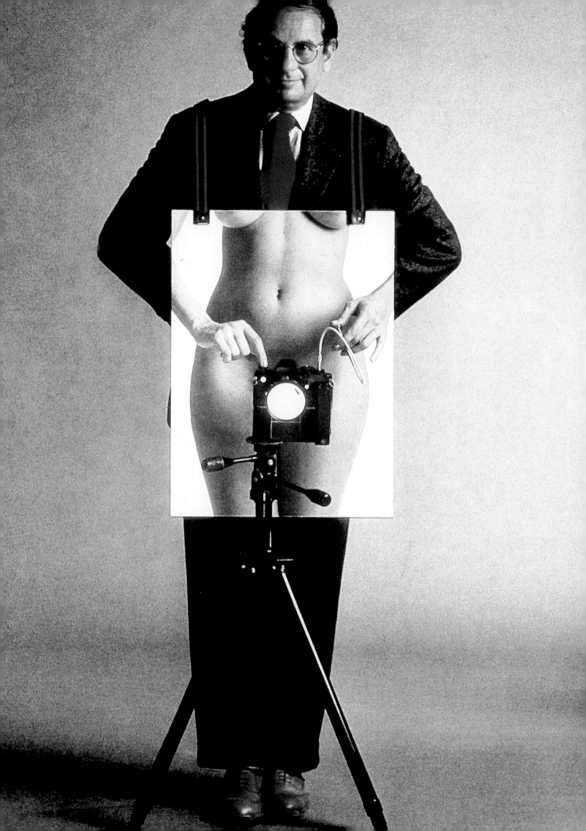

Milton Glaser

Herb Lubalin Award
1991

Rochelle Udell

Herb Lubalin Award
1992

Leo Lionni

Herb Lubalin Award
1993

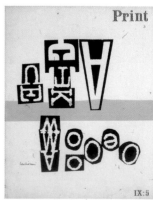

Ruth Ansel

Herb Lubalin Award
1994

George Lois

Herb Lubalin Award
2004

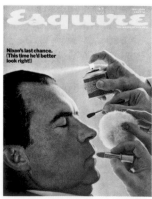

Magazine
of the Year

The Magazine of the Year A-ward is pre-sented to the art director who dem-on-strates the most effec-tive and imagina-tive use of de-sign, typogra-phy, il-lustra-tion and photog-raphy within the con-text of a cogent

and effec-
tive edito-
rial message.
It is the
most antici-
pated award
the Soci-
ety grants
as part of
its Annual
Competi-
tion.

The Annual
Competi-
tion jury se-
lects fifteen
finalists;
the top five

winners are all
awarded Gold
Medals for
Excellence, and
one is chosen
Magazine of the
Year. The top
winner is an-
nounced at a spe-
cial presentation
during the
Society's annual
Awards Gala.

The first award
was given in 1998;
the award has
been given each
year since that
time.

Magazine of the Year
1997

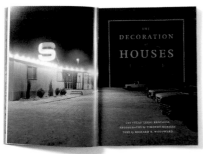

2wice

Art Director
J. Abbott Miller

Designers
Paul Carlos, Luke Hayman

Photographer
Jay Zukerhorn

Studio
Design/Writing/Research,
New York

feet

Publisher
Dance Ink Foundation

43

An interview with Abbott Miller

SPD: When did you first get interested in magazine design?

Miller: Once I was asked to design one, which was a small dance magazine called *Dance Ink*. I really had never had to think in a magazine-like way before that project.

SPD: Who was/were your mentor(s)?

Miller: My teachers at Cooper Union: George Sadek, for an insistence on typography and words as the most beautiful and meaningful things in the world; Hans Haacke for questioning the social and political role of design; Nicki Logis for providing a vocabulary for thinking in three-dimensions; and P. Adams Sitney, for film theory, Herman Melville, and Gertrude Stein.

SPD: Who is the person who had the most influence on you?

Miller: Ellen Lupton, who was always the smartest person in my classes at Cooper Union, and who, many years later, became my wife. Her influence is everywhere in my thinking.

SPD: What outside of magazines inspires you?

Miller: Architecture and photography and industrial design.

SPD: How do you lead your staff?

Miller: By treating them as equals. Their contributions are critical to the outcome.

SPD: What's the best career move you've made?

Miller: Opening my own studio at an early point in my career.

SPD: What's the worst career move you've made?

Miller: Trying to work for people I did not respect and who did not respect design.

SPD: Who is your favorite publication designer and why?

Miller: Fernando Gutiérrez, for the subtlety, restraint, scale, and charisma of his design.

SPD: Who is your favorite fine artist and why?

Miller: Marcel Duchamp because he re-wrote the terms of artistic production and recast the role of the artist.

SPD: Which designer do you most admire?

Miller: El Lissitzky.

SPD: Can you choose your all-time favorite work of design you've done?

Miller: The 16 issues of *2wice* magazine I've done.

SPD: What is the key to producing constant, memorable work over a number of years?

Miller: Maintaining an appetite for doing good work, and having the opportunities to do so.

SPD: What is the future of magazine design?

Miller: I think the future of magazine design belongs to photography.

SPD: If you had to switch careers, what would you be doing?

Miller: Architecture or film.

SPD: Should art directors have complete autonomy?

Miller: What in the world would

"complete autonomy" be in the context of an extraordinarily social organism like a magazine?

SPD: What is the hardest thing about producing a magazine on a creative level?

Miller: Identifying content that is meaningful and worthwhile.

SPD: How important is it for a design director to actually design instead of direct?

Miller: It's really important in the projects I do because they are not heavily formatted, and they are generally intimate projects I am working on with just one other person.

SPD: What professional accomplishment are you most proud of?

Miller: That I have managed to straddle the editorial/art divide, and create projects where these two sides are inseparable.

SPD: What's the most important lesson you've learned in your career?

Miller: That "your career" is the wrong way to think about it. The issues are: what are you making and putting out in the world, and have you made it better, more interesting, more beautiful, more effective because of how you've designed it, produced it, distributed it?

SPD: Is it better to be loved or feared?

Miller: As a parent loved, as a teacher feared.

45

Magazine of the Year
1998

The New York Times
Magazine

Art Director
Janet Froelich

Designers
Catherine Gilmore-Barnes,
Nancy Harris, Joele Cuyler,
Andrea Fella, Claude Martel

Photo Editor
Kathy Ryan

Photographers
Alexei Hay, Jake Chessum,
Tom Schierlitz, Larry Towell,
Lauren Greenfield

Publisher
The New York Times

An interview with Janet Froelich

SPD: When did you first get interested in magazine design?

Froelich: I began as a fine artist-a painter-and in the late seventies became involved with a group of radical women artists producing a publication called *Heresies-A Feminist Publication on Art and Politics*. It was a collective, and everyone did everything, in earnest, tortured all-night sessions. Through it I discovered that I loved type, page design, and working with the ideas that were generated by artists and writers.

SPD: Who was/were your mentor(s)?

Froelich: Since I studied fine art, and not graphic design, to my regret I never really had a design mentor. Over the years I have learned from an eclectic group of fine artists, editors, and designers, and I owe a huge debt to the historical work I leaned on in the process of teaching myself this craft. Herb Lubalin was the first designer I tried, seriously and unsuccessfully, to emulate. I endlessly copied pages of his *U & lc*.

SPD: Who is the person who had the most influence on you?

Froelich: Adam Moss. His ideas were breathtaking, he had incredible respect for the reader, and he taught me to think differently about magazines.

SPD: What outside of magazines inspires you?

Froelich: I've always felt a powerful connection to the world of fine art, to the painters and photographers who stretch the way we think visually. I'm also inspired by the renaissance of design that we've witnessed over the past decade.

SPD: How do you lead your staff?

Froelich: By being passionate about design. By listening to their ideas. By consistently acknowledging their contributions.

SPD: What's the best career move you've made?

Froelich: Staying at *The New York Times Magazine*.

SPD: What's the worst career move you've ever made?

Froelich: Staying at *The New York Times Magazine*.

SPD: Who is your favorite publication designer and why?

Froelich: This has been a great forty years of magazine design, and there's a lot of work out there to admire. This book is full of work I wish I'd done.

SPD: Who is your favorite fine artist and why?

Froelich: I can't name one artist or one designer, to me that's like a parent naming their favorite child. There are so many reasons to love so much work. I find myself full of wonder at the richness of it all.

SPD: Can you choose your all-time favorite work of design you've done?

Froelich: For obvious reasons I am proudest of the cover we did for 9/11 ("The Towers of Light"). It isn't as much design as it is a powerful idea, and those twin beams of light became the actual, annual memorial to the events of 9/11. Every year for the past four years I have looked up at the sky, at those beams, and felt a personal connection to the memorial.

SPD: What is the key to producing constant, memorable work over a number of years?

Froelich: Equal parts of luck, passion and not taking yourself too seriously.

SPD: If you had to switch careers, what would you be doing?

Froelich: I always wanted to sing. But I don't have much of a voice.

SPD: Should art directors have complete autonomy?

Froelich: When my son was very small he said he wanted to be "dictator of the world". It must have seemed so wonderful to this small person to imagine having that kind of power over everything. He's grown now, and I'm sure he would find it terrifying to have so much responsibility. True collaboration is the part of this field that I find the most satisfying.

SPD: What is the hardest thing about producing a magazine on a creative level?

Froelich: Listening to all the disparate voices that matter-editors, publishers, writers, photographers-and holding onto an authentic graphic voice. Hiring well.

SPD: How important is it for a design director to actually design instead of direct?

Froelich: I love to design. For me, it's crucial. But hey, everybody's different.

SPD: What professional accomplishment are you most proud of?

Froelich: That I'm still designing, and still loving it.

SPD: What's the most important lesson you've learned in your career?

Froelich: Not to take anything too seriously. My first boss, at *The Daily News*, reminded me that in the end it's just fish wrap.

SPD: Is it better to be loved or feared?

Froelich: Loved AND feared would be pretty cool.

Magazine of the Year
1999

Fast Company

Art Director
Patrick Mitchell

Designers
Patrick Mitchell, Emily
Crawford, Gretchen Smelter,
Rebecca Rees

Illustrators
Brian Cronin,
Andrea Ventura

Photo Editor
Alicia Jylkka

Photographers
Michael McLaughlin, Sian Kennedy,
Anton Corbijn

Publisher
Fast Company

An interview with Patrick Mitchell

SPD: When did you first get interested in magazine design?

Mitchell: In college. We had a very small design department at Ole Miss, and our professor-we only had one!-allowed us to choose our own projects. Every project I did was magazine-based.

SPD: Who was/were your mentor(s)?

Mitchell: Hans Teensma, who hired me for my first magazine job at Musician magazine. He taught me how to handle all of the things that come flying at art directors, and how to argue with editors with grace and style—to compromise without compromising. And, in too many ways to mention, Fred Woodward.

SPD: Who is the person who had the most influence on you?

Mitchell: Kim Mitchell (my wife), my parents, Steve Jobs, Mike Hodges (my college design professor), Bill Taylor & Alan Webber, George Gendron, Roger Black.

SPD: What outside of magazines inspires you?

Mitchell: My wife and kids, Rockport, Massachusetts (where I live), Manhattan, nighttime, nighttime in Manhattan, all kinds of music, Chris Ware, the Caribbean, Errol Morris.

SPD: How do you lead your staff?

Mitchell: From the middle. We're all in this together.

SPD: What's the best career move you've made?

Mitchell: I think they've all been pretty good, but I'd have to say aborting my first attempt at my

own business to go to work for *Fast Company* was the best.

SPD: What's the worst career move you've made?

Mitchell: I've actually been pretty happy with all of them.

SPD: Who is your favorite publication designer and why?

Mitchell: Dave Eggers. I love what he does with words, both writing them and designing with them, as well as the overall obsessive/compulsive look of his work.

SPD: Who is your favorite fine artist and why?

Mitchell: Thomas Hart Benton. He could see the nobility in the mundane.

SPD: Which designer do you most admire?

Mitchell: The sons and daughters of Tibor are all doing pretty inspiring work. I'm also a fan of Bill Cahan, and several Scandinavian designers.

SPD: Can you choose your all-time favorite work of design you've done?

Mitchell: One single thing? No, but I'd have to say there were a few years at *Fast Company* when everything was clicking.

SPD: What is the key to producing constant, memorable work over a number of years?

Mitchell: It happens when all of your collaboration works. Magazine design works when the editors, designers, and readers all share the same vision.

SPD: What is the future of magazine design?

Mitchell: What am I, Nostradamus? I wish I knew.

SPD: If you had to switch careers, what would you be doing?

Mitchell: If I had to switch careers I'd probably end up roaming the streets with a shopping cart. There's nothing else I want to do.

SPD: Should art directors have complete autonomy?

Mitchell: No, they should just have the same amount of autonomy an editor-in-chief has. If an art director keeps his customers, the editorial mission of the magazine and the readers as the priorities, there's no need for him to report to anybody else.

SPD: What is the hardest thing about producing a magazine on a creative level?

Mitchell: They just keep coming.

SPD: How important is it for a design director to actually design instead of direct?

Mitchell: Very. You can't direct if you can't design. The funny thing is, when you've finally gotten the design to a point where you can direct other people doing it, it's usually time to move on.

SPD: What professional accomplishment are you most proud of?

Mitchell: Having *Fast Company*—a business magazine—mentioned in the same breath as *Rolling Stone*, *Esquire*, *The New York Times Magazine*, *Details*, and other magazines known for great design.

SPD: What's the most important lesson you've learned in your career?

Mitchell: That magazines will tell you what they're supposed to look like.

SPD: Is it better to be loved or feared?

Mitchell: I'm a lover, not a... uh...fear-er.

Magazine of the Year 2000

Esquire

Design Director
John Korpics

Designers
John Korpics, Hannah Mc-
Caughey, Rockwell Harwood,
Erin Whelan

Photo Editors
Fiona McDonagh, Lisa Abrams

Photographers
Matt Mahurin, Nigel Parry, Dan Winters,
Sam Jones, Jayne Hinds Bidaut,
Kurt Markus, Hugh Kretschmer,
Teun Hocks

Publisher
The Hearst Corporation—Magazine
Division

An interview with John Korpics

SPD: When did you first get interested in magazine design?

Korpics: I answered an ad in the *Philadelphia Inquirer* for a designer at *Philadelphia* magazine. Oddly enough, when I got the job, I immediately became interested in magazine design.

SPD: Who was/were your mentor(s)?

Korpics: In a strange way it was Bill Regardie, the man who owned the first magazine that I was art director of (the modestly titled *Regardie's*). He would sit in his office experimenting with mind altering substances, then he'd scream for me to come in so he could tell me he wanted to remove the logo completely from the cover this month. He was (and I think still is) sort of like the Hunter S Thompson of Washington DC. He spent a year running stories with the sole intent of getting (then DC mayor) Marion Barry thrown out of office. I think I did 4 Marion Barry covers, each one more negative and biased than the last one, all to further Bill's agenda. He was larger than life, and there were many times when I was terrified of him, but he gave me a chance at 24 to be an art director, and he showed me that the rules could always be thrown out and reinvented, which was a valuable lesson.

SPD: Who is the person who had the most influence on you?

Korpics: My high school art teacher, Claude Falcone. I was trying to be a fine artist, and he looked at all of my work and sat me down in his cluttered office and said "Have you ever thought about graphic design?" Changed my life.

SPD: What outside of magazines inspires you?

Korpics: I love art museums and television. I get a lot from both.

SPD: How do you lead your staff?

Korpics: I play to their strengths. Everybody has something they do well. If a person is particularly strong, a lot of times the magazine's look will adjust to allow them to do what they do best. This way, every time a new person comes in, there is the possibility that the magazine will evolve a little, and stay fresh. I love that.

SPD: What's the best career move you've made?

Korpics: I have no idea. I've had jobs I hated and jobs I loved, but in some way, they all contributed to me being where I am right now.

SPD: What's the worst career move you've made?

Korpics: The job I hated the most, without a doubt, was *Musician* magazine. I was completely alone. I assigned everything, designed everything, did all the billing, all of the pre-production, proofing, press checks, and returned all the art with tear sheets, while sitting in a small closet sized cubicle wedged between a guy who farted all day, chewed on his unwashed ponytail and practiced his drumming on a drum pad, and a guy who talked as fast as an auctioneer and never shut up. I did the whole thing on a Mac 2x that crashed so much that I still to this day hit Apple S every 5 minutes, and I did it all for $7,000 an issue, most of which went to shoot the cover. I lasted 1 year and I developed a minor drinking problem.

SPD: Who is your favorite publication designer and why?

Korpics: Rockwell Harwood, because beneath all of those scary tattoos, he's just a big teddy bear.

SPD: Who is your favorite fine artist and why?

Korpics: I love a lot of the abstract expressionists. I like really bold graphic stuff like Robert Motherwell. I love Richard Diebenkorn because it all looks like layouts to me. Jackson Pollock. I really love Miro and Klee. DeKooning, Picasso. Stuff like that.

SPD: Which designer do you most admire?

Korpics: Paul Rand.

SPD: Can you choose your all-time favorite work of design you've done?

Korpics: Nope.

SPD: What is the key to producing constant, memorable work over a number of years?

Korpics: Let me know when you find out.

SPD: What is the future of magazine design?

Korpics: If I had to guess I would say Minimalism. I think we're coming out of a trend where a lot of magazines are over-designed. There's no need for a lot of what's being done right now. It goes beyond establishing a brand or a visual identity and becomes about the individual goals of the designer. Unless busy and overdesigned is somehow inherent to the identity of a magazine, which can be the case, the design should simply enhace the identity, not overwhelm it. So to sum up, every magazine will soon look like *The New Yorker*.

SPD: If you had to switch careers, what would you be doing?

Korpics: Singing in a band and playing guitar.

SPD: Should art directors have complete autonomy?

Korpics: Are you insane? Well, maybe I should....

SPD: What is the hardest thing about producing a magazine on a creative level?

Korpics: The hardest thing for me is when your editorial product is uninspired, to still try and make the visuals creative.

SPD: How important is it for a design director to actually design instead of direct?

Korpics: I don't think it matters. If a magazine looks good, then however you got there is the best way to do it.

SPD: What professional accomplishment are you most proud of?

Korpics: When I won the Oscar for my work in 'The Pianist'. That and my SPD awards.

SPD: What's the most important lesson you've learned in your career?

Korpics: I never set goals for myself. I like to see where the road takes me.

SPD: Is it better to be loved or feared?

Korpics: It depends on how much text they're trying to get in.

Magazine of the Year
2001

Details

Creative Director
Dennis Freedman

Design Director
Edward Leida

Art Director
Rockwell Harwood

Photo Editors
Alice Rose George, Amy Steigbigel,
Janine Foeller

Photographers
Michael Thompson, Steven Klein,
Tom Munro, Larry Sultan

Publisher
Condé Nast Publications, Inc.

An interview with Rockwell Harwood

SPD: When did you first get interested in magazine design?

Harwood: When I dropped out of SVA after a year and decided I needed to move the career thing along a little quicker. There were a lot of people in my class going for the same type of job. So I figured it out. So far.

SPD: Who is the person who had the most influence on you?

Harwood: Alexander Liberman. Banged out the first layout I ever did. Diana LaGuardia was the first to hire me editorially.

SPD: What outside of magazines inspires you?

Harwood: Everything outside. Infinite examples of good design that do not pertain to the obligatory solution.

SPD: How do you lead your staff?

Harwood: I try not and play the whole hierarchy thing. We discuss ideas and go for the best execution. Whether it be design or photography.

SPD: What's the best career move you've made?

Harwood: Shaking hands with Patrick McCarthy, Dan Peres, Dennis Freedman, Eddie Leida and taking the job at Details.

SPD: What's the worst career move you've made?

Harwood: Skydiving from the ground up.

SPD: Who is your favorite publication designer and why?

Harwood: I thought Darrin Perry

was very talented. His watch at ESPN was one of a kind.

SPD: Who is your favorite fine artist and why?

Harwood: Fred Tomaselli. Defining art is narcississitic. Just go and see a show.

SPD: Which designer do you most admire?

Harwood: Erik Nitsche and Herman Rorschach.

SPD: Can you choose your all-time favorite work of design you've done?

Harwood: I can't. I don't keep a portfolio so there is nothing to reminisce about.

SPD: What is the key to producing constant, memorable work over a number of years?

Harwood: When I get there I will be the first to share.

SPD: If you had to switch careers, what would you be doing?

Harwood: Film.

SPD: Should art directors have complete autonomy?

Harwood: Yes. No. Well...what do you think?

SPD: What is the hardest thing about producing a magazine on a creative level?

Harwood: The bar. Every time you push it, soon it becomes the norm.

SPD: How important is it for a design director to actually design instead of direct?

Harwood: To myself it is important. I like to design and I like to think.

SPD: What's the most important

lesson you've learned in your
career?

Harwood: Don't sell an idea based
on one direction and then deliver
something completely different.
Work towards it.

SPD: Is it better to be loved or
feared?

Harwood: Feared. Everyone loves
fear, that's why it is so attractive.
Got it Flanders?

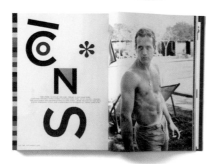

GQ

Design Director
Fred Woodward

Designers
Fred Woodward, Paul Martinez,
Matthew Lenning, Ken DeLago,
Gillian Goodman

Photo Editors
Jennifer Crandall, Catherine
Talese, Kristen Schaefer,
Michael Norseng, Eve Ekman

Creative Director, Fashion
Jim Moore

Photographer
Mark Seliger

Fashion Editor
Madeline Weeks

Publisher
Condé Nast Publications,
Inc.

An interview with Fred Woodward

SPD: When did you first get interested in magazine design?

Woodward: In the winter of 1976, I was studying graphic design at Memphis State, having transferred less than a year earlier from Mississippi State, where I had studied practically everything else. I was working a few afternoons a week after classes, mostly pasteup, for Jack Atkinson, who ran a small design business out of the attic of his midtown Arts and Crafts bungalow. I showed up for work one day, and Jack met me at the door. He had just received a call about designing the prototype issue for a new city magazine. Jack normally had a very calm, kind of bored-with-it-all air about him, but not that day. We drove to the college library and stayed until it closed, looking at back issues of New York magazine. I remember that as we walked across campus to his car that night, I asked Jack what an art director did. The next day, I was doing it.

SPD: Who was/were your mentors?

Woodward: Jack pulled out after three issues-it just didn't make business sense for him. I continued to do the magazine alone over my summer break from school. I'm sure they were interviewing everybody in town, but I was pretty oblivious and just kept working as though the job was mine. A few days before the fall semester was about to begin, Bob Towery, the publisher and owner, offered me the job. That was the end of my schooling and the beginning of my education. I always wanted a mentor, but was almost always an art director-not a very good one, but an art director just the same. I learned by doing, by having the freedom to make my own mistakes,

and by looking at (studying) magazines better than my own. There are many people to whom I owe a great debt. Here are a few: Harry Coulianos at GQ, Milton Glaser and Walter Bernard at New York, Herb Lubalin at Avant Garde and Eros, Mike Salisbury at West and City, Art Kane at Viva, Marty Pedersen at Nautical Quarterly, Roger Black at Rolling Stone and New West, Mary Shanahan and Bea Feitler at Rolling Stone, Robert Priest at Esquire, and Neville Brody at The Face. I wanted to work at CBS Records because of John Berg and Paula Scher. When I moved to Texas in the early '80s, I was inspired and encouraged by the likes of Woody Pirtle, Jack Summerford, and Jerry Herring. A little deeper into my career, I backtracked a bit and learned from the work done by the great ones, Alexey Brodovitch at Harper's Bazaar and Henry Wolf at Bazaar, Esquire, and Show. George Lois's Esquire covers. Paul Rand and Bradbury Thompson and Lester Beale. And along the way, the work of contemporaries like Fabien Baron and David Carson helped to make me bolder. I had been working two or three years when I sent off my very humble portfolio, unsolicited, to Rolling Stone, the magazine I loved most. It wasn't that I expected to be hired, more that I was just trying to find out how I was doing. Or maybe I was sending out the exploratory probe to find out if my particular kind of life-form could be sustained in that faraway, largely unknown environment. Anyway, I got it back after not too long a wait, meticulously wrapped in brown kraft paper and accompanied by a handwritten note on official Rolling Stone stationary from the associate art director, Greg Scott. It was a thoughtful assessment of the work-honest, but not brutally so. He concluded by saying that it seemed to him that instead of spending my time wishing I could come to New York and sweep floors at some estab-

lished American institution of a magazine, that perhaps I wasn't making the most of the unique opportunities I already had right where I was. With a few sentences, he took my head off, filled it up to the brim, and screwed it back on straight and tight. Twenty-five or so years later, I'm still amazed he took the time-still grateful that he did. Alan Cober was one of the first illustration gods who was gracious enough to work with me. He would call after receiving the copies I would FedEx him fresh from the printer and always, always sign off at the end of a lengthy conversation with "You're the best there ever was, kid." I knew it was just idle talk-just like I knew he never stopped drawing during our calls-but he said it so sweetly and so often that I started believing him. If only just a bit. I could keep going for another day and a half, but I'll stop here.

Woodward: Who is the person who had the most influence on you?

Fred: Van Chancellor, my seventh-grade basketball coach, who instilled in me early on the virtues of a powerful work ethic...and celibacy. Pistol Pete Maravich. I always wanted to be as good a man as my dad and his dad, but my mom and my grandmother probably had more sway over me.

SPD: Other than magazines, what inspires you?

Woodward: Anything done so well that it gives me that little buzz and reminds me I can do better. The first time I felt it was watching my dad fix a flat tire. There was no wasted motion and no complaint-just a man who took a hard job and made it look easy.

SPD: How do you lead your staff?

Woodward: At my best, by example. By practicing the golden

all in it together-no matter how deep it gets.

SPD: What's the best career move you've made?

Woodward: Hopefully the next one.

SPD: What's the worst career move you've made?

Woodward: Probably the next one.

SPD: Who is your favorite publication designer and why?

Woodward: Brodovitch, because without him, we'd all still be layout artists.

SPD: Who is your favorite fine artist and why?

Woodward: Picasso, because he never stopped changing, and he never got old. Brancussi, because he never changed, and made time for a little golf. Richard Avedon, Irving Penn, and Helmut Newton, because they made their art from the commercial-magazine assignment-a great reminder of what's possible every day. Dylan, because it takes a train to run, it takes a river to cry.

SPD: Which designer do you most admire?

Woodward: Milton Glaser.

SPD: Can you choose your all-time favorite work of design you've done?

Woodward: No, sorry.

SPD: What is the key to producing constant, memorable work over a number of years?

Woodward: A healthy fear of failure. You've got to get behind the mule every morning and plow. Baby needs a new pair of shoes.

SPD: What is the future of magazine design?

Woodward: No idea, really-just hope there are magazines to design for another ten to fifteen years. I'm supposed to finish the issue I'm working on by next Friday.

SPD: If you had to switch careers, what would you be doing?

Woodward: Photographer. Director. Stay-at-home dad. Stir-fry chef in the Conde Nast cafeteria.

SPD: Should art directors have complete autonomy?

Woodward: Yes.

SPD: What is the hardest thing about producing a magazine on a creative level?

Woodward: Not having complete autonomy.

SPD: How important is it for a design director to actually design instead of direct?

Woodward: Pretty important-especially if you work alone. Incrementally less so, with each talented designer you have on staff. Come to think about it, I've never seen a winning coach, in any sport, score a single point.

SPD: What professional accomplishment are you most proud of?

Woodward: The AIGA Medal. To have been the youngest inductee into the Art Directors' Hall of Fame. To have remained competitive over the long haul. This last year at SPD.

SPD: What's the most important lesson you've learned in your career?

Woodward: You have to be able to take a hit. If you can't get it printed, nobody will know you did it. There's always next month. Don't look back. It's better to burn out than to fade away. It don't mean a thing if it ain't got that swing.

SPD: Is it better to be loved or feared?

Woodward: I would rather be loved, but whatever it takes.

Magazine of the Year
2003

Martha Stewart Kids

Creative Director
Gael Towey

Design Director
Debra Bishop

Editor-in-Chief
Margaret Roach

Art Directors
Jennifer Wagner, Brooke
Reynolds, Jennifer Dahl

Illustrators
Calef Brown, Greg Clarke
Lane Smith, David Sheldo
Ross Macdonald

Photo Editors
Stacie McCormick, Jamie Báss Perotta

Photographers
William Abranowicz, Sang An,
Christopher Baker, Frank Heckers,
Gentl + Hyers, Stephen Lewis,
Tosca Radigonda, Victor Schrager,
Philip Newton

Stylists
Jodi Levine, Ayesha Patel,
Tara Bench, Anna Beckman,
Shannon Carter, Sarah Conroy,
Charlyne Mattox

Publisher
Martha Stewart Living
Omnimedia

Magazine of the Year
2004

Kids

Creative Director
Gael Towey

Design Director
Debra Bishop

Editor-in-Chief
Jodi Levine

Art Directors
Jennifer Wagner, Brooke
Reynolds, Robin Rosenthal

Illustrators
Marc Boutavant, Greg
Clarke, Jessie Hartland,
Calef Brown, Mary Lynn
Blasutta, Harry Bates

crazy **halloween** hairdos!

yummy treats for school

10 kooky pumpkins

plus... lots of warm and cozy ideas for fall

$1

Photo Editors
Stacie McCormick, Jamie Bass Perotta

Photographers
Sang An, Victor Schrager, Stephen Lewis,
Tosca Radigonda, Gentl + Hyers

Stylists
Anna Beckman, Charlyne Mattox,
Sarah Conroy, Megan Hedgpeth,
Tara Bench, Silke Stoddard

Publisher
Martha Stewart Living
Omnimedia

An interview with Debra Bishop

SPD: When did you first get interested in magazine design?

Bishop: I have to confess I was not really interested in working on magazines as a young designer. I wanted to do record covers, posters, and book covers, but when I was asked to work at *Rolling Stone* it seemed like I could apply the same kind of aesthetic there. It was after working there for a while that I realized the beauty of editorial design.

SPD: Who was/were your mentor(s)?

Bishop: I am lucky to have had a lot of good teachers. My SVA instructor and first boss was Paula Scher, then Fred Woodward at *Rolling Stone* and then Gael Towey at *Martha Stewart*.

SPD: Who is the person who had the most influence on you?

Bishop: All of the people I mentioned in your previous question have expertise that still influences me on a daily basis. For instance, when I make a mistake, I often think of Paula because she used to say there needed to be one mistake in everything she worked on. She liked the human element. From the moment I stepped foot in her class she instilled in me a healthy obsession with typography. But what I am most influenced by is her ability to exploit her quirky personality and sense of humor to make great art. All that aside, the people I have been most influenced by are my father, my husband, my children and my shrink.

SPD: What outside of magazines inspires you?

Bishop: I would say that my children inspire me a great deal and the things that I remember as a child. Also, comic books, packaging, ephemera, old type books, photographs, T.V. and movies.

SPD: How do you lead your staff?

Bishop: I believe in going into battle with the troops.

SPD: What's the best career move you've made?

Bishop: 1. Moving to New York. 2. Doing good work and making extreme eye contact with Paula Scher in her portfolio class so she would eventually notice me enough to hire me.

SPD: What's the worst career move you've made?

Bishop: Working at Riley and Mc-Cormick Western Wear in Calgary.

SPD: Can you choose your all-time favorite work of design you've done?

Bishop: I like the type design I did for the "new music" section in *Rolling Stone*, featuring Kurt Cobain, circa 1992, pre-computer and hand done with Xeroxes and a waxer. It takes me a few years to be able to look at my work with a kind eye.

SPD: What is the key to producing constant, memorable work over a number of years?

Bishop: It's important to feel confident so that you are willing to take risks, but don't get too comfortable, even though you are longing to be. Fear is often a good catalyst.

SPD: What is the future of magazine design?

Bishop: I don't know, but it's kind of piggy to keep up the paper usage isn't it? I think we need to find a new medium that doesn't abuse nature but that is tactile.

SPD: If you had to switch careers, what would you be doing?

Bishop: I like designing better than anything but I wouldn't mind trying other graphic design vehicles. No pun intended, but lately I've been interested in motorcycle design. Not the mechanical part but the body and paint.

SPD: Should art directors have complete autonomy?

Bishop: There is no reason that art directors should not be able to self govern the very job that they were hired to do and that only they are qualified to do. Nothing great is designed by committee.

SPD: What is the hardest thing about producing a magazine on a creative level?

Bishop: Nothing great is designed by committee.

SPD: How important is it for a design director to actually design instead of direct?

Bishop: I think it is important to walk the walk.

SPD: What professional accomplishment are you most proud of?

Bishop: I am proud of being part of creating the *Kids* magazine. We wanted to raise the standard that existed at the time and show that children's content has enormous potential to be smart and beautiful.

SPD: What's the most important lesson you've learned in your career?

Bishop: 1. An idea is only a point of departure. 2. An idea is only as good as its execution (note to editors). 3. Never show unfinished work.

SPD: Is it better to be loved or feared?

Bishop: It is best to be respected.

A Brief History:

A few notable events in the
publication design industry
since SPD's beginnings.*

1965

The Society of Publica-
tion Designers (SPD)
is founded as a profes-
sional organization to
promote excellence in
publication design.

The American Society
of Magazine Editors
(ASME) is founded
as a professional
organization to preserve
the mutual interests of
magazine editors.

Nova, a progressive
British women's monthly,
begins publication
with Harry Peccinotti
as art director.

Allen Katzman and
Walter Bowart co-found
the *East Village Other*, an
alternative biweekly
paper. The publication
is a wellspring for

undeground comic strips
and political collages.

1966

Twiggy bursts onto the
scene. The working-
class waif soon lands
on magazine covers
ranging from *Vogue*
and *Seventeen* to *Newsweek*,
redefining forever the
ideal of female beauty
in magazines.

Dot Zero, an architecture
and design journal, is
launched. Contributors
include Mildred Con-
stantine, Jay Doblin,
Ralph Eckerstrom, and
Massimo Vignelli.

*The New York Herald
Tribune*, the first news-
paper to be designed
like a magazine,
ceases publication after
a newspaper strike.

1965
Winston Churchhill dies
Malcom X is assassinated
First US forces arrive in Vietnam

1966

1967
BBC Radio 1 launched

1968
Vietnam War: My Lai Massacre
Martin Luther King Jr.
is assassinated

Glaser   Brodovitch

1967

Life publishes the cover story "The Great Poster Wave: Expendable Graphic Art Becomes America's Biggest Hang-Up," about the psychedelic and "personality" poster explosion in America.

Jann Wenner's *Rolling Stone* begins publication in San Francisco. The first designer is John Williams, and the first art director is Robert Kingsbury. The magazine's focus is to view the world through the prism of rock-and-roll.

The Advocate, then the nation's only gay and lesbian national newsmagazine, is launched as *The Los Angeles Advocate*

by Bill Rand and Dick Michaels.

Deaths:
Henry R. Luce (b. 1898) was the co-founder of *Time* and Time Inc. and launched *Life*, *Fortune*, and *Sports Illustrated*.

1968

The Hearst Corporation begins publication of *Eye*, a slick, glossy mainstream monthly magazine designed to exploit a growing youth culture interested in music, fashion, drugs, and sexual liberation.

Avant Garde, a richly designed magazine publishing essays, fictional pieces, and reportage, is unveiled under the editorial leadership of Ralph

Ginzburg and the art direction of Herb Lubalin.

Clay Felker and Milton Glaser launch *New York* magazine from the rubble of the defunct *New York Herald Tribune*. The format established by *New York*, modeled after "dinner-table conversation of the well-informed," continues to be emulated in cities across the country.

Graphic design pioneer Alexey Brodovich retires to France. In his 24-year reign as art director of *Harper's Bazaar* (1934-1958), and with his work at the short-lived, industry focused *Portfolio*, Brodovich became the first great designer of the photographic spread.

The Evergreen Review's "Che Guevara" cover and subway poster illustrated by Paul Davis enrages the Cuban exile community. An angry mob gathers outside the New York offices of Grove Press, and one of the protesters throws a grenade.

Screw magazine's first issue is published by Al Goldstein and Jim Buckley.

Will Hopkins succeeds Allen Hurlburt as art director of *Look*.

Audience, a hardcover cultural periodical, begins publication under the art direction of Seymour Chwast and Milton Glaser. It becomes an outlet for the Pushpin style of eclectic, comic, and narrative illustration.

1969
Man walks on moon
Woodstock

1970
National Guardsmen kill four at Kent State

1971

1972
First pocket calculators

Silverstein

Avant Garde

1969

The Saturday Evening Post, well known for its Norman Rockwell covers, ceases regular weekly publication after 148 years. The general interest magazine placed an emphasis on current events and well-written fiction.

Andy Warhol and Gerard Malanga launch *Interview*, one of the country's first celebrity-focused magazines. Warhol's fascination with fame is reflected in the magazine's focus on interviews of celebrities by celebrities.

1970

Louis Silverstein redesigns much of the Sunday *New York Times* throughout the 1970s, giving the Gray Lady a modernized facelift.

ITC releases Herb Lubalin and Tom Carnase's Avant Garde Gothic typeface, based on their *Avant Garde* magazine logo.

Jet and *Ebony* publisher John Johnson launches *Essence*—a lifestyle magazine for modern African American women.

1971

Twen magazine, created by founder and self-taught art director Willy Fleckhaus, ceases publication after 129 issues. The magazine presented fresh, provocative and trendsetting content aimed at twenty-somethings.

Publication Design, destined to become a bible for magazine art directors, is published by Allen Hurlburt.

1972

Life folds after 36 years.

Ms. magazine, founded by Pat Carbine, Gloria Steinem, and others to focus on the women's movement, begins publication. Art director Bea Feitler reintroduces Victorian woodtypes as a signature style.

After 10 years, George Lois designs his last cover for *Esquire*. The provocative, controversial images of Lois's work catapulted newsstand sales and fueled many heated debates.

1973

Herb Lubalin art directs *U & lc.*, the ITC magazine showcasing new typefaces. Lubalin is notable for his bold and creative use of type with which he gave visual form to ideas.

1974

Bar codes are first used at Marsh Supermarket in Troy, Ohio, forever changing (or defacing) the magazine cover.

People begins publication as a mainstream gossip and personality weekly.

1975

Legs McNeil and John Holmstrom co-found *Punk* magazine. McNeil claims he coined the name after hearing Telly

Lubalin   Brody

Savalas use the line "You lousy punk!" on the show *Kojak*.

Steven Jobs and Steve Wozniak design the Apple I computer.

1976

The first laser photo-typesetter is introduced by Monotype Corpora-tion, a technology that quickly eclipses hot typesetting.

Under the art direc-tion of April Greiman and Jayme Odgers, *Wet* magazine— utilizing new wave design and typog-raphy— is published in Venice, California.

1977

Walter Bernard re-designs *Time*, recasting

the publication with an orderly typographic format that merges conceptual illustration and photography.

The Apple II is in-troduced as the first personal computer with the capacity to render color graphics.

1978

Life is relaunched by Time Inc. as a monthly.

1979

Condé Nast acquires *GQ*—formerly *Apparel Arts*, a trade publication for the men's tailoring industry.

1980

Art Spiegelman and Françoise Mouly

showcase a sophisticated form of sequential art and visual storytelling in the newly published *RAW* magazine.

As the new art director for *Esquire*, Robert Priest introduces American magazines to concep-tual illustrators from London's Royal College.

Terry Jones begins *iD*, a fashion magazine documenting street fashion. Jones uses the thrust to shoot fashion as photo-journalism and to introduce a visual language of impulsive graphics.

1981

Adam Osborne introduces the first portable computer. The Osborne I weighs 24

pounds, costs $1,795 and is equipped with a five inch screen, a modem port, two 5 1/4" floppy drives, a bundled software package, and a battery pack.

Founding editor Sharon Lee Ryder launches *Metropolis*, a magazine about the disciplines of design. Carl Lehman-Haupt creates the original look of the magazine and officially becomes art director several years later.

Neville Brody becomes art director of *The Face*. His typographic style influences the look of culture and fashion magazines.

Deaths:
Herb Lubalin (b. 1918), a graphic designer hailed as the typographic genius

75

Star Wars released

Saturday Night Fever released

1978

1979

1980

Mount St. Helen's erupts

Rubik's cube craze

CNN launched

Feitler

of his time, was notable for his work in both advertising and editorial design. Lubalin's achievements were seen in everything from symbol and typeface design to posters and packaging, as he sought to do away with the distinction between type and image.

1982

USA Today hits the streets in the Baltimore/Washington area. It is the first daily newspaper to use full color and present "quick-read" news, a move that few in the industry expect to succeed.

Annie Flanders launches *Details* on newsprint out of her Manhattan apartment. Originally a celebrity-focused downtown publication, the magazine sets the stage for magazines like *Black Book* and *Nylon*.

Deaths:
Bea Feitler (b. 1938), one of the first prominent female graphic designers, was appointed co–art director of *Harper's Bazaar* at the age of 25. In addition, she was founding art director of *Ms.*, oversaw two redesigns of *Rolling Stone*, and redesigned the revival of the 1930s classic *Vanity Fair*.

1983

Condé Nast revives *Vanity Fair* using Bea Feitler's redesign. Editor Richard Locke and art director Lloyd Ziff oversee the magazine's newest incarnation.

WBMG, a magazine and newspaper design consultancy in New York, is formed by Walter Bernard, former art director of *Time*, and Milton Glaser, cofounder of Pushpin Studios.

The computer is named "Machine of the Year" by *Time*, replacing for that year the magazine's annual "Man of the Year" award.

1984

The March issue of *National Geographic* is the first in the U.S. to use a hologram on its cover.

Rudy VanderLans and Zuzana Licko found *Emigré* magazine, a cultural journal to showcase artists, photographers, poets, and architects.

1985

Elle (U.S.) begins publication.

Roger Black redesigns *Newsweek* with a goal of making it more visual. One of the features of the redesign forces editors to run much shorter stories.

Bob Guccione Jr. founds *Spin* magazine. The publication covers the emerging alternative music scene, filling the void in U.S. coverage of underground bands.

Step-by-Step Graphics magazine is launched to focus on the career

1981   AIDS virus identified

1982   Spielberg's E.T. opens   US Embassy in Beirut bombed

1983

1984

S P Y

Thompson   Woodward

development of graphic designers and illustrators.

Adobe introduces Illustrator, a vector or point-based drawing program using Bézier curves.

SPD honors Cipe Pineles Burtin with the Herb Lubalin Award for Lifetime Achievement, see page 18.

1986

Spy magazine, the brainchild of editors Kurt Andersen and Graydon Carter, debuts. Design director Stephen Doyle creates the original format with art direction by Alexander Isley. The magazine sets out to deconstruct not only magazines but social mores, social climbers and socialites.

SPD honors Bradbury Thompson with the Herb Lubalin Award for Lifetime Achievement, see page 20.

1987

Fred Woodward, formerly of *Texas Monthly* and *Regardie's*, is appointed art director of *Rolling Stone* with Gail Anderson as deputy art director. Woodward's use of imaginative typography and iconic photography influences a generation of magazine designers.

Roger Black forms Roger Black Incorporated, a company that designs newspapers and magazines internationally.

As art director of *Arena* magazine, Neville Brody

moves away from frenzied design and focuses on minimal typography.

SPD honors Will Hopkins with the Herb Lubalin Award for Lifetime Achievement, see page 22.

1988

Beach Culture, an obscure California surfing magazine designed by David Carson, becomes a showcase for his radical typographic experiments, which are based in part on Macintosh effects

SPD honors Frank Zachary with the Herb Lubalin Award for Lifetime Achievement, see page 24.

1989

Adbusters magazine is founded by Kalle Lasn to expose and satirize dubious practices in mass advertising.

Sixteen magazines around the world take part in the "Fax for Freedom" project in support of the Tiananmen Square protesters. Participating magazines print a manifesto against the Chinese government and a list of phone numbers where readers can fax the page in protest of the regime.

SPD honors Henry Wolf with the Herb Lubalin Award for Lifetime Achievement, see page 26.

1985 | Famine in Ethiopia | Reagan and Gorbachev meet at summit

1986 | Space shuttle Challenger explodes | Worst nuclear accident at Chernobyl

1987

1988 | Armenian earthquake, over 150,000 killed | Terrorists explode Pan Am flight over Scotland

Toscani   Carson   Pineles-Burton

1990

James Truman comes to *Details* as editor-in-chief, with Derek Ungless as art director. *Details* is repositioned as a nontraditional men's magazine.

Adobe releases the first edition of Photoshop, an imaging program that allows designers and photographers to easily manipulate photographs.

Entertainment Weekly is launched by Time Inc., an outgrowth of *People* magazine's "Picks & Pans" section with Michael Grossman as design director. The magazine is the first large consumer weekly to be designed on a Macintosh.

1991

Founder Oliviero Toscani and editor Tibor Kalman present the premiere issue of *Colors*, which features a jaundiced view of war, religion, race, travel, and shopping.

Martha Stewart Living is launched by Time Inc. under the art direction of Gael Towey. The publication reinvents the woman's lifestyle magazine with inspiring natural photography.

Frank Zachary, editor-in-chief of *Town & Country* since 1972, retires at the age of 77. Prior to that post, Zachary was art director of *Holiday* and founding editor of *Portfolio* with art director Alexey Brodovich.

SPD honors Milton Glaser with the Herb Lubalin Award for Lifetime Achievement, see page 28.

Deaths:
Cipe Pineles Burtin (b. 1910), an early and influential female voice in the graphic design industry, led the creative team of *Glamour* where she was the first autonomous female art director of a mass-market American publication. Burtin also led the creative forces of *Seventeen*, *Charm* and *Mademoiselle*.

1992

Tina Brown, fomer editor of *Tatler* (London) and *Vanity Fair*, becomes the editor of *The New Yorker*. She introduces photographs, color, and other graphic elements to the weekly.

David Carson launches and art directs *RayGun*, where he creates experimental and often controversial designs.

Most magazines begin to convert to the Quark Publishing System.

Fabien Baron redesigns *Harper's Bazaar*, where his return to elegant typography recalls the iconic designs of Alexey Brodovich.

SPD honors Rochelle Udell with the Herb Lubalin Award for Lifetime Achievement, see page 30.

1993

Quincy Jones and Time Inc. launch *Vibe*, a music

1989 | Thousands of students are killed in China's Tiananmen Square

1990 | Nelson Mandela freed
Iraq invades Kuwait and seizes petroleum reserves

1991 | South Africa ends apartheid

1992 | LA riots after Rodney King verdict

Wallpaper* The New York Times

magazine focused on hip-hop and urban culture. Creative director Gary Koepke and art director Richard Baker lead the magazine's creative team.

Time launches its online version, a move that soon becomes the industry standard.

SPD honors Leo Lionni with the Herb Lubalin Award for lifetime achievement, see page 32.

1994

John F. Kennedy Jr. launches *George* with the goal of stimulating interest in the American political system. The first cover features the bare-midriffed Cindy Crawford dressed as George Washington.

SPD honors Ruth Ansel with the Herb Lubalin Award for Lifetime Achievement, see page 34.

1995

Rochelle Udell is hired by Condé Nast Publications to take over as editor-in-chief of *Self*, making her one of the few art directors to take on an editorial role.

1996

Designed with neo-Modern simplicity, British-based *Wallpaper** is launched as the lifestyle magazine of Generation Next.

Slate is introduced as one of the first high profile online-only magazines.

1997

Under the design direction of Tom Bodkin, *The New York Times* starts using color in all sections.

Nest, A Quarterly of Interiors, is launched as the brainchild of novice publisher, editor, and art director Joe Holtzman. Its diverse, cultlike fan club adored the magazine for its visual excess and unrefined typography and individuality.

Maxim, one of the first "laddie" magazines, begins publication in the U.S.

1998

Editor-in-chief John Papanek launches

ESPN: The Magazine under the art direction of F. Darrin Perry.

2wice magazine is awarded SPD's first Magazine of the Year Award under the design direction of J. Abbott Miller.

1999

Art Spiegelman creates "41 Shots, 10 Cents" cover for *The New Yorker*, a critique of the New York police shooting of unarmed suspect Amadou Diallo, 41 times. Off-duty police officers stage a protest demonstration in front of *The New Yorker*'s offices.

The New York Times Magazine is awarded SPD's Magazine of the Year under the design direction of Janet Froelich.

79

World Trade Center bombed

Bill Clinton succeeds George H. W. Bush as president of the USA

1994

Rwandan genocide begins, 800,000 slaughtered

Kurt Cobain, lead singer of Nirvana, is found dead. Seattle, Washington

1995

Murrah Building in Oklahoma City is bombed, 168 killed

O.J. Simpson is found not guilty

1996

Dolly the sheep, the first mammal to be successfully cloned, is born

Deaths: Alexander Liberman (b. 1912), editorial director of Condé Nast from 1962 to 1994, served as art director of *Vogue*, where he brought in otherwise unknown photographers such as Irving Penn.

2000

Life, founded in 1936, folds for the second time in 64 years.

Oliviero Toscani, of *Colors*, becomes creative director of *Talk*.

O, The Oprah Magazine launches with founding editor Oprah Winfrey and founding design director Carla Frank. It is considered the most successful launch in history, selling out

1.5 million copies of the first issue.

Time Inc. launches *Real Simple*, a magazine dedicated to making women's lives easier, under the leadership of editor-in-chief Susan Wyland and creative director Robert Valentine.

Fast Company is awarded SPD's Magazine of the Year under the design direction of Patrick Mitchell.

2001

George folds, less than two years after JFK Jr. dies in a plane crash.

Fred Woodward leaves *Rolling Stone* to become design director for *GQ*. Woodward succeeds in making the publication

appealing to younger audiences without alienating older readers.

Martha Stewart Kids for parents and children is launched. Conceived by editor Jodi Levine and art director Debra Bishop, the magazine showcases smart how-to content and graphic wit.

The U.S. Supreme Court, in the case of *The New York Times* v. *Tasini*, confirms that the copyright laws of the United States apply to cyberspace.

Esquire is awarded SPD's Magazine of the Year under the design direction of John Korpics.

2002

Led by design director Joe Dizney and design

consultant Mario Garcia, *The Wall Street Journal* gets a dramatic new look for the first time since 1942.

Wenner Media reformats *US Weekly* to a tabloid glossy.

Details is awarded SPD's Magazine of the Year under the design direction of Rockwell Harwood.

Deaths: Rudolph de Harak (b. 1924) was a renowned graphic designer praised for his clear communication and elegant typography.

2003

GQ is awarded SPD's Magazine of the Year under the design

1997 | Princess Diana dies in a car crash

1998

1999 | The human population surpasses 6 billion | The Euro is introduced in 12 European Union member states

2000

Antupit

Froelich

Lois

direction of Fred
Woodward.

Deaths:
Sam Antupit (b. 1932)
art directed *Esquire*,
Harper's Bazaar, *Show*,
Vogue, *Mademoiselle*, and
House & Garden and
founded Common
Place Publishing.

2004

Life is reborn as a week-
end insert distributed
in newspapers nation-
wide with Richard Baker
as creative director.

Janet Froelich
becomes creative
director of all of
The New York Times'
magazine division.

SPD honors George
Lois with the Herb
Lubalin Award for

Life-time Achievement,
see page 36.

Martha Stewart Kids is
awarded SPD's Magazine
of the Year under the de-
sign direction of Debra
Bishop.

Deaths:
Richard Avedon
(b. 1923), a celebrated
fashion photographer
discovered by Alexey
Brodovich, art director
of *Harper's Bazaar*. Avedon
became a staff photog-
rapher for *Harper's Bazaar*,
Vogue, and the first-ever
staff photographer for
The New Yorker.

Henri Cartier-Bresson
(b.1908), the French
photographer hailed for
his ability to capture a
moment, was considered
to be the father of
photojournalism.

F. Darrin Perry
(b.1965) a ground-
breaking designer
for *Wired* and *ESPN:
The Magazine*.

Helmut Newton (b.
1920), an influential
German-Australian
fashion photographer,
was famous for his
nude studies of women
printed in *Playboy*,
French *Vogue* and many
other publications.

2005

Many large publish-
ing companies convert
from Quark software
to Adobe InDesign,
providing significant
changes to production
quality control.

Kids, formerly *Martha
Stewart Kids*, is awarded
SPD's Magazine of

the Year under the
design direction of
Debra Bishop. The
magazine is the first
in the history of the
award to be honored
two years in a row.

John Korpics, design
director of *Esquire*, moves
to *InStyle* to take on the
role of creative director.

Deaths:
John Johnson (b. 1918)
founded *Ebony* and *Jet*
magazines and was the
first African American
to make Forbes list
of the "400 Richest
Americans."

Henry Luce III (b. 1925),
son of media-mogul
Henry R. Luce,
pulished *Fortune* and
Time and founded
the Time-Life music
division.

81

George W. Bush is inaugurated

September 11th attacks on the
World Trade Center

Apple introduces the IPOD

2002

Space Shuttle Columbia disintigrates

2003

2004

Madrid train bombings

Tsunami kills 275,000 people

Henry Wolf (b. 1925)
was an influential art
director, graphic
designer and photogra-
pher for *Esquire*, *Harper's
Bazaar* and *Show*.

*Portions of SPD Timeline
are adapted from Graphic
Design Time Line by Steven
Heller and Elinor Pettit,
published by Allworth Press.
Copyright © 2000.

82

1970-

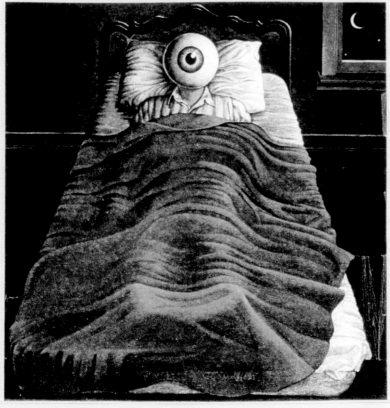

001 The New York Times Magazine, 1973

002 The New York Times Magazine, 1973

003 McCall's, 1973

004 The New York Times "The Week in Review", 1973

The New York Times Magazine

JULY 22, 1973/SECTION 6

The Story So Far

By J. Anthony Lukas

Chief Newman, my coach, an American Indian, produced some very fine teams at that small, little college at Whittier . . . . There were no excuses for failure. He didn't feel sorry for you when you got knocked down. He had a different definition of being a good loser. He said: "You know what a good loser is? It's somebody who hates to lose. . . ."

—Richard M. Nixon,
at Pro Football Hall of Fame dinner,
July 30, 1971.

I N the raw winter of 1970, Richard Nixon looked like a loser. From balmy San Clemente and Key Biscayne, White House aides strove earnestly to put the best possible face on the returns in that November's midterm elections. But back in Washington a consensus was hardening, like ice on the Mall's reflecting pool, that the election constituted a serious setback for the President and an ominous portent for 1972.

The G.O.P. did gain two seats in the Senate and lost only 12 in the House—less than the party in power generally does at midterm. But it also lost 11 governorships and some key state legislatures. Except for Tennessee, the ballyhooed Southern strategy failed to gain the Republicans any ground below the Mason-Dixon line. And they did badly in many of the largest states — notably California, Ohio, Pennsylvania, Michigan, Texas and Florida — where the 1972 election would almost certainly be decided. When 28 Republican Governors and Governors-elect gathered that December among the snowy peaks of Sun Valley, Idaho, their standing joke was that they should have met at Death Valley. Gov. Edgar D. Whitcomb of Indiana, which gave Mr. Nixon his biggest majority in 1968, said the President was in trouble even there. Columnists Rowland Evans and Robert Novak wrote later: "In November, 1970, the Presi-

dency of Richard Nixon had hit bottom."

The gloomy post-mortems that winter often focused on the President's strident "law and order" campaigning, particularly his harsh Phoenix speech ("No band of violent thugs is going to keep me from going out and speaking with the American people") rebroadcast on election eve — only to be followed immediately by Senator Edmund Muskie, measured and calm in a Maine living room, asking the voters to repudiate the Republicans' "politics of fear." Now, many Republicans felt the voters had done just that. Gov. David Cargo of New Mexico warned that his party had "lost the election because the strategy was completely negative."

Publicly, the Southern White House stuck with its upbeat appraisal, but behind the palm fronds it began reassessing its strategy. A few days after the election, the President met with his senior aides at Key Biscayne to—in one aide's words—"go over the game films." Later that month, a smaller group, headed by Attorney General John Mitchell, closeted with him again. From this session emerged a unanimous conclusion: Nixon must drop his partisan image and henceforth be The President. Four days into the new year, Mr. Nixon publicly proclaimed his new persona in a televised interview with four network correspondents. "This is a noncampaign year," he told his interlocutors, "and now I am going to wear my hat as President of the United States."

But if the President was to assume an air of statesmanlike high-mindedness for the next two years, then others would have to carry on the tough partisan brawl build- (Continued on Page 8)

CONTENTS OF THIS SPECIAL ISSUE: PAGE 4

The future, as somebody predicted, isn't what it used to be. Nothing has changed man's conception of the future as much as the frightening specter of population explosion and attendant cataclysmic theories. Out of speculation about the population explosion evolved the so-called doomsday theory, warning that man is rushing to self-destruction—fear supported by several academics of national reputation.

Population statistics also prompted Buckminster Fuller to write *Operating Manual For Spaceship Earth*, and undergirds the concern that the Earth is not a planet of infinite resource or capacity to absorb human and technological wastes, but rather a spaceship whose capacities are fast approaching the maximum.

Many futuristic theories regarding population lack the perspective of history. As expert Herman Kahn observes, there has always been more continuity than change, what has gone on for the last millenium should continue for at least another 27 years. Any projection beyond seven years is highly suspect, in Kahn's view. The key is to understand trends and probabilities and create options with enough vision to avoid disaster.

Overrated as the phrase may be, "population explosion" accurately describes what will happen in Metro Atlanta in the next 27 years. Planners crystal ... *continued on page 162*

If population projections are on target, the people impact on the Atlanta region will be enormous 27 years from now, when

One Will Give You Three

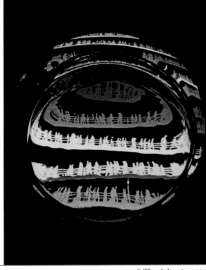

006 The Atlantic, 1973

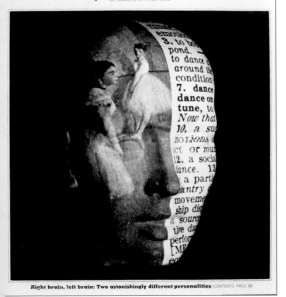

The New York Times Magazine

SEPTEMBER 9, 1973 / SECTION 6

Right brain, left brain: Two astonishingly different personalities/CONTENTS: PAGE 30

007 The New York Times Magazine, 1973

87

Saturday Review of FAILURE

Death of a family

By Bob Kuttner / National Editor / The Village Voice

One afternoon last winter, Nicolas H. Charney, editor-in-chief and chairman of the board of Saturday Review Industries, invited his staff to a slide show. The topic was not the charms of San Francisco, though most present were certainly new to the area. "Nick decided we should learn something about the look and feel of magazines," one senior editor recalls, "so he produced a sixth-grade audio-visual show. Don Wright, the art director was at the back of the conference room running the projector. Nick was on a folding metal chair providing the voice-over."

Charney went on for nearly three hours, discoursing on good graphics and bad graphics, contrasting "old" magazines with new. *Look* had died because it was not with-it graphically, Charney told the audience, which included several former *Look* staffers. Other examples of yesterday's magazines were ordered up: *Harper's*, *Atlantic* and *The New Yorker*, which would last perhaps

008 Folio, 1973

009 Popular Photography, 1973

010 Mineral Digest, 1973

011 Oui, 1973

012 Horizon, 1973

013 Oui, 1973

014 Life, 1974

015 The 5 Minute Hour, 1974

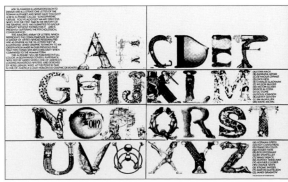

018 Art in Virginia, 1974

019 Minneapolis Tribune Thursday Section, 1974

SUMMER CAMPS FOR GROWN-UPS

ESCAPE CAMPS FOR WOMEN

FOR FRUSTRATED FURNITURE BUYERS

EXPLORING THE WILDERNESS

NEWS FROM CAVITY COUNTRY

McCALL'S MONTHLY NEWSLETTER FOR WOMEN

Right Now

JUNE 1974

When Dr. William Masters and Virginia Johnson published their book on *Human Sexual Inadequacy* in 1970 they estimated that half of the marriages in the country were in sexual trouble. Other more recent studies put the number as high as 60 or even 70 per cent. Yet, since then Masters and Johnson seem to have proved that most couples can overcome their problems in a relatively short but concentrated program of therapy. According to a five-year follow-up study of people treated in their own St. Louis clinic they report a success rate of 74.5 percent.

In response to the obviously huge demand for help more and more local sex clinics and therapy centers are opening up all over the country to treat couples on an outpatient basis. Most of them haven't been in existence long enough to measure their results, but they tend to use the basic techniques developed by Masters and Johnson and get the same fairly speedy "cures." For they find that sexual problems are more often caused by ignorance and poor conditioning than by deep-seated neuroses that require years of psychoanalysis.

What is it like to undergo therapy at one of these clinics? The first step is generally separate interviews with a therapist, who takes down a complete sexual history and asks questions about all aspects of a person's sexuality. If the clinic uses co-therapists, the wife meets with the female member of the team first while the husband talks to the male therapist. Then each confers with the counselor of the opposite sex. Finally, all four sit down together for a discussion of the problems, attitudes and misconceptions that were revealed in the separate interviews.

After the discussion in which husband and wife often reveal to each other hidden fears and fantasies they have never talked about before they are assigned homework to be done in the privacy of their own bedroom. No reputable therapist expects anybody to perform sexual acts...

HOW SEX CLINICS CAN HELP

Designed by Hinrichs Design Associates, Inc.

021 National Geographic World, 1974

022 Oui, 1974

023 Distillers Corp.-Seagram's Ltd., 1974

024 New York, 1974

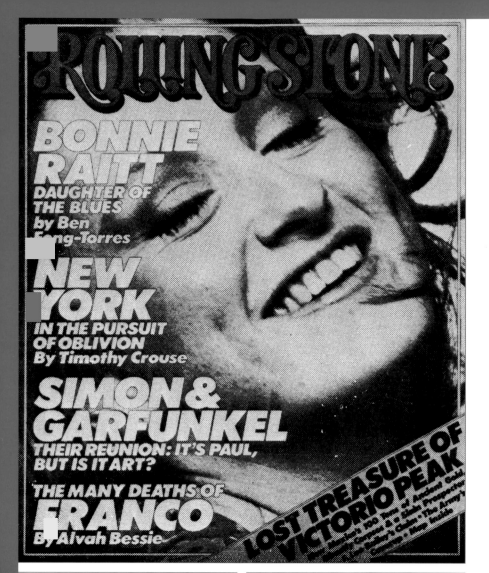

ROLLING STONE

BONNIE RAITT
DAUGHTER OF THE BLUES
by Ben Fong-Torres

NEW YORK
IN THE PURSUIT OF OBLIVION
By Timothy Crouse

SIMON & GARFUNKEL
THEIR REUNION: IT'S PAUL, BUT IS IT ART?

THE MANY DEATHS OF FRANCO
By Alvah Bessie

LOST TREASURE OF VICTORIO PEAK

025 Rolling Stone, 1975

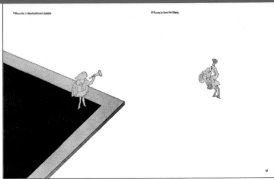

026 Printing Salesman's Herald, 1975

027 Champion International Corp. 1974 Annual Report, 1975

028 Audubon, 1975

029 Oui, 1975

030 U & lc, 1975

031 Pastimes, 1975

032 Playboy, 1976

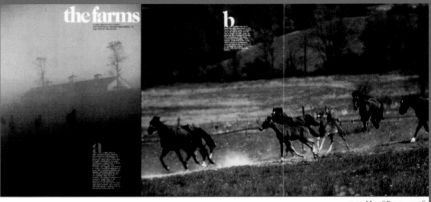

033 Hoof Beats, 1976

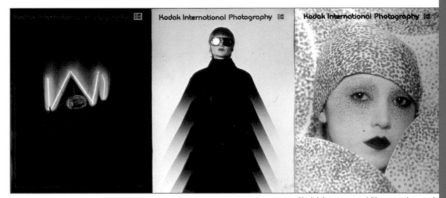

034 Kodak International Photography, 1976

035 Quest 77, 1976

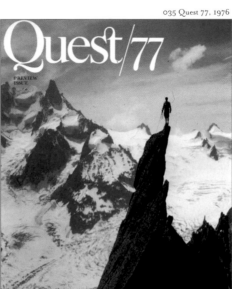

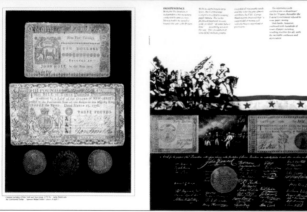

036 The Arthur Young Journal, 1976

037 U & lc, 1976

038 California Business, 1976

EMERGENCY MEDICINE
DECEMBER 1976

By Frank J. Weinstock, M.D.

blackout

The eyes are really rather fantastic organs. They each receive an image, turn it upside down, flip it back over again, perceive, and combine the images—in color in daytime, black and white when it's dark—all, literally, in less than a blink of an eye! It's not surprising, therefore, that occasionally the system malfunctions. While a sudden loss of vision may not actually stem from the eyes themselves, it's frequently the first manifestation of a change there or somewhere else.

Sound complicated? It is, of course. But really, there's often quite a lot you can do to minimize the visual loss—and sometimes reverse it altogether—if you handle the problem quickly and correctly. And if there's nothing that can or / *continued*

23

This exquisitely chromolithographed little-girl doll in her lacy underwear came equipped with a wardrobe that would have been exactly what every little girl in America would have wanted around 1900: a sailor suit for everyday, an afternoon frock, a "Scottish" outfit with matching tam-o'-shanter, a "Sunday best" with beribboned and befeathered bonnet, and, most delightful of all, a fancy-dress shepherdess costume.

The Metropolitan Museum of Art, Gift of Miss Doris V. Reichard, 41.114.1-9

THE TENTH ANNIVERSARY ISSUE

Rolling Stone

DR. HUNTER S. THOMPSON
Fear & Loathing : The Banshee Screams for the Buffalo

ANNIE LEIBOVITZ
A special fifty-page color collection of Greatest Hits · Plus A Decade in the Life

041 Rolling Stone, 1977

JERRY BROWN and RALPH NADER in suits and ties, LINDA LOVELACE in crotchless red underwear.

"Before I opened the box I gave her a fifteen-minute preamble. 'Now Linda, this is a little far out. Isn't anything real different. A fantasy.' I was scared stiff she would flip out. But I opened the box and she just died. She loved it, and put it on immediately. She sent her art director out to get red nail polish to match the underwear."
— A.L.

RODLANO STONES, Los Angeles, July 1975

Sociobiologist Irven DeVore talks with Scot Morris about the selfishness built into our genes. It is not the survival of the fittest that humans and other animals strive for: it is for the reproduction of the individual's genes.

The New Science of GENETIC SELF-INTEREST

Scot Morris: The evolution of behavior has become a hot issue lately. The conference you organized at the American Anthropological Association last November aroused quite a stir: huge attendance, radical protest, even an attempt to pass a resolution condemning social biology.

Irven DeVore: The hullabaloo is because many people oppose the notion that human behavior is in any way directed by our genes or that our destinies may be somewhat preordained by our biology.

Morris: Is this theory really something new and important, or is it just a repetition of the same old argument that biologists and environmentalists get into every few years?

DeVore: Yes it is new: we're still calling it by several names: sociobiology, behavioral biology, psychobiology, and so on. And it is important, probably the most important development in understanding behavior since Darwin It has already revolutionized the understanding of animal behavior and is well on its way to revolutionizing the social sciences.

Morris: Psychology and ethology have gotten along pretty well without it up to now, though. Why do you say it's so important now?

DeVore: Because it's a complete "paradigm shift," in Thomas Kuhn's terminology, for a whole new way of looking at behavior, especially the most puzzling behaviors that defy traditional explanations.

Morris: Like what, for example?

DeVore: Like murder and infanticide: systematically killing other members of your own species. Lorenz and others

had convinced people that aggressive animals stop short of killing their own kind—or if they do, it's because of some breakdown in their ritualized fighting system caused by some unusual stress, or even that the killing was somehow for the good of the species as a whole.

Morris: As a means of population control, for example?

DeVore: Yes. But we now know that it occurs in species that aren't overpopulated, or may even be on the verge of extinction. Male lions sometimes eat lion cubs, for instance. Murder is a comparatively rare event in any species, so no one had reported it in lions until relatively recently, after field studies that had been running continuously for eight or 10 years. Reports on animals killing their own kind are now coming in so fast that it's almost routine. I was just reading about some studies on the murder rates in bears and mountain lions. But we've heard similar reports about many species: chimpanzees, gorillas, baboons, elephant seals, wild dogs, hyenas, gulls, you name it.

Morris: What happened to the "Peaceable Kingdom"?

DeVore: It was an illusion, apparently. Contrary to what the popular writers saying a few years ago—that humans are the most aggressive, vicious animals on earth, the "killer ape" with the mark of Cain—we may turn out to be one of the more pacific animals of all warfare aside.

Morris: What kind of killing has been observed?

DeVore: There are many instances of adult males killing each other, but even more revealing is the widespread infan-

ticide. Not just leaving the young to die, but deliberate killing, usually by a male who has just taken over a group of females and young after driving out the resident male. And the new male continues to kill any young born in the next few weeks or months—that's true in lions and in the langur monkeys of India, for example. One would have to construct a very tortured argument to show how this behavior is "good for the species as a whole." It is manifestly bad for the young who are killed, of course, and it's bad for the females who lose all the time and energy they have invested in their offspring. But that's not to say it isn't good for the males who do the killing, those offspring aren't his. Infanticide can increase the male's own reproductive success and help him leave more offspring.

Morris: For instance?

DeVore: Female langur monkeys, for example, ordinarily come into estrus about every two years. But if a nursing mother loses her infant, she comes into estrus and conceives within two months, instead of six to eight months. So the killer male comes out ahead of the game if he can get the females pregnant and keep out other males until his infants grow big enough to avoid being killed by the next invading male.

Morris: What about human beings? Is there any comparable kind of behavior in human societies?

DeVore: Oh yes. It's rare, but it does happen. Most often the parents will kill a newborn because there's another infant that's not yet old enough to be weaned. But the other kind occurs too. An anthropologist among the Eskimo recently reported an incident in which a

HANGING LOOSE AT 1,500 FEET, UPSIDE-DOWN ROY CLARK PRAYS, 'SEAT BELT, DO YOUR STUFF'

Photographs by George Long

043 People, 1977

044 People, 1977

Billy Carter

HE MAY BE A ROYAL PAIN TO SOME, BUT HIS BIG BROTHER IS STILL AMUSED

045 Field & Stream, 1977

THE KILLING OF A WILD RIVER

BY DOYLE KLINE

Doyle Kline, who lives in the Southwest, has a background in resource management

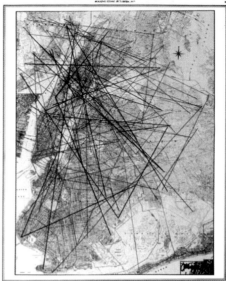

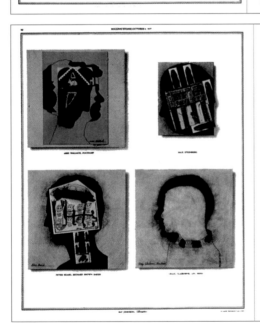

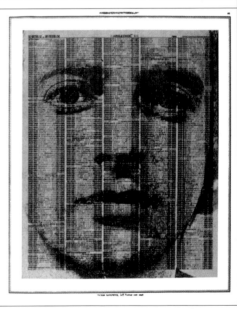

046 Rolling Stone, 1977

Lovely To Look At, Delightful To Hold

Accessories are expected to look good and serve the purpose for which they are intended. But once in a while an accessory comes along that is so beautiful, so appealing to the touch, that it can stand as an art object in its own right. Here are four as beautiful to behold as to wear.

047 The New York Times, 1977

$3.00

AMERICAN PRESERVATION

THE MAGAZINE FOR HISTORIC AND NEIGHBORHOOD PRESERVATION
OCTOBER · NOVEMBER 1977

GALVESTON'S EAST END DISTRICT:
A TEXAS TREASURE OF 19TH CENTURY HOMES

PRESERVATION'S MOST VEXING PROBLEM
THE DISPLACEMENT OF LOW-INCOME PERSONS

048 American Preservation, 1977

The Yellow Pie Everybody Eats Down In Key West Page C7

A Skinny Little Box You Can Count On Page C11

A New Play By Thomas Babe at the Public Page C16

Books: Feenie Ziner Turns Maternal Love Into An Adventure Page C19

FOOD STYLE ENTERTAINMENT

The Living Section

The New York Times

L   C1

WEDNESDAY, JANUARY 18, 1978

The Chicken: Inexpensive, Elegant

cheap cheap!

By CRAIG CLAIBORNE

TAKE IT from this prophet: If you want to know the name of the best buy among meat and poultry the rest of the year it inevitably will be chicken.

Chicken has traditionally succored the poor in years that are lean. By contrast it has for centuries delighted the palates of the royally robed as well, in the form of such dishes as supremes de volaille Polignac (chicken breasts with mushrooms and truffles in cream sauce) and poulet reine sauté à l'archidiuc (sautéed chicken in a madeira-flavored cream sauce).

As chicken broth it has, for countless generations, been nourishment and balm for mind and body and made those who imbibe feel whole again. If proof were needed as to the appeal of chicken for the masses, consider Colonel Sanders and Kentucky Fried.

It is true in ages past in certain cultures — particularly primitive

Continued on Page C4

Prawns in Peking, Mooncake in Canton

By CHARLOTTE V. SALISBURY

Continued on Page C8

Fashion: Serious About Summer

By BERNADINE MORRIS

Parrot is star of Oscar de la Renta summer show.

Continued on Page C12

051 Metropolitan Museum, 1978

PHOTOGRAPH BY HIRO

053 Playboy, 1978

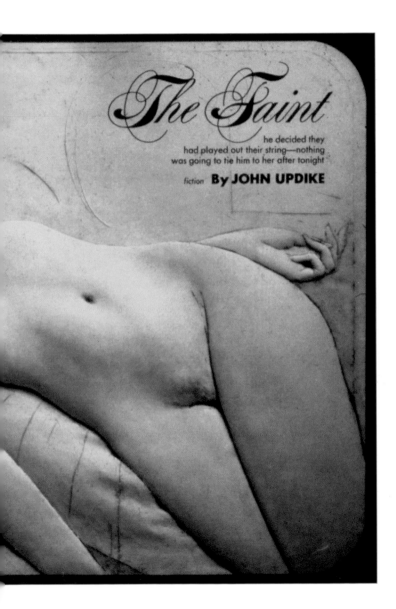

The Saint

he decided they
had played out their string—nothing
was going to tie him to her after tonight

fiction **By JOHN UPDIKE**

054 Life, 1979

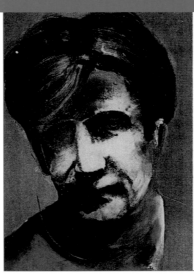

THE
EXECUTIONER'S
SONG

By NORMAN MAILER

*you remember how gary gilmore died. now
here's the tale of how he lived...and the
story of the people whose lives he changed*

055 Playboy, 1979

THE SHAPES WHO
TURNED US ON

HINC

So many good stories begin with the narrator, nearing journey's end, stopping to ask for directions and discovering in the response he elicits a clue to whatever it is he seeks. The inquiries of David Balfour in Stevenson's *Kidnapped* not only found him the House of Shaws, they raised the hackles on the young man's neck, so darkly did the townspeople react to the mention of his uncle. □ Rolling down into Southwest Harbor on Maine's Mount Desert Island, we couldn't resis storybook entrance as we pulled into the Gulf station at the bottom of the hill. "Can y direct me to the Hinckley yard," we asked a group of grizzled shellbacks who were sitt inside. □ "Finestkind" offered an ill-disguised Main Line drawl. A middle-aged mega politan transplant in pink-faded Alligator shirt, sun-and-soap-bleached khakis, and studi squalor deck shoes strolled toward me with that knowing Dean Witter look, nodded head and repeated with even more conviction — "Finestkind." □ A good entrance, thought, for at the risk of belaboring that already shopworn Down East encomium, Hinckley yard and the yachts that have come off its stocks have indeed been finestkind

At right, a Hinckley craftsman applies gold leaf to the topside stripe that forms one of the smaller distinctions of Hinckley-built yachts. The stripe is symbolic—in the fact that it's pure

gold and that a man sees to it with pride and with skilled hands—of many larger and a few smaller things that go into a completed Hinckley. A typical result is shown at right, a Hinckley 50, a welter 50 reaching powerfully through Maine-coast seas with an obviously happy crew enjoying the ride. The Hinckley yard is

perfectionist in its standards, building much of the hardware and systems put into the boats and boasting truthfully that "Hinckley builds more of the total boat ... in an industry which manufactures most of its boats less quality enough but fails far short of perfection for reasons related to marketing and

mass-produced ... the Hinckley yard is a phenomenon ... old fashioned ... but fashioned with but dedicated to perfecting and using the most modern materials available. The th that result are perhaps the best production boa the world

Editor's Note: We thought it would be interesting to compare the Hinckley Bermuda to a similar stock boat of high quality but lesser price. (Obviously lesser price since B-40 is the biggest-ticket 40′ auxiliary on the market here or in Europe.) The o choice was the Gulfstar 40, a boat that we and many others had found impressive. asked John Atkin to survey a typical B-40 and a typical G-40, and to give us a pair survey reports with his impressions, his own interesting asides, and a comparat analysis of both boats. The two surveys are published here. They are interesting as a focus on Hin ley workmanship within the context of comparison with a similar boat produced by a ma production-line builder, and as a focus on the Gulfstar 40 as an attempt by a major builder achieve Southwest Harbor standards and still build a boat they could sell. The fact that the G proved a marketing disappointment is no reflection on its worth as a boat or as an experiment Gulfstar. It was an excellent cruising/racing auxiliary. The Gulfstar 40 listed this past spring $83,500. The Bermuda 40 listed for $133,500. Both boats had similar lists of standard equipme

GULFSTAR 40

Coming to terms with the actual quality of fiberglass reinforced plastic from hulls simply observing them is nearly like judging the quality of an enameled bathtub. And there is great similarity in other respects! Both lack character. You'd need to "belt" a bathtub to see if it were made from cast iron or pressed tin, or would to discover the material, and you'd need to belt a particular fiberglass yacht to come to terms with its thickness, the quality of the laminate, what fibers were incorporated, and all manner of factors that make up the structure. To inquire, there are "glass" boats with lather decks that "squeak" from the failure of the "glass and core to bond; there are topsides that are frightening in their ability to flex; there are good and bad methods of seating hardware and joining deck to hull—and so on—that radiate quality or shoddiness. Like getting married, an involvement with a fiberglass boat should not be taken lightly. Either can sound out poor little worth or squeak it to sand down around your ears.

The Gulfstar 40 is a totally different

concept from the Bermuda 40. There are ten years separating the origins of the "B-40" and the "G-40"—ten years in which hulls have changed from those designed to beat the CCA rule to those designed to beat the IOR. And their hulls are a drastic change in material. The quality of hardware has been influenced by "production standards," along with the advice of cost accountants, those dreadful characters who manage to spoil most everything by "making it cheaper." Never better—just cheaper. Cost accountants and "marketing analysts" should all be put adrift in a big fiberglass ark in the middle of the Pacific to fend for themselves. Out of the kindness of my heart I might let them take along one of their plastic bilge pumps, with the expectation that they will allow themselves completely mud-hauling to get the thing to stay together.

Stepping aboard the Gulfstar 40, once is not impressed by what I can only call the "fragrance of quality" that exists aboard the Bermuda 40. There is a world of suttle difference, and the quality of the work can scarcely be compared. The comparisons down on the two-year-old G-40 discussed here, for example, are in the process of being pulled apart by the sun, and there is only minimal exterior joinerwork; "peaks"—as captained in corners, primarily, in the process of layup—exist on the cockpit seats, after end of the trunk cabin, etc.; the aluminum overhead casting lacks any degree of finish, although I don't question its strength; the dorade vents are fitted with flexible PVC plastic cowls; cockpit hatches are installed with two bronze strap hinges either ored, two of which were broken and all of which needed to be refastened.

I want to say at this point that the

Gulfstar 40 generally reflects high ty and good structural integrity. planes mate of the "contemporary duction stands" of the major the yachts that I have the opportun survey. But this exercise is not on surveys; it is a comparison. The stock boat has arvelegs shut by a synthetic, fine extending forward to the cabin, either side of the on ionway, while the B-40 has a sliding hraves and that seems high This is the sort of thing that make gating shape two yachts a very di land interesting task. Both are rate, but I must say that the B "first-rater."

G-40 hardware is made by S. Merriman, etc., and it is all of high ity. There are top-action Barient winches on the halyards. The ma is extruded aluminum coated with hard, glossy finish, which is very some. The extruded main boom with jiffy-reefing equipment which simply well-made and strong. The stainless-steel roll thwarts—one side—made up to stainless fastenings

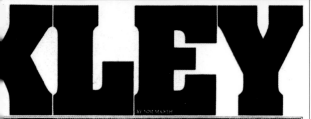

BY NIM MARSH

B

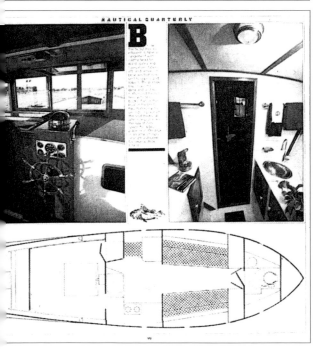

New U.S. Power to
STRIKE
from
THE AIR

It is a sleek irony of our atomic world that military power now has that one patriotic task once banned: understanding even while the U.S. and the Soviet cannot struggle to reach agreement about the limitation of arms. There now the major feature upon us how to control a given surplus, it seems a serious and bitter revelation of weight if frightful by a new creature it certainly breakthroughs, not war technology advances is apparent cornucopia on the great inventions of arms limitation. Serious spin-counters for pursuers face and in the following pages literature technology moves as it applies a — it are power. These are not talent at such. In I some we already not model by some advanced strategies at the gathering or pilaster-gelagen.

The mounted figure at left at the radar watchful-res operation of our F-14 Tomcat the Navy's 60250 million fighter in sight formation behind four are another F-14 support fighter are a filament its aircraft force plane. The control board F-14 with the hot 71000 again at move the control of aimed a arming of 50 different threeweek three-flight shape against other fighters at sharp liquids an ground targets. It had three missile air-miss one of which can fire and weapons guided missives a few than a mission at six aircraft meeting ranges 100 different miles. The technology of the F-14 is our samples even our action after craning date carriers the plane staff has a number of bags or is marked was. Seventh tactant, armed force fighters become on the F-14 as being marked for positive.see page 191

Photographs Co/Incorrendas

19

SR-71 Blackbird

F-18 Hornet

E2C Hawkeye

057 Life, 1979

1980-

058 Nautical Quarterly, 1980

059 U & lc, 1980

U&lc.

UPPER AND LOWER CASE. THE INTERNATIONAL JOURNAL OF TYPOGRAPHICS · PUBLISHED BY INTERNATIONAL TYPEFACE CORPORATION · VOLUME SEVEN · NUMBER THREE · SEPT. 1980

Something for Everybody...

Z is the most neglected character in the English language. E is by far the most popular. For each Z used in the formation of words the following proportions have been fairly accurately established for the usage frequency of the other 25 letters.

E-60,T-45,A-42.5,I, N,O,&S-40,H-32,R-31,D-22,L-20,U-17,C &M-15,F-12.5,W&Y-10,G&P-8.5, B-8,V-6,K-4,Q-2.5,J&X-2&Z-1.

E for Enigma:
The beginning & eternity, The end of time & space, The beginning of every end, The end of every place.

Reading from left to right and from top to bottom this word square was worked out by an anonymous puzzlist. The degree of difficulty increases with the size of the square. Try it sometime.

**NESTLES
ENTRANT
STRANGE
TRAITOR
LANTERN
ENGORGE
STERNER.**

TO WIDOWERS AND SINGLE GENTLEMEN

WANTED

BY A LADY, A SITUATION TO SUPERINTEND THE HOUSEHOLD AND PRESIDE AT THE TABLE. SHE IS: AGREEABLE, BECOMING, CAREFUL, DESIRABLE, ENGLISH, FACETIOUS, GENEROUS, HONEST, INDUSTRIOUS, JUDICIOUS, KEEN, LIVELY, MERRY, NATTY, OBEDIENT, PHILOSOPHIC, QUIET, REGULAR, SOCIABLE, TASTEFUL, USEFUL, VIVACIOUS, WOMANISH, XANTIPPISH, YOUTHFUL, ZEALOUS. ADDRESS ALL INQUIRIES TO: XYZ, SIMMONS LIBRARY, EDGEWARE ROAD, LONDON

LONDON TIMES, 1832

A
VILE
Young lady on
EVIL
Bent. Lowered her
VEIL
With sly intent,
"LEVI"
She said, "It's time to play. What shall we do to
LIVE
Today?"
"My Dear," said he, "Do as you please. I'm going to eat some
IVEL*
Cheese."

*This cheese is presumed to have been made in the valley of the Ivel River.

continued on page 37

060 U & lc, 1980

061 Nautical Quarterly, 1980

NAUTICAL QUARTERLY

NEWFOUNDLAND

PHOTOGRAPHS BY SAM ABELL

Photographs like these are rare, although their images are not. If there is any message in the photographs on the following nine pages beyond their quality of exquisite simplicity, it may be one appropriately real and simple: that our eyes see things like them every day. But our eyes see without holding, they are active and distracted, tools for our minds, focusing a moment and then moving on. The camera holds the image, and in the holding makes it something else. The something else is a moment frozen and made classic, a more profound kind of seeing than our active eyes normally deliver. These are seacoast photographs, classic images of the kinds of things that flavor small-boat cruising: men working at the fishing trade, fog and gannets, shapes and colors of boats and buildings. In cruising we see things like these in passing, and in the fast cuts of recollection we see them again in a romantic tumble, a nostalgia that makes us smile and plan for next year. A good cruise. Photographs like these make plain the hard beauty of the world. It is a beauty worth the eye and mind seeing and recalling the way the camera does, worth concentrating a minute's attention on the look of a beached whaleboat, the white-blue-green of clouds-water-grass, whenever we cruise along a coast.

These photographs were made by Sam Abell on a trip to the island of Newfoundland. A young and largely self-taught photographer, Abell was born in Sylvania, Ohio, in 1945 and graduated from the University of Kentucky in 1969 with a degree in English. He has been a contract photographer for National Geographic since 1970. He says of these Newfoundland photographs: "Some photographers I know seem to absorb aspects of their assignments like actors from the roles they play; this happens especially early in our careers, and eventually it helps shape our seeing. The island of Newfoundland, austere at first and lyrical at last, was that place for me. From it I took a directness and simplicity of seeing I had not brought with me, and if in the interplay of light and line and color there is a notion of mystery it is because I look for just that."

Living in the Coronary Culture

BY Michael Halberstam

Try too hard,
worry too much,
lift too strenuously,...
and *bim-bam!*
you're dead of a
heart attack.
This brutal possibility
affects not only
the victim himself
but also our society,
our literature,
our commerce, and
what we laughingly call
our living patterns

WHEN NINETEENTH-CENTURY AU-
DIENCES WAITED EAGERLY FOR
THE NEXT BURST OF GENIUS FROM
the likes of Byron, Dumas, and Puccini,
they were unaware that they were participating in an enormous exercise in medical epidemiology. Rather, they celebrated
such authors and composers because
their works were a distillation of life,
and an overwhelming fact of the lives
depicted by artists in the last century
was the slow, painful wasting away of
talented, artistically sensitive young
men and women. These charming
youths lived poetic, bohemian lives.
They died romantic deaths.

The truth is, they died of pulmonary
tuberculosis. So many fictional heroes and
heroines—as well as their authors—died
of TB that illusion and creativity became
almost synonymous. The poetic look

062 Esquire, 1981

063 Nautical Quarterly, 1981

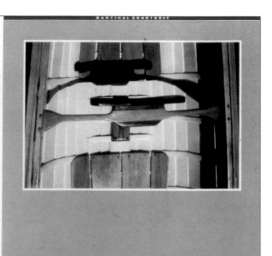

PAINTINGS BY MIHANOVIC

HARD AND SOFT

Marine paintings—whether of clipper ships, yachts or fishboats—tend to be action-packed—a Gloucester schooner rail down on the race to market, a 12 Meter on a spinnaker run, *Tueping* in the Trades with her studding sails out. The paintings on these six pages are different. They are serene and mysterious, their principal action the soft breathing of the Adriatic on the bright coast of Yugoslavia.

It is subtle action to capture, subtler still when a cobbled bottom as precise and intricate as a mosaic slides off under a lambent surface. The artist is Zvonimir Mihanovic (pronounced Machano-vitch), a Croatian born in Yugoslavia in 1946, whose first painting brought him First Prize in Yugoslavia's Salon of Young Artists in 1962. He studied subsequently at the Academy of Fine Arts in Zagreb and the Brera Academy of Fine Arts in Milan, and traveled in 1972 and 1973 to museums in London, Boston, New York and Washington to study paintings of classical realism.

His own realism is an old tradition of meticulous detail and compelling moodiness, although there is a suggestion of the "hardedge" realism of recent decades. These paintings have very solid reality—all the heavy essence of the concrete with few distractions. Even the light has a weighty, stone-slab quality.

It is the light of the eastern Med, the almost-physical light that travelers in the Greek islands have so often remarked. The boats are the typical double-enders of the Adriatic's fisheries, full-bodied carved types with lines that go back to Homer's time, along with dinghies and tenders of the same chunky build. Solid, serene boats on solid, serene water, but with an odd softness of mood and weather.

Mihanovic has done other types of paintings in his two decades of major work, but marine paintings like these are now his preoccupation, indeed his passion. A man at the Wally Findlay Gallery in New York, where Mihanovic paintings were first shown in the U.S. in January and February of 1981, describes him as "absolutely in love with the Adriatic." Mihanovic has a home and studio in Paris, but he spends the long Yugoslavian summer aboard a houseboat in the Adriatic. His paintings are oils on large canvases, and each represents a month to six weeks of work. There were 20-odd paintings in his recent show in New York—two years of work—and it is expected that there will be as many paintings about a year from now when his new work is shown at Wally Findlay's Beverly Hills gallery. He is on the Adriatic as this is written, seeing and wonderfully putting on canvas the hard surfaces and softer depths of coastal images like these.

First of four symposium articles in this issue

Charles E. Reed, MD

Occupational asthma

A challenge in patient management and community care

Consider

Is a seasonal pattern among the symptoms of occupational asthma take?

What mechanisms of action have been implicated for occupational asthma?

How should occupational asthma be managed?

Asthmatic reactions to substances encountered on the job are a common and growing problem for workers and employers. The physician can help by carefully seeking and considering potential occupational causes in asthma cases and by working with employers on preventive measures.

"Occupational" asthma would seem to refer to the asthma provoked by exposure to some agent present in the work setting. This, of course, is true, but the term has wider meaning.[1] Agents that cause occupational asthma sometimes escape the occupational setting to affect individuals who work or live nearby; for example, in Brazil, France, and the United States, small epidemics of asthma from castor bean, an extraordinarily potent allergen, have occurred among children living downwind from facilities producing castor oil. Also, people may encounter occupational allergens while pursuing a hobby such as electronics, painting, or photography.

The definition of occupational asthma, while requiring some broadness, does need to be restricted to exclude nonspecific aggravation of chronic asthma by irritating fumes or dusts encountered at work. This distinction may seem more pedantic than real, but it has important practical implications for understanding the mechanisms of the attacks, management of individual patients, and application of industrial hygiene principles to minimize risk.

The study of deliberate exposure to occupational allergens in the clinical research setting has led to recognition of unexpected patterns of airway response that offer valuable clues to understanding not only occupational asthma but also the pathogenesis of asthma in general.

continued

© 1981 Mayo Foundation

Cuban Writers In Exile

By Charles Greenfield

For more than two decades now, Cuba, that exasperating, complicated social laboratory 90 miles from Key West, has clung to America's heel like some tenacious crab unwilling to let go.

On a much smaller scale, its relationship with its own writers has been equally turbulent. In the honeymoon days of the '60s, most Cuban writers, flushed with memories of recent revolutionary success and fervent to the point of overlooking the messy purges and blatant propaganda, were reluctant to rock the boat. By the '70s, serious writing had come virtually to a halt: trials of "reactionary" or "CIA sponsored" intellectuals, hollow confessions full of contrition and mea culpa, increased censorship often self-imposed, prison and solitary confinement, silence,

brutality and sometimes death.

Today the intimidation continues. More than ever *El Exilio* seems the only choice left open to artists who — from the days of the poet and father of Cuban independence at the end of the last century, José Marti, to newly arrived Mariel refugee and poet-novelist Reynaldo Arenas — seek a voice for their anguish.

LYDIA CABRERA

"When Jicotea (the turtle) began to grow up, his mother asked him wisely:

Son, you've got a good head on your shoulders and it's getting time to learn a trade. What do you

want to be: a cook? a baker? a confection...
— No, mother . . .
— A locksmith? A barber?
— No, mother.
— A general?
— No, mother.
Then the old mother said very seriously:
— Son, do you want to be a rascal?
— Oh yes, mother dear!
The mother and son then smiled at each ...
'Thank God! a chip off the old block,' she ...
herself."

— Ayapa: Stories of Jicote...

Through the window the usual harsh ... is beginning to weaken and Cuba's matri...

ILLUSTRATION © 1981 BRAD HOLLAND

066 The Plain Dealer Magazine, 1981

The hundreds of billions of dollars that Arab and other foreign investors have poured into the U.S. have given them a potential stranglehold over our own destiny.

THE SELLING OF AMERICA

BY ERNEST VOLKMAN
ILLUSTRATION BY MARVIN MATTELSON

067 Penthouse, 1981

068 Foremost-McKesson Annual Report, 1981

069 Foremost-McKesson Annual Report, 1981

and services consist of well-recognized brand names and established market franchises. They include Mueller pasta, Foremost dairy products, Sparkletts and other bottled water brands, Armor All protectant for automotive and home applications, Liquore Galliano, Mount Gay rums, a number of wine labels and the prescription claims services of Pharmaceutical Card System.

Our value-added distribution services distinguish our operations from those of most of our competitors by providing a range of values to our customers and suppliers far beyond the simple logistics of distribution. Buying from manufacturers and selling in smaller quantities to retailers, we make products available at the right time and place. At the same time, we provide valuable services such as marketing, planning, research, display and advertising support, computerized retail business systems and special packaging.

These core businesses — proprietary products and services and value-added distribution — will be the primary focus of our future growth.

Conceptually, our growth strategy can be thought of as a series of concentric circles built from these core businesses.

Our first priority is ensuring the future growth of the company is to continue to promote greater internal efficiencies while increasing the market share of current operations. In this area we will commit additional resources to improving working capital efficiencies, developing computer systems, making productivity improvements and to the effective marketing of our current product lines.

We expect to achieve further important gains in efficiency by extending our present electronic data processing technology to all of our distribution systems. The Drug & Health Care Group pioneered this development, using computers to reduce its own operating costs and improving its retail customers' profitability through its Economost, Econoscan and Econotone electronic order entry systems. About 90% of its business is now generated by these programs.

By adopting similar technology, the Chemical and Wine & Spirits groups offer attractive opportunities for more intensive computer use. The Chemical Group will incur start-up expenses of over $2 million in fiscal 1982 for an advanced marketing and product information system. A major computer expansion already under way in Wine & Spirits will provide that group with an advanced automated order system

> **G**iven our capital resources, our diversity and the position of market leadership we enjoy in all of our major business segments, we have a wide choice of options as we pursue our goals.

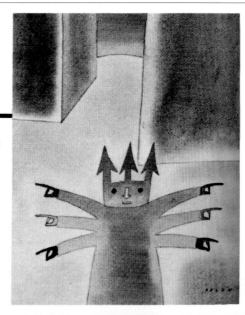

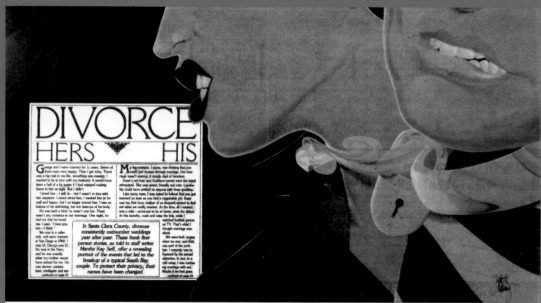

070 Cal Today, 1981

071 Life, 1981

VOICES **REAGANOMICS**

We are threatened with an economic calamity of tremendous proportions, and the old business-as-usual treatment can't save us. —Ronald Reagan

The idea that has been established over the past 10 years, that almost every service that someone might need in life ought to be provided, financed by the government as a matter of basic right, is wrong. We reject the notion. —David Stockman

Wall Street is full of Keynesians. They still cannot understand how a tax cut will be anything other than inflationary. I'm going to educate them. —Treasury Secretary Donald Regan

I do believe a lot of your assumptions are bull-oriented. —Rep. Thomas Downey to Donald Regan

By morning I'll be hung in effigy. The screams will be heard from border to border and coast to coast. —Ronald Reagan, just before sending his proposed spending cuts to Congress

This isn't a budget document—this is a document of reaction, with all the whims and prejudices of a little group of willful men. —House Majority Leader Jim Wright

Don't just stand there, undo something. —Murray Weidenbaum, chairman, Council of Economic Advisers

It's like rubbernose shots. It's really going to hurt, but I know if we don't get it, we are going to die. —Wisconsin Governor Lee Dreyfus, on Reagan's budget

The most costly roll of the dice ever proposed for this nation. —AFL-CIO President Lane Kirkland, on the Reagan budget

Only an ostrich could have missed the contradictions in Reaganomics. —economist Walter Heller

When it comes to giving tax breaks to the wealthy of this country, the President has a heart of gold. —Speaker Tip O'Neill

We won't stand still when our programs are gutted, our jobs taken away and our dreams deferred. —Urban League President Vernon Jordan

I have no early morning for you. Sell everything. Market top has been reached. —stock analyst Joseph Granville

I never found that Wall Street is a source of good economic advice. —Ronald Reagan

Do you realize the greed that came to the forefront? The hogs were really feeding. The greed level, the level of opportunities, just got out of control. [The administration's] basic strategy was to match or exceed the Democrats, and we did. —David Stockman, on the tax-cut battle in Congress

They still won't believe us, but we are going to balance this budget by 1984. —Ronald Reagan, September

I did not come here to balance the budget—not at the expense of my tax-cutting and defense programs. If we can't do it in 1984, we'll have to do it later. —Ronald Reagan, November

Our proposal is not a "rich man's windfall," as some have falsely charged. —Ronald Reagan

Kemp-Roth was always a Trojan horse to bring down the top rate.... It's kind of hard to sell "trickle-down," so the supply-side formula was the only way to get a tax policy that was really "trickle-down." —David Stockman

I think there's a slight recession, and I hope a short recession. —Ronald Reagan

All of us—the administration, the Congress and the American people—are going to be bone tired from the budget battles over the next few years. —Ronald Reagan

None of us really understands what's going on with all these numbers. —David Stockman

VOICES **AMERICA**

075 The Boston Globe, 1984

ETHIOPIA
Famine and flight

A guerrilla from the
Tigray People's Liberation
Front crosses the
cracked surface of the
dried-out Gash River
in Tigray Province.

Stan Grossfeld and
Colin Nickerson in Ethiopia
Photo by Gary Fairman

Design by Lucy Bartholomay

The Boston Globe

ETHIOPIA

Famine and flight

'The great dying has begun.
The more people who stay here, the
more people who will die.'

Refugees, above, fleeing to food
relief camps in Sudan, move down
a dried-out riverbed in Tigray
Province, Ethiopia.

This special section is
an account of suffering people
as seen by Globe staff reporter
Colin Nickerson and Globe staff
photographer Stan Grossfeld,
who returned to Boston
from a two-week journey into
rebel-held Tigray Province
in Ethiopia.

As seen in most works of science fiction the attempt to dismember man through transfer of his human functions to the machine-city runs aground on an irreducible, undeniable human core.

creative dynamic at its core as the opposition between closure and openness itself. Here, to embrace the city as finality is, as its name implies, a dangerous. And yet there are many forms of exile in this work, and all of them — from city or garden, earth or outer space, past or future — are separations that instantly command a return. In another example the propensity of science fiction to adapt the site — an impulse to its own purpose, seeking to bring open sidedness out of man's primordial desire to enclose and end, can be measured in the landscape of Clifford Simak's classic novel *City*. Here, suspended between a waning mankind sealed in his city-tomb of Geneva, and the measuring rise of an ant society spreading their monoliths: at-edge of "building" across the face of the earth, the open world of robots and dogs contemplates its future. It is better than one should lose a world than go on killing. There is yielding, but no end of ends. In the course of this novel men have gone to Jupiter and changed their bodies to adapt to its conditions, dogs have learned their was into another dimension and back — in all of its city enclosures there is always a door leading somewhere else to be found. Through out 10,000 years of interchange between its various races and between urban and agrarian options, there has always been displacement, but never finality, no lasting utopian or dystopian, but always new worlds for old.

Few critics of traditional utopia share the open-ended ness, let alone the open-mindedness of science fiction. Frank and Fritzie Manuel for instance in their monumental *Utopian Thought in the Western World* view science fiction negatively, as the sign of a waning of the "utopian propensity" in our scientific century. They state their case thus: "What distresses a critical historian today is the discrepancy between the piling up of technological and extatile instrumentalities for making all things possible, and the pitiable poverty of goals." In the eyes of science fiction however the goals of the utopian propensity seem quite clear. Brutal — disembodied, brain, Orwell's totalitarian machine, the end of all human sense of man, biologically and spiritually. It is precisely because our goals have become unthinkable that science fiction's fascination with means is so important, for it incarnates, in the midst of our endings, the will not to end, the survival of at least a hope for progress at the heart of the defeatism that informs

076 Arts & Architecture, 1984

077 The New York Times Magazine, 1984

The New York Times Magazine

WHAT WE REALLY KNOW ABOUT RUSSIA
By Leslie H. Gelb

078 Industrial Design, 1984

079 Fortune, 1984

080 The Boston Globe Magazine, 1984

DRAW THE COWBOY

Test your art skills! No tracing allowed!

I remember seeing this drawing for the first time in the back of a Batman comic book when I was six. It was an ad for one of those art correspondence schools. I couldn't read all the promises it made, but that didn't matter. I had to draw that cowboy. My mother drew it too. Later, we entered hers—in my name. After a few very long weeks the reply came. I was too young for the school, it said, but the drawing showed real talent. And even though it was my mom's talent, not mine, I kept on drawing.

I guess almost every kid who thought he could draw did this; it was an introduction to both the commercial and the competitive sides of art. We've asked twenty of the finest illustrators around to draw that same cowboy. We're pretty excited about the results, but then, for most of these artists, it wasn't their first time.
—Fred Woodward

081 Texas Monthly, 1984

PALE FIRE

BY
Wendy
Goodman

PHOTOGRAPHED
BY
Tony
McGee

*Linen shift by Shamask
Couture, about $100 at
Alms [840 Madison
Avenue, at 70th] and Saks
Fifth Avenue. Model: Lara
Young, of Elite Model
Management.*

*Nineteenth-century French
hand-painted screen from
Rose Cumming, Inc.*

MARCH 5, 1984/NEW YORK 43

082 New York, 1984

083 Mother Jones, 1984

084 Mother Jones, 1984

Portraits in POWER

Photography by HELMUT NEWTON

THE TEXAS ESTABLISHMENT IN ITS NATURAL HABITAT. "Isn't it wonderful that foreign places always look the way you imagine them," Helmut Newton said one night while walking through a livestock barn at the Travis County Stock Show. "You go to Tahiti, and it looks just like a Gauguin. You go to Texas, and it's a scene from *Dallas* or *Giant*."

For Newton, a European who has captured the public imagination by translating private, often dark fantasies into compelling photographs, Texas meant power—tycoons, people who were larger than life. He had photographed royalty, the rich, the famous, and some of the most beautiful women in the world. He had shocked the worlds of fashion, art, and photography when he published photos of fashion models coming down the runway, first dressed, then nude. Personally a charming, cultivated man, he brought the kink of sadomasochism to fashion photography and made pictures that were art. But nothing struck Newton as more exotic than Texas, and nothing was more romantic than the Texas millionaire.

086 New York, 1985

FAST FOOD

CAVIAR PETROSSIAN PARIS

THE BEST BUILDING TOP

TENOR

PLACE TO TAKE OUT-OF-TOWNERS

THE BEST BARBER

THE BOXER AND THE BLONDE

This is the story of Billy Conn, who won the girl he loved but lost the best fight ever

BY FRANK DEFORD

BILLY CONN

Lou turned the boxer a "Gaelic pink," and Hollywood had a part for him

088 The New York Times Magazine, 1985

089 Rolling Stone, 1985

PHOTOGRAPH BY ALBERT WATSON

CLINT EASTWOOD

PRECISELY TWO DECADES AGO, A FRIEND OF MINE INSISTED I GO SEE A MOVIE about the American West, a film made in Italy and shot partially in Spain. At the time, it was intellectually acceptable to be passionate about Italian films that limned the sick soul of Europe; the idea of an Italian western was oxymoronic – at best, like, oh, a German romantic comedy. What's more, in America the western as a genre seemed bankrupt, and going to see *A Fistful of Dollars*, which featured an international no-star cast headed by Clint Eastwood, some second-banana cowboy on an American TV series called *Rawhide*, promised to be entertaining in a manner the director, another unknown named Sergio Leone, probably never intended.

My friend was a graduate student in philosophy, and she'd seen the movie three times because she thought it was "existential." The Clint Eastwood

character was called the Man with No Name, and he went around rescuing people for no stated reason and outdrawing ugly, sweating bad guys who insulted his smile.

A lot of the violence was stylized, tongue-in-cheek comic-book mayhem, and you couldn't take it very seriously, though several critics did just that, describing the film as "simple, noisy, brutish." This sort of abusive critical reaction didn't keep audiences away, but it did rather dampen the enthusiasm of philosophy majors who had seen unsatterings of Sartre in the Man with No Name.

Clint Eastwood starred in two more of the movies that came to be called spaghetti westerns, then he swelt back to Hollywood in 1967 to make *Hang 'Em High*, another popular success in spite of critical reactions like "crude,

THE ROLLING STONE INTERVIEW • BY TIM CAHILL

A guy leans over the partition that divides our banquette from his and calls out: "Hey, Donald, I want a piece of that deal"

At first Trump was enthusiastic about discussing The Subject. But then he had severe second thoughts about it. He wanted to cancel the lunch

PHOTOGRAPHS BY GEORGE LANGE

091 Manhattan, Inc., 1985

Lincoln West will be "the biggest project in the history of the city. It'll be the most spectacular project ever..."

Trump was worried about revealing the full extent of his involvement in the delicate—and explosive—subject. "I'm dealing at a very high level on this."

NOVEMBER 1985 143

Trump has strong feelings about the Coliseum deal Zuckerman made. But they are closer to ridicule than regret

Trump is a bit like the Ancient Mariner here at "21," a stranger at the feast. Will the dove of peace become his albatross?

MANHATTAN, INC.

NOVEMBER 1985 143

141

092 Life, 1986

142

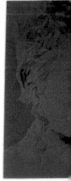

THE
CREATIVE
IMITATION

RICH
ORIENTAL
OVERTONE

094 Connoisseur, 1986

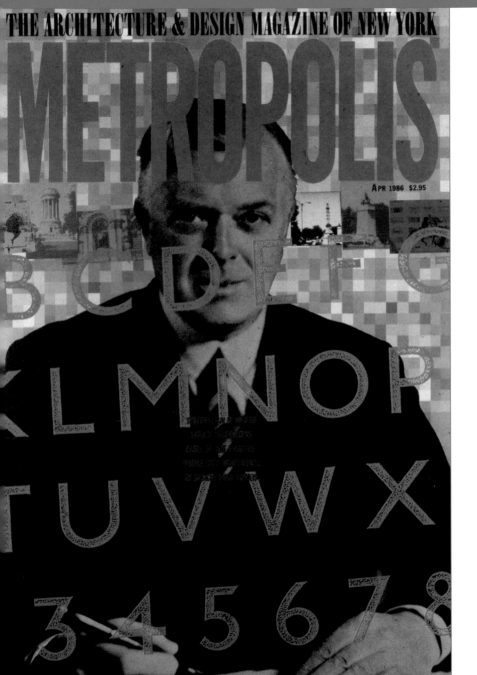

THE ARCHITECTURE & DESIGN MAGAZINE OF NEW YORK

METROPOLIS

APR 1986 $2.95

095 Metropolis, 1986

096 New York, 1986

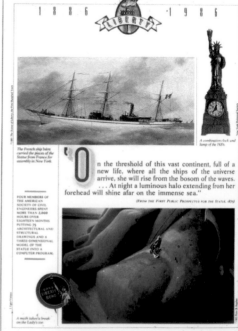

Venice

By Erica Jong

I IS LIKE NO OTHER PLACE ON EARTH. You arrive from Tokyo, New York, Paris, Delhi, Seattle, Rio, Rome, and the first thing you notice, descending from whatever vehicle has brought you — train, plane, automobile — is that your feet rock a little with the rhythm of the slowly moving surface. For this is the lagoon city (or rather it is two cities: one above and seemingly solid, one below and reflected in the waters), and that slight wobble tells you everything about its essence. It is the city of mirrors, the city of mirages, of once solid and liquid, at once air and stone. The stones themselves are thick with history, and those cats that dash through the alleyways must surely be the ghosts of the famous dead in feline disguise.

Many noted artists, after all, died here. Wagner, Browning, Diaghilev — though some, like Dante, merely died of medicine contracted on their last visit. These illustrious deaths have given the city a certain spooky patina and a faintly macabre reputation — like New Orleans, only more so. Or maybe it is the time-stopped nature of the place, the fact that in many miles still look exactly as they do in Carpaccio or Bellini paintings (except for the television antennas, of course) which gives the sense that you can turn a corner and walk into the past — so its accompanying photographs by Michael O'Neill illustrate.

The first time I came to Venice I was 19 and a student of it bells began in Florence. I came alone, by second-class railway carriage, clutching a small spiral notebook in one hand and a

Erica Jong has just completed a novel set in Venice.

THE MEETING OF THE
MASKS, CARNIVAL TIME,
PIAZZA SAN MARCO.

PHOTOGRAPHS BY MICHAEL O'NEILL

ball point pen in the other, for I already knew that Venice existed in part for English-speaking writers to write about. Shakespeare, Byron, Browning, Ruskin, James, all had succumbed to its spell.

I came down the steps of the railroad station and was at once astounded and elated by the gleaming band of water at their feet. (I had yet to see the dead cats floating in the canals, or the rare sewage, or the masses of detergent bubbles, or the plastic bottles.)

I was breathless with the idea and the reality of Venice, and their breathlessness has never quite left me — despite the fact that I now prize La Serenissima far too well to be a rhapsodist merely of her beauties. Still, on my many return visits, I have never failed to re-experience that first burst of elation, that start of recognition, part physical, part literary.

On my first trip to Venice, I remember sitting in the Piazzetta reading Byron, amazed to be just a stone's throw from the place that inspired these words:

I stood in Venice, on the "Bridge of Sighs";
A Palace and a prison on each hand:
I saw from out the wave her structures rise
As from the stroke of the Enchanter's wand:
A thousand Years their cloudy wings expand
Around me, and a dying Glory smiles
O'er the far times, when many a subject land
Look'd to the winged Lion's marble piles,
Where Venice sate in state, throned on her hundred isles!

And then a very Venetian thing happened. A young man, attracted by my dreamy expression, the poetry I was reading...

the notebook, or something sensual in the ancient stones themselves, came up to me bearing a bunch of violets.

He was a tourist, too, a Croatian doctor from Australia, and he was shy — not the sort of parvenu who accosts American college girls with violets. As we spent the day touring the palaces, the works of art, I realized that only Venice could have released him from his shyness. Venice does that to people. Just as it releases their longings, it also allows unpredictable things to happen.

One summer night two years ago, I was dining with friends at a little outdoor restaurant on a canal in Dorsoduro. A friend offer to try his boat, a brightly colored Torcello fishing boat, stopped to join us for coffee, and then invited us for a ride along the back canals at midnight. One of our party was a violinist from the Fenice Theater, and he took on his fiddle, sat crosslegged on the prow of the boat and played Mozart for us. As we rowed through the maze of little canals, the oars dipping and splashing in the inky water, the music filling the air, Venetians opened their windows and came out on their balconies to shout, "Bravo!"

The mythical Venice may be hard to grasp on a sunny day in midsummer when this city of 100,000 seems to recede to that number with the tourists milling about the Piazza San Marco, feeding scruffy pigeons, having their pockets picked, listening to wheezy bands playing "New York, New York" or the mediocre renditions of 1960's rock music in the Piazzetta. But

IN WATER, PIAZZA SAN MARCO

PROTECTING FURNITURE IN A FLOODED PALAZZO.

097 The New York Times Magazine, 1986

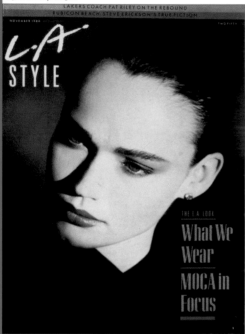

LAKERS COACH PAT RILEY ON THE REBOUND
RUBICON BEACH, STEVE ERICKSON'S TRUE FICTION

NOVEMBER 1986

L.A. STYLE

THE L.A. LOOK

What We Wear

MOCA in Focus

A HOLLYWOOD STORY FROM

Rubicon Beach

FICTION BY STEVE ERICKSON

THE EDGARS' HOUSEKEEPER, Catherine, managed to put the kitten behind her back just as Llewellyn Edgar walked into the service area looking for clean laundry. Llewellyn was athletic-looking like his wife; in a couple of years he'd be forty but he didn't show his age. He had light longish brown hair and a mustache. Catherine steeled herself to the impact of his regard.

A NEW GENERATION OF JUDGES AND OFFICIALS
has declared all-out war on the Mafia in Sicily. The
battle is being waged in the courts, in the political arena
and in the streets of Palermo, Sicily's principal city. Two
photographers, Letizia Battaglia from Palermo and
Franco Zecchin, a Milanese, in the course of working for
a Sicilian daily newspaper, L'Ora, joined the campaign,
seeking to inform and educate the public about the
Mafia. For the last six years, they have
been documenting the violence and
corruption synonymous with the Mafia and
recording the arduous struggle to make
justice, at long last, prevail on the island.

SICILY and the MAFIA

Photographs by Letizia Battaglia and Franco Zecchin

Secretly weeping, Vincenzo Sabia, a Mafioso, attends a defiant pose during the trial that led to his conviction on drug charges. At right, nuns mingles with tears at the funeral of a Sicilian banker who was killed for favoring the wrong Mafia faction.

For years, the Mafia
seemed to act with
impunity. Empowered
by new, tougher laws,
and using informers
willing to break the
traditional code of silence,
Italian prosecutors are on the
offensive, risking their lives
to save their countrymen's.

Defendants in a 1983 trial, above, in Palermo. When the jury returned verdicts that were unprecedentedly severe, the Mafia's mythic invulnerability began to crumble, and its grip on Sicily to loosen.

At left: A trial in the town of Caltanissetta of a man accused of the murder of Rocco Chinnici, a judge in Palermo. It was one of many attacks that have been made on officials and judges. Case is still pending.

Right: The body of Benedetto Grado, who was murdered a year after his son. Both were victims of the escalating clash between rival Mafia factions over the soaring revenues from the international drug trade.

099 The New York Times Magazine, 1986

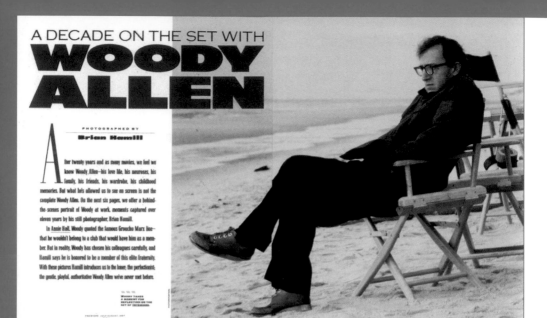

A DECADE ON THE SET WITH
WOODY ALLEN

PHOTOGRAPHED BY
Brian Hamill

After twenty years and as many movies, we feel we know Woody Allen—his love life, his neuroses, his family, his friends, his wardrobe, his childhood memories. But what he's allowed us to see on screen is not the complete Woody Allen. On the next six pages, we offer a behind-the-scenes portrait of Woody at work, moments captured over eleven years by his still photographer, Brian Hamill.

In Annie Hall, Woody quoted the famous Groucho Marx line—that he wouldn't belong to a club that would have him as a member. But in reality, Woody has chosen his colleagues carefully, and Hamill says he is honored to be a member of this elite fraternity. With these pictures Hamill introduces us to the loner, the perfectionist, the gentle, playful, authoritative Woody Allen we've never met before.

WOODY TAKES A MOMENT FOR REFLECTION ON THE SET OF INTERIORS.

100 Premiere, 1987

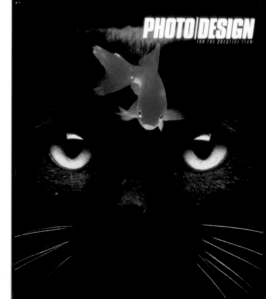

101 Photo/Design, 1987

PRESIDENTIAL ✦ SWEEPSTAKES

GEORGE
BUSH

THE VICE PRESIDENT RODE
TO THE TOP WITH
RONALD REAGAN. WILL HE NOW
FOLLOW HIM DOWN

BY JAMES HORWITZ

PRESIDENTIAL ✦ SWEEPSTAKES

ALBERT
GORE

THE SENATOR'S ROOTS
MAY BE ON A TENNESSEE FARM,
BUT AT HEART HE'S
A WASHINGTON ANIMAL

BY GARRETT EPPS

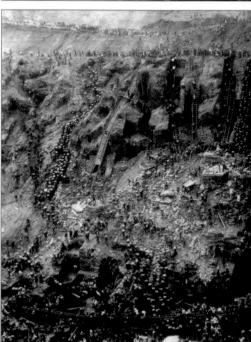

103 The New York Times Magazine, 1987

152

T he Serra Pel-
ada mine is divided into 6,400 small
claims whose owners glean most of
the profits. An elected committee
administers the mine and the town;
it has so far accredited 61,000 workers. Laborers, who are paid a stan-
daily wage, often receive a small percentage of their finds. The mine is
being worked entirely by hand. And
it is constantly changing in shape as
laborers carve into the plots, wash
the earth and haul it up to be dis-
carded or plundered. The sound of
Serra Pelada is a persistent, work-a-
day hum, punctuated at times —
when the land slides, when a worker
falls, a fight breaks out or someone
strikes gold — by screams.

PANNING *for gold, Brazilian miners hardly differ from the 49'ers in California more than a century ago.*

ING *sacks of earth from the crater earns laborers a daily wage and, perhaps, a percentage of their finds.*
NY STEP, *workers mount crude wooden ladders, left, to haul their loads out of the 600-foot-deep pit.*

153

104 Art Center Review #2, 1987

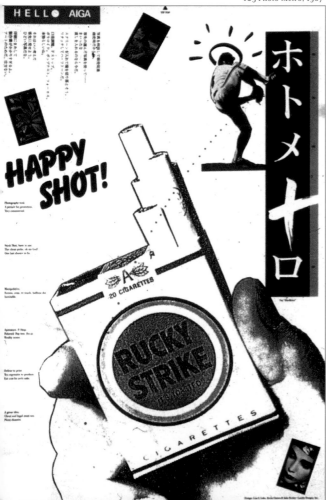

IMAGES

1967 · 1987

YOKO ONO AND JOHN LENNON *by Annie Leibovitz*

JANUARY 22ND, 1981

106 Rolling Stone, 1987

JACK NICHOLSON

I still get high. I still like to have a good time with the women. That's not where it's at today.

*P*EOPLE *lately are very nostalgic for the Sixties. Do you feel that way?*

No. I don't feel like it's the past. It doesn't seem a distance removed or a big change. We're only one turn up and down with hair on twenty years. And that's about the depth of it. I always feel public perceptions are a little distorted anyway. I didn't like the nostalgia that they had in the Sixties for the Thirties and Forties. I'm not a nostalgic kind of person, although I'm very sentimental.

So there's nothing you're nostalgic about?

I'm nostalgic for my former weight.

You must see some differences between the Sixties and the Eighties besides fashion.

Let me put it this way. In 1967 you could hear Krishnamurti in the Oak Grove, at Ojai. Now he's on channel C in New York City between the porno shows.

Do you think the sexes have changed significantly in the last twenty years?

I think the biggest thing in terms of youth culture is AIDS. I think AIDS is a real issue. I think the Persian Gulf versus solar electricity and the environment is a real issue. I think lying to yourself about substance control and creating a criminal class that corrupts the legal system is a real issue.

Whether a Democrat, which I am, or a Republican, which I am not, is elected next year, I don't think it's as critical as any one of those things. I think conglomeration as a real quality-of-life issue. If you know what America looks like today, you know one other than Coca-Cola to be deciding what is germane about a movie and what is not. I tend this in order for me to function. And it isn't goin' that way.

Which way is it going?

Demographics. It's annihilating. And there's no remuneration. My livelihood is being eaten alive by demographics.

By that do you mean television versus movies?

I say it about sports, I say it about life. It's a demographic principle. Don't bet against it if it's good for

PHOTOGRAPH BY HERB RITTS

television. That's what America's become, I think. The phrase *free television* is the greatest lie that we live under in the world. Free television. I read that Procter and Gamble had a $900 million advertising budget, and this is one company.

So your biggest problem with American culture is TV?

Well, I've written it in my work. In *Drive, He Said,* the radical is watching the astronaut parade on television, and he's taken a lot of drugs to beat the draft, and he stands up, pulls a sword off the wall, holds it over the television and says, "This is the instrument of the death of our times." Then he hits it with the sword and throws it out the window.

And he is very satisfying for you.

Yeah. This is how I feel. I'm an anachronism. I feel like an old fart in the theater that comes out and says, "Ooh, are these talking pictures? This is a tragedy." Do you know what I mean? But you know, television is not going to go away. Talented people are going to work in it to make livelihoods and so forth. There's no denying that, so my point of view is kind of hopeless. I mean, I know I'm not gonna win. People become moved. They don't believe anything happened if they don't see it on television. It just doesn't exist.

Did you watch the Iran-contra hearings on television? What did you think of them?

I thought they were fantastic. If I had to hit Washington as an outsider, I wouldn't be an outsider because of these hearings. Because you can be in the papers, you can be anywhere, but you can't be to me in front of a camera, 'cause I know what you're thinking. It's thirty years of very specialized training.

What did you think of Oliver North?

I think he's a character actor. He's a great front man. All the outlaws like Oliver North – and I'm an outlaw personality, so I'm supposed to like him. I like a person who just says, "Hey, I'm sorry, but I gotta get this done." This is movie thinking in a way. This is the way you have to work as a production person in movies. It's all well and good, but come Thursday, you've got to get that one and that leads and that strees or else that's it. There's no in-between.

Do you support any of the Democrats currently running for president?

Not specifically. The top candidates in the Democratic party today – Hart, Kennedy and Cuomo – all declared themselves out of the race. You know, that's

107 Goucher College Annual Report, 1988

"There are no weird stories about rats," George Laws said. And then he told some. We sat at the edge of the teeming ratopolis in a basement where the city's rathunters unwind after a day going into holes with rats. The air was choked with smoke, music and the legend of that four-legged shadow of man. If rat stories did not seem weird to Laws, a foreman of exterminators for the city of New York, it was because nothing rats do surprises him. If the stories seemed weird to me, it was because I had just started collecting them. Not the commonplace assertions: that for every one of us there is one, or two, or four of them (perhaps 30 million rats in the city of New York?), or that they can squeeze through holes the size of a quarter, or that they pop up in toilets. Old news. The idea was to view the range of human experience involving rats, to dip a bucket into that polluted river! "Plastic means to a rat like a rattle to a baby," said Laws. "Any hole a rat can put his head through, he can put his body through." "They don't have no bone, just **BY PHILIP WEISS** gristle," said someone else. This was a rat myth. "The head's the only bone. She'll cut a hole for her head and cut it no wider and pull the rest of her body through." "Like a liquid?" "Not liquid. I wouldn't use that word." "You can put down bait from now till doomsday, you'll never kill them all." "How's that stuff work?" "His own blood drowns him. See him moving slowly, trembling just like a person having a heart attack." "Eat chicken like we eat chicken, eat bacon just like we eat bacon." "Man has been living wrong as far as sanitation is con-

They live in our walls. They wait for our trains. They are our food. They furnish their nests with our detritus. They chew through our sheet metal, our food survive our dogs. They are here when we're gone. They'll be here when we're gone. They are our enemy, our shadow, our next-door neighbor. They were here before we were. They were here pipes and our concrete. They a

109 Italian Vogue, 1988

TRASPARENZA

*Protagonista di infiniti
ricorrente nella moda.
Vela e svela i caratteri della
è vetro, cellophane, perspex,
la più inafferrabile
suggestioni moderne.*

*giochi visivi. È un tema
nell'arte e nel design.
seduzione. La trasparenza
garza e chiffon. Ma anche
e misteriosa delle
di Mariuccia Casadio*

110 Italian Vogue, 1988

111 Italian Vogue, 1988

112 Italian Vogue, 1988

161

113 Fannie Mae–Home Annual Report, 1988

114 Arena, 1988

115 Life, 1988

163

CITY OF LOST BOYS

Driven from Sudan's
farms and villages by
civil war, famine and
poverty, some 10,000
children scratch out a
precarious existence on
the streets of Khartoum

116 Life, 1988

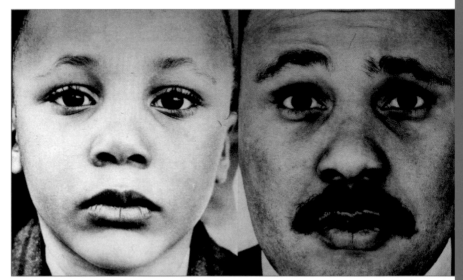

117 Rolling Stone, 1988

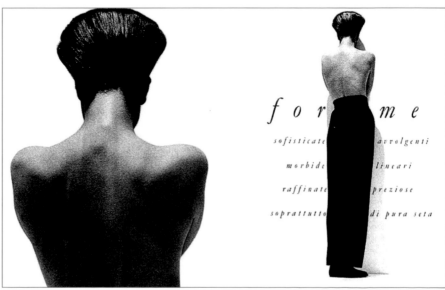

for me

sofisticate *avvolgenti*

morbide *lineari*

raffinate *preziose*

soprattutto *di pura seta*

118 Italian Vogue, 1988

FOUR CENTURIES OF HARVESTING SUGAR

CUBA

Photographer Sebastiao Salgado captures the toil and camaraderie in the country's cane fields

His documentation of vanishing ways of work has now taken Salgado to a sugar plantation near Havana. First cultivated in the late 1500s, sugarcane accounts for 75 percent of Cuba's exports. Though the industry has been mechanized since the 1959 revolution, a third of the crop still is harvested by hand. From December through May, 100,000 men slash from sunrise to sunset. Most leave regular jobs for the fields. The pay is better than the national average of $180 a month, and the labor is considered patriotic. "They believe the worker is the real base of their system," says Salgado. A man can cut 5,000 pounds of cane in eight hours. A machine does three times that amount in 15 minutes. Clearly, the days of the machete-wielding army are numbered.

The technique—chop and slash—and the tools are still the same. "These men love the macho ambience," says Salgado, "and the cutting."

Tractors and oxen are used to scoop up felled cane. Fields are burned the night before harvest to rid the cane of leaves—goggles are worn because of ash and cinder.

Coarse working preburn hair and skin from sugar made sticky by the island's humidity. Workers in a refinery clean turbines that burn spent cane stalks to produce steam.

In the field since five a.m, workers head back to barracks at set p.m. Music often follows... dinner. When asked what they do when not working Salgado says "Others sing."

119 Life, 1988

Privatizing
Public
Services

Many U.S. state and local governments now contract out
for public services. It's a good solution … but not for everyone,
an E&W engagement finds

by Stanley
Ginsberg

The photo at right is Charles Herman, a firefighter with Rural/ Metro Corp., a private fire company employed by the city of Scottsdale, Arizona.

(body text illegible)

Parsons Municipal Services Inc. operates the nation's first privately built, owned, and operated wastewater

treatment facility in Chandler, Arizona. Above, worker Rusty Radhan is shown cleaning an empty clarifier; next page, bus driver Peter Monzcoe, of Decamp Bus Lines, which handles municipal service in the Montclair, New Jersey, area.

(body text illegible)

Stanley Ginsberg is a business journalist who frequently writes on public policy issues.

The diversity of contracted services is vast, like the opposite

Neither Black nor White

(body text illegible)

A Matter of Money

(body text illegible)

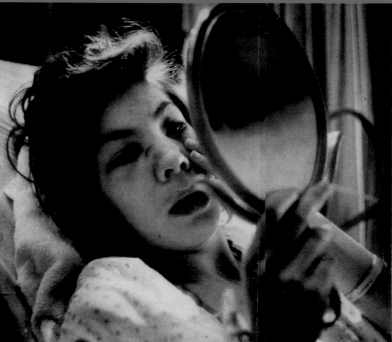

STOP! FOR GOD'S SAKE STOP!

Four million women are beaten by their partners each year. In Minnesota, battered women are fighting back

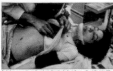

As doctors uncover the marks on her battered body, Duaté Armani calls out the name of the boyfriend who had run over her with his car. For the 24-year-old woman (the names of some of the people in this article have been changed) it was the culmination of three years of physical abuse. Left: Two days later she says, "Well, I guess I don't love too bad."

PHOTOGRAPHY DONNA FERRATO TEXT GEORGE HOWE COLT
REPORTING KAREN BRAILSFORD, ANNE HOLLISTER

121 Life, 1988

"I hate you! Don't you ever come back to my home," screams an eight-year-old boy at his father, in cases around the man for domestic abuse. Fifteen minutes earlier, the boy had dialed the police emergency number and yelled that his dad had a knife and was beating his mother. As the officers struggled to subdue the man, his son tried to pull them away. The boy and his mother moved out—but only for three weeks before they returned to the father.

M

THE HOLD HE USED WAS TAUGHT IN VIETNAM. HE TOLD ME IT KILLS WITHOUT LEAVING MARKS

'HE WAS SO SWEET. HE BOUGHT EACH OF MY DAUGHTERS A RED ROSE'

A 1984 STUDY SHOWED THAT ARREST IS THE MOST EFFECTIVE DETERRENT TO MEN WHO BATTER

He hasn't **CAN** had a big hit album in years. The other Beatles are suing him. **PAUL** But with 'Flowers in the Dirt,' his strong new record, **McCARTNEY** and plans for his first world tour in more than a decade, the **GET** ex-Beatle is doing his best to toughen up his image and climb back **BACK?** to the top.

BY JAMES HENKE

122 Rolling Stone, 1989

PART TWO: LIVING WITHOUT ENEMIES

Gorbachev wasn't just revolutionizing his own society; he was transforming ours as well. Since Stalin's day, the Soviets had played the perfect enemy. The evil Russian bear defined our national purpose and gave us a global mission. But here was Gorbachev declaring peace. Could we look at him and still see the face of the enemy? And what posed the greater threat, having an enemy or not having one? BY LAWRENCE WRIGHT

PEACE

123 Rolling Stone, 1989

April 10 1989 Volume 70 No 16

CONTENTS

A MONSTER FROM THE DEEP
No, that's not the creature from the Black Lagoon, it's Tennessee's Raymond Brown just before breaking the surface in the breaststroke leg of a 400-IM heat at the NCAAs (page 82)

Cheers! America's Best New Restaurants of 1989

Plus: Glenn Close, Marlon Brando, Ann Beattie, Tom Robbins, and More

Esquire

Man At His Best
November 1989 Price $2.50

How to Raise a Perfect Kid
A fearless handbook for fathers and fathers-to-be

126 Mohawk Paper Mills, 1989

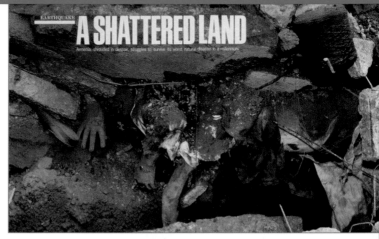

A SHATTERED LAND

Armenia, shrouded in despair, struggles to survive its worst natural disaster in a millennium

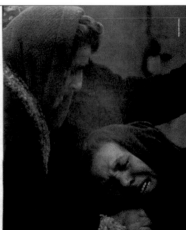

American safari: Eight ways West

T RAILS THROUGH MOUNTAIN MEADOWS AND CASCADING rivers invite you West this spring and summer. In our special issue, eight of America's finest writers are your guides to the adventures and beauties of the intermountain West, bordered by the Rockies on one side and the Cascades on the other. You can lose yourself, even by car, in the romantic solitude of the mountains and plains. Fish the rivers or float them in raft, seek out the wildlife; ride horseback, or lead the whole day through. In our on-page Traveler's File (page 195) we tell you in detail how to set about enjoying the grandeur and surprise of an American safari, when you can catch communal celebrations in Idaho, Montana, and Wyoming, and when there's the best chance of finding sunshine, cool air, and blue skies. Go West!

W WE TRAVEL WEST
in a motel
with a car
outside
chocked with
camping gear?
The Traveler
suggested we
drag it all
behind the
car on a
dirt road
so our wives
would dread
we used it

d DRIVING
offers peace,
solitude,
inaccessibility
(you can't
hit a moving
target).
Whimsicality
returns. Why
not continue
on down to
Mexico, hike
out the
Seri Indian
territory, and
camp on
a mountain
ridge under
a glorious
full moon?

PHOTOGRAPHS By RICHARD MISRACH

1990-

129 Rolling Stone, 1990

130 Beach Culture, 1990

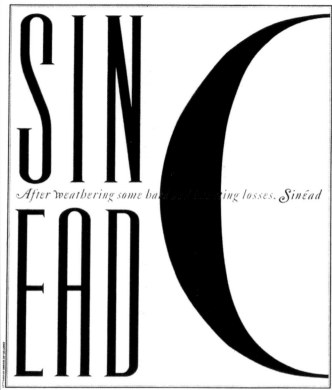

SIN EAD

After weathering some har̶ ̶a̶n̶d̶ ̶d̶a̶u̶nting losses, Sinéad

'CON NOR

O'Connor has emerg̶e̶d̶ ̶a̶s̶ ̶the decade's first new superstar

PHOTOGRAPHS BY ANDREW MACPHERSON

178

Faces

In an era of Polaroids and video cameras, this is still a place where having one's picture taken is a serious event.

I am a product of the border. My mother was from Juárez, my father from El Paso. I remained last year to follow in the tradition of *los ambulantes,* the itinerant photographers who work plazas and festivals throughout Mexico. The Mexican people on both sides of the border make great subjects. They just stand before the camera, unposed, as if to say, "Look at me. This is who I am." ▼ This is something we Americans have largely lost. In fact, we seldom have our picture taken anymore; even at our most sacred ceremonies—the wedding, the bar mitzvah, the graduation—we are videotaped.

When we do stand before the camera, we have learned to wear a mask. The photographer who asks us to smile is really saying, "I can't bear to see the real you." Afraid to reveal ourselves, we wear the mask. ▼ When we look at the pictures of our grandparents, in their wedding photo, for example there are not smiling. They are solemn, they are sincere. They have taken their wedding seriously. The photograph is not *coity-true*—it is capturing Mexicans still act this way before the camera. They do not smile—on *scenia.* For them, having their picture taken is still an event of great importance.

▼▼▼

Photography and Text by MAX AGUILERA-HELLWEG

of the

LUIS ALBERTO NIÑO VARGAS
▼▼▼
Twelve-Year-Old Boy, Ciudad Miguel Alemán

Border

JOSÉ LUCIANO AND GLORIA VERONICA GUEVARA
▼▼▼
Young Lovers, Ciudad Miguel Alemán

CRISTINA ESTRADA AND DAISY
▼▼▼
Familia, Nuevo Progreso

LEVI VALDEZ
▼▼▼
Laborer, Juárez

ROSA RAMIREZ
▼▼▼
Bar Dweller, Juárez

Reshaping the Global Economy

Staggered by the Persian Gulf crisis, jolted by the changes in the Eastern bloc, the world economy is in a state of fundamental flux.

Where the new lines of competition will be drawn is not yet clear — except that old military and political allegiances are being replaced by new economic ties. Some believe the new order will consist of three powerful centres — Europe, Japan and North America; others predict Europe and North America will be clearing houses for the Japanese juggernaut. But an idea too conveniently the Eastern bloc to capitalism is a key factor in the final architecture of the new economic world.

How clear, then, that just when socialist notions of Eastern gripe begin to shed their Marxist mantles, capitalist countries risk their only philosophical destiny: and economic point of not one appear to be tripping into a recession. After seven years of uninterrupted growth, the United States economy is freed shed by a real downturn. Consumption, traditionally the engine of American expansionism, can no longer be taken for granted. And the savings and loan debacle, coupled with poor showings by banks and the concerns brought on by insurance companies have led observers and investors to question the likelihood of a renewal for the American economy.

Further north, Canada, 75 per cent of whose international trade is with its powerful neighbour, is in no better shape. As Canadian leaders have acknowledged, the Canadian economy

By Serge Marti

L'Europe, remise par les changements survenus en Europe orientale, l'économie mondiale est dans un état de fondamentale...

133 Global, 1991

134 Life, 1990

There are places in America where childhood has ceased to exist. Where children taste crack before they taste life, then are born in a narcotic stupor. Where guns have replaced toys and a baseball bat is just another weapon. North Philadelphia is one such place, so surreal that police wear a badge that reads: "The land of Oz, where the abnormal is normal." A living nightmare, but one we must confront: Our kids are dying here.

CHILDREN OF THE DAMNED

Photography: Eugene Richards
Reporting and Text: Edward Barnes

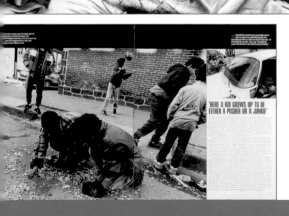

'HERE A KID GROWS UP TO BE EITHER A PUSHER OR A JUNKIE'

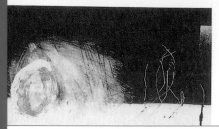

Purpose and Expected Outcomes

You will save a good deal of time and energy if you can first develop a clear sense of class purpose, of what you want students to achieve. Your chair will have given you an overview of departmental policy and suggested or required course content. Asking questions and getting answers *at the outset* is an absolute necessity. It may help to consult a syllabus or a course outline put together by an experienced instructor who is teaching, or has taught, the same or similar material. Talking with fellow teachers prior to setting goals and developing a week-by-week outline can help you plan and give you a better idea of how your course fits in with others in the department.

VIII. Ethics and Standards

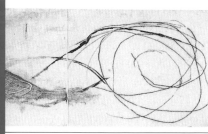

Clear as the meanings of such serious, high-minded terms as *ethics* and *standards* may be to most of us, a brief mention of the moral side of teaching as it applies to your experience at Art Center may be helpful. Let's examine some instances where personal integrity and preservation of standards are put to the test in the everyday business of teaching.

135 Teaching At Art Center Book, 1990

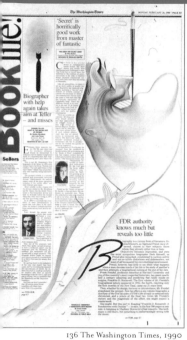

136 The Washington Times, 1990

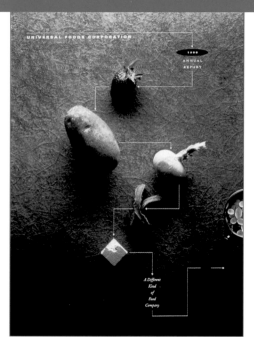

137 Universal Foods Corporation, 1990

138 Associated Press Annual Report, 1990

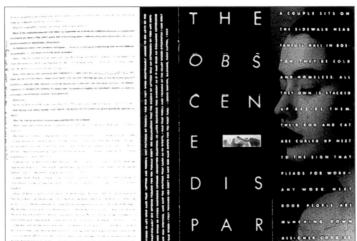

139 26–A Journal About Type & Typography, 1990

PERHAPS

ROMANIA'S
A Photo Essay by

LOST

James Nachtwey

CHILDREN

IN THE

First the dictator decreed that the children be born. Then his regime institutionalized them in degrading conditions.

ALTHOUGH

Five months after the revolution the situation is still disastrous, says a French doctor.

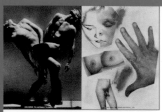

141 Ads Against AIDS, 1991

"Comedy is not pretty," Steve Martin once observed. Photographer Arthur Grace experienced that painful truth about 20 years ago when he tried stand-up for a week. As they say in the trade, he died every night. Still, he remained intrigued by the comic's craft. For more than a year Grace focused his camera on some of America's funniest men and women. In his book *Comedians* the portraits are as revealing as a punch line

"DAMN! They Gonna Lynch Us!"

That's what it felt like to Rodney Glenn King's passenger Pooh Allen when L.A.'s finest pulled the car over that terrible night in March. As it turned out, all that was missing was the rope

By Mike Sager

Pooh and Glenn and Freddie G. was kickin' it late that night outside Pooh's house, all three sitting in the car. The stars were out and the radio hummed blues into the cool March air. It was a typical Saturday on the wrong side of Altadena, near the border between the Bloods and the Crips; some homeboys, some reefer, some Old English 800, something ready to go down.

Glenn was behind the wheel of the white Hyundai, a four-door that belonged to his grandma. He stared out the windshield, worrying his sparse mustache. Freddie G. groaned in the backseat, his crippled leg snug in a metal brace. Pooh lounged behind Glenn, light-skinned, a little heavy, head angled forward to keep his Jheri curl from getting scrunched. It had been a long night. Sort of a reunion.

Glenn had been trying to hook up with Pooh all week. Tonight, he'd just come on by the house. Pooh was playing with his baby girl, half-watching television.

"What's up?" said Glenn. He'd walked over, slid Pooh some skin. He'd known Pooh since Little League. Through the years they'd lost touch on and off, but that's how it was in the neighborhood. You move a while, you move back, you pick right up. Glenn was

C omedy exists somewhere between ballet and door-to-door sales, although the French consider it an art form. But they also consider pastry an art form.

ROBIN WILLIAMS

I t's a profound evil. If it's been doing it so long it's almost second nature. You wake me up in the middle of the night. I can do forty minutes.

ALAN KING

GOLDEN GATE THEATER, SAN FRANCISCO, 1990

T here's something significant, talking about men and women in comedy. It's just that thing of standing up and being in control. First of all, very few women see themselves in that role, consciously or not. They just don't. To make people laugh is to be powerful, and women are not supposed to be powerful.

LILY TOMLIN

I

JERRY LEWIS

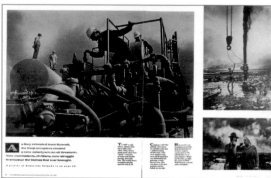

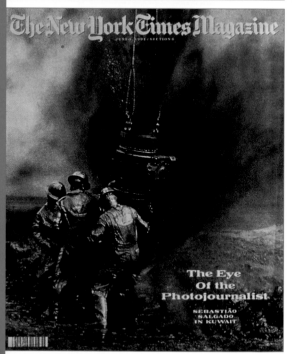

144 The New York Times Magazine, 1991

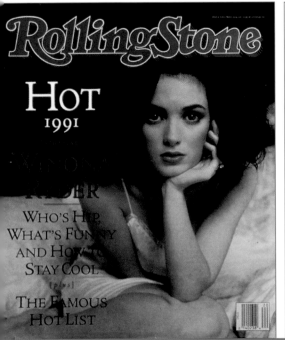

146 Rolling Stone, 1991

RS 617

'ALL THE NEWS THAT FITS'

ROCK & ROLL

COVER: Photograph of Metallica by Mark Seliger, Paris, September 1991. Grooming by Pada.

MILES DAVIS *Illustration by Philip Burke*

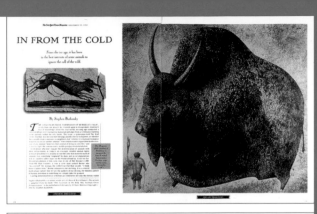

TIME

EVIL

**Does it exist — or
do bad things just happen?**

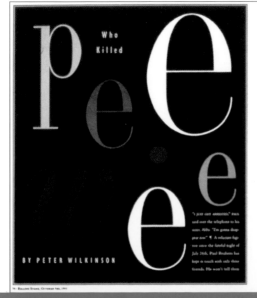

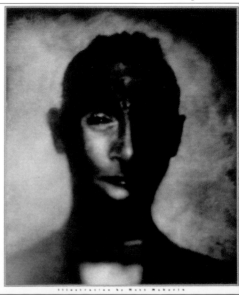

151 Rolling Stone, 1992

EYE
WITNESS

ALFRED EISENSTAEDT—born in Germany in 1898 and still going strong—is by no means a dense photographer. He is a public, credentialed photojournalist, a member of a magazine from its inception, who has specialized in famous people (politicians and notables) and poses are these taken on important and interesting events. His pictures, usually occasioned by his discriminating convictions, have been collected into several books. Graphically liberal volumes of ample visual that, today, seem to raise and alter the same. When these tonell a main occupation has been to document the people and the happenings that were the news of their time, the tens of the shots presented into the win too etching forever. The convention of his carteas with dance makers, dating from early to late years, created images of a heroic and a dance that are hard to resist.

TOBI TOBIAS

Left and above: Paris Opéra, early 1990s

dream
George C. Wolfe's
girls

is a smooth show
about a mythic music man.

Despite its title, this is not one of those funnily scripted revues that hit Broadway so often and so seem large ado—a villain production interests to watch. It is through the job is a new fangled, an attitudes of stiffness rfeatures this right, lighting effects, and clever framing, because. Although it too sounds stylistically at Tommy Tune's Grand Hotel. The Musical and, to a lesser intent, but rather has been its production fine Lookout Dangerously (strange and, Vincent parties important front) and Oan Oo The round James theatre famous, without really being its scrub-like any of them or this like a theatre. With its charismatic approaches to the stage set nothing but there have cannily been deconstructions. Always of seduction of Tyler fabulous—Peter Frankl's this. And let his face is that.

For almost all the next, time our people, Wolfe uses his own methods and lavishes these, a careful unbelievable seems around the Tren Undor terms—as Living actors. Always, there is just one lecture, and it takes up the entire space available. There is nothing to

Wolfe constructed
and then directed it.

Wolfe's conscious wisdom has a tad directing that own play or about to likely to produce success as conception the conceiving into own invet-erabelties in this case it couldn't be any wider way. The knit and her appearances are their seem of a carvas, and runs it's driven. If when one get in love, and so get us lost to gee′—a lot an occure for the visuals.

NANCY DALVA

For thousands of years we've been decorating our faces. But why? Tina Gaudoin debates the politics of MAKE UP

Never mind the adage men don't cry. In this culture (by and large), men don't wear makeup. Elementary? Well, think about it. In 1991 American women spent $4.7 billion on maquillage and millions of hours on the choice of products and their application. For most of us, that's probably dollars and time well spent. Nonetheless, it begs the question: Why, and for whom? Is makeup part of our mating ritual? A pleasure enhancer? Or is it our protection (physically and metaphorically) against the outside world? Do we wear it for ourselves or for others? And, perhaps most important, are we in danger of becoming makeup-dependent?

"If we did away with the cosmetics companies and advertising completely, women would reinvent the industry. Making up is quite literally in our genes; it's part of our genetic reproductive strategy," says Helen Fisher, Ph.D., an anthropologist at the American Museum of Natural

153 Harper's Bazaar, 1992

Wild

remember a time
when genders
were bent, rules
broken, inhibitions
shed, and all the
best girls were
pretty wild?

The Buffalo Girl tangles
with Sergeant Pepper.
This page: Velvet coat,
about $2495; white
organza blouse, about
$655; and black rayon
shorts, about $195. All
from Ozbek. Hat, Phillip
Treacy; necklace, Alan
McDonald, both for Ozbek.

154 Harper's Bazaar, 1992

195

155 The Washington Post Magazine, 1992

EXECUTIVE
GROOMING
101

In this introductory course,
Professor Alan Flusser will
instruct students in exactly what it takes to be a successful executive in American
today. Pencils, and monkey wrenches required. By Joanne Alan Lader

There is no mystery about inward being in a strong   you thinking about inward stress onward brings
field it is naturally determined to what the mind it   as I sit through the opening hours of "Project-
—George Ott   ing a Positive Executive Image," course No. 2374-002 at the American Management Association's Washington
center on First Street SW. This is a two-day executive grooming seminar intended to teach you the ways of
corporate America, so that you can blend in, become accepted and climb the ladder leading over up.

PHOTO ILLUSTRATION BY GEOF KERN

156 Parenting, 1992

157 Details, 1992

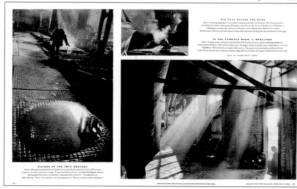

KAZAKHSTAN'S
DARK
SATANIC
MILLS

A PHOTO ESSAY
BY
SEBASTIÃO
SALGADO

The New York Times Magazine

DECEMBER 6, 1992 / SECTION 6

SOMALIA 1992

A PHOTO ESSAY BY JAMES NACHTWEY

159 The New York Times Magazine, 1992

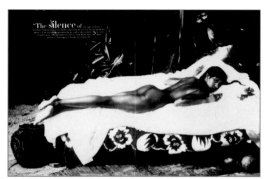

"**in
my**solitude here,
I have what is needed
to recharge my forces.
Here, poetry exudes from
everywhere.... One has only
to drift away into a dream
to find inspiration."
—Paul Gauguin

Photographed by Peter Lindbergh

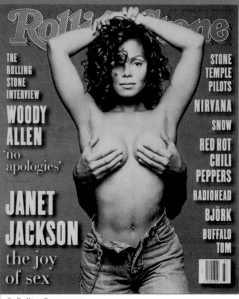

161 Rolling Stone, 1993

162 Rolling Stone, 1993

163 The New York Times Magazine, 1993

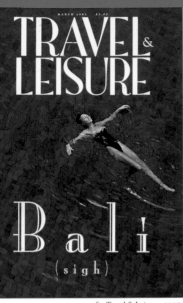

164 Travel & Leisure, 1993

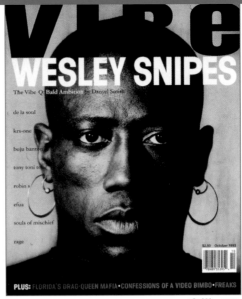

165 Vibe, 1993

166 GQ, 1993

167 Travel & Leisure, 1993

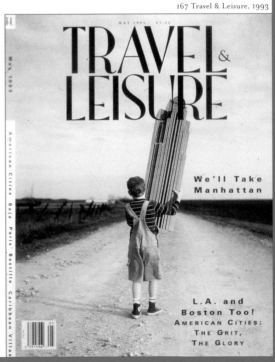

FAR AND AWAY

The wilds of west Ireland are the perfect setting for this season's rough and rugged fashions

W Fashion

168 W, 1993

202

169 Men's Journal, 1993

170 The New York Times Magazine, 1993

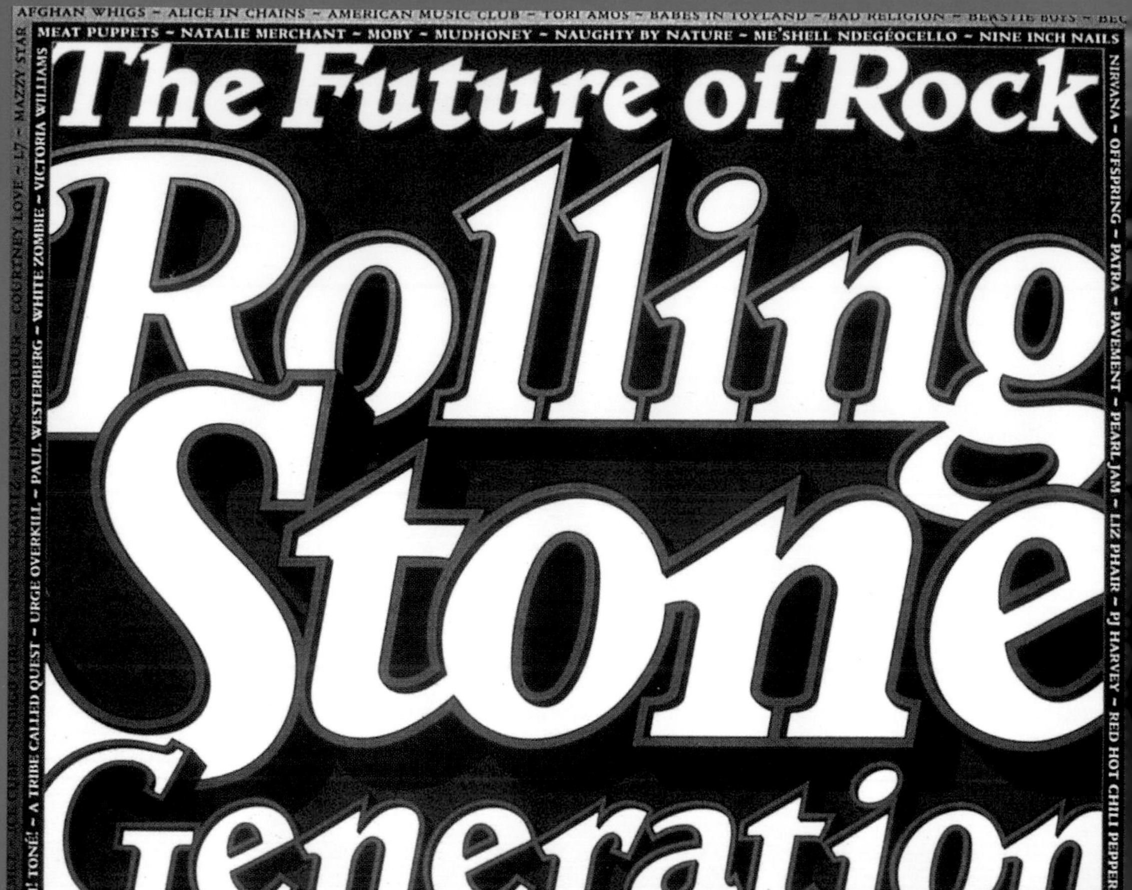

The Future of Rock

Rolling Stone

Generation

'Next

COLLECTORS' ISSUE

171 Rolling Stone, 1994

Seal / MeShell NdegéOcello

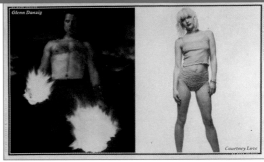

Glenn Danzig / Courtney Love

Frank Black / Babes in Toyland

Liz Phair / Henry Rollins

Juliana Hatfield

RWANDA

[The Death of a Nation]

Text: William Owen

Design in the a

"Multimedia" may well be one of the most overused words of

Text: Anne Burdick

ReVerb is a four-woman, one-man design team in the heart of
Los Angeles. In their conceptually based work, artificial disti
between "high" and "low" melt into an alternately grating a
concoction that reflects the discord and simultaneity of life in

A sense of
ruptur

A COLLAGE
writings of
Jean Cocteau

repackaged versions of old forms: electronic books, interactive magazines, interactive cinema – old wine in new bottles.

Interactive and multimedia are by no means synonymous. Does interactive simply mean making choices, and if so, is the act of choice creative in itself? Is the interactive machine a conveyance – a medium – or something of a higher order, a tool for production? And in relation to who is it interactive – a conversation, a book, a painting, a movie? We inevitably judge the new media within the context

of our experience of traditional forms of art and literature and often fail to make the distinction between the form of the work and its conveyance: between the novel and the printed page, the painting and the canvas, the movie and celluloid. Clearly the conveyance is dumb, but the notion that these forms involve no dialogue between artist and viewer and that the act of consumption is passive is false. In fact, the dialogue is simply inherent, it takes place through a process of public and private discussion, works of critical theory and media attention.

digital reproduction

it mean for designers, what has been achieved so far and where are we heading?

174 El Mundo, 1994

Sheer fabric at the shoulders allows the bride to be bare but will discreet. This long silk-monoelline dress by Donald Deal has tiny BOWS on the bodice, at the waist, and to back ($2,400). Earrings from Verdura. Opposite: STARS take the place of a veil (these are cluster pins from Verdura). Strapless sheath of silk taffeta with lace knots down the bodice from Donald Deal ($4,500).

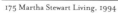
175 Martha Stewart Living, 1994

In deep, Nadja Auermann and Alexander Bangaud kick to kiss on St. Barts. Opposite page: Cream silk dress, Martine Sitbon. This page: White silk jersey blouse, about $575, worn over a white romper, about $325. Both, Anne Klein by Richard Tyler. Photographs by Patrick Demarchelier.

Avedon began his career at *Harper's Bazaar.* A Whitney Museum retrospective chronicles the life of this unparalleled artist. On these pages he comes home again. By Amy Fine-Collins Produced by Wendy Goodman

Next: It's Short & Sexy, Sensuous Knits, Wild Colors, Dreamy Dresses, Hard or Soft Fitness Meryl Streep: Margaritas, Movies, and Her Life Avedon's One Man Show: The Bazaar Years

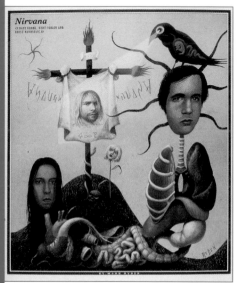

177 Rolling Stone, 1994

178 Rolling Stone, 1994

179 Harper's Bazaar, 1994

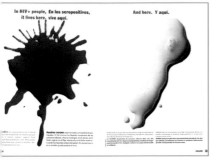

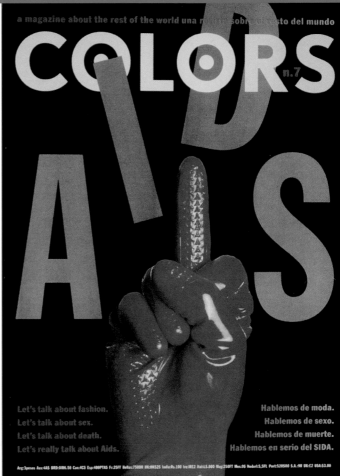

181 The Boston Globe, 1994

The Boston Globe

LOST FUTURES
Our *forgotten* children

This child, who suffers from a blood disease, is used by his family as a beggar in picturesque Halong Bay in Vietnam.

Text and Photographs by Stan Grossfeld

THEY ARE THE WORLD'S most precious resource. They will inherit the earth and carry on the work of humankind into the 21st century.

They are our children: our babies, our toddlers, our teens. Most of them will be up to the challenge, as their ancestors have been through the ages. But for millions of children in this country and around the world, there is no future; they are already living in hell on earth.

In 1994, the spotlight focused on the horrors of Rwanda and Bosnia. But crack babies are being buried each week in paupers' graves in the shadow of the Empire State Building; children are being worked to death in India's factories; and thousands of HIV-positive infants lie suffering in Romania.

This portfolio is the result of two years of reporting and photography in the dark and hidden corners of 18 countries where too many children live unwanted and die unmourned.

The streets of *despair*

Trapped *in a* hellhole

xx Life After Death

Courtney Love

xx Photograph xx
by Mark Seliger xxx
x xxxxxxxxxxxxxxxxxx x

183 Anchorage Daily News/Impulse, 1994

polo is my life

Fear and Loathing in Horse Country

Queer for
Power, Slave
to Speed . . .
Adventures
in the Pony
Business

by hun

"Arms, my only ornament,
my only rest, the fight."
—Cervantes,
DON QUIXOTE

I

Whooping It Up With the
Horse People: Trapped in
a World of Beasts...The
Genius of Genghis Khan
and the Beauty of Sweet
Belinda...On Fire With
the Polo Fever...
Polo meant nothing to
me when I was young. It
was just another sport
for the idle rich —
golf on horseback — and
on most days I had bet-
ter things to do than
hang around in a flim-
sy blue-striped tent
on a soggy field far
out on the River Road
and drink gin with
teen-age girls. But

illustrations by ralph steadman

184 Rolling Stone, 1994

HOW TO GIVE
ORDERS
LIKE A MAN

BY DEBORAH TANNEN

A UNIVERSITY PRESIDENT WAS EXPECTING A VISIT FROM a member of the board of trustees. When her secretary buzzed to tell her that the board member had arrived, she left her office and entered the reception area to greet him. Before ushering him into her office, she handed her secretary a sheet of paper and said: "I've just finished drafting this letter. Do you think you could type it right away? I'd like to get it out before lunch. And would you please do me a favor and hold all calls while I'm meeting with Mr. Smith?"

When they sat down behind the closed door of her office, Mr. Smith began by telling her that he thought she had spoken inappropriately to her secretary. "Don't forget," he said, "You're the president."

Putting aside the question of the appropriateness of his admonishing the president on her way of speaking, it is revealing — and representative of many Americans' assumptions — that the indirect way in which the university president told her secretary what to do struck him as self-deprecating. He took it as evidence that she didn't think she had the right to make demands of her secretary. He probably thought he was giving her a needed pep talk, bolstering her self-confidence.

I challenge the assumption that talking in an indirect way necessarily reveals powerlessness, lack of self-confidence or anything else about the character of the speaker. Indirectness is a fundamental element in human communication. It is also one of the elements that varies most from one culture to another, and one that can cause confusion and misunderstanding when speakers have different habits with regard to using it. I also want to dispel the assumption that American women tend to be more indirect than American men. Women and men are both indirect, but in addition to differences associated with their backgrounds — regional, ethnic and class — they tend to be indirect in different situations and in different ways.

At work, we need to get others to do things, and we all have different ways of accomplishing this. Any individual's ways will vary depending on who is being addressed — a boss, a peer or a subordinate. At one extreme are bald commands. At the other are requests so indirect that they don't sound like requests at all, but are just a statement of need or a description of a situation. People with direct styles of asking others to do things perceive indirect requests — if they perceive them as requests at all — as manipulative. But this is often just a way of blaming others for our discomfort with their styles.

> Directness
> is not necessarily
> logical or effective.
> Indirectness
> is not necessarily
> manipulative or
> insecure.

The indirect style is no more manipulative than making a telephone call, asking "Is Rachel there?" and expecting whoever answers the phone to put Rachel on. (Only a child is likely to answer "Yes" and continue holding the phone — not out of orneriness but because of inexperience with the conventional meaning of the question. (A mischievous adult might do it to tease.) Those who feel that indirect orders are illogical or manipulative do not recognize the conventional nature of indirect requests.

Issuing orders indirectly can be the prerogative of those in power. Imagine, for example, a master who says "It's cold in here" and expects a servant to make a move to close a window, while a servant who says the same thing is not likely to see his employer rise to correct the situation and make him more comfortable. Indeed, a Frenchman raised in Brittany tells me that his family never gave bald commands to their servants but always communicated orders in indirect and highly polite ways. This pattern renders less surprising the finding of David Bellinger and Jean Berko Gleason that fathers' speech to their young children had a higher incidence than mothers' of both direct imperatives like "Turn the bolt with the wrench" and indirect orders like "The wheel is going to fall off."

The use of indirectness can hardly be understood without the cross-cultural perspective. Many Americans find it self-evident that directness is logical and aligned with power while indirectness is akin to dishonesty and reflects subservience. But for speakers raised in most of the world's cultures, varieties of indirectness are the norm in communication. This is the pattern found by a Japanese sociolinguist, Kunihiko Harada, in his analysis of a conversation he recorded between a Japanese boss and a subordinate.

The markers of superior status were clear. One speaker was a Japanese man in his late 40's who managed the local branch of a Japanese private school in the United States. His conversational partner was a Japanese-American woman in her early 20's who worked at the school. By virtue of her job, her age and her native fluency in the language being taught, the man was in the superior position. Yet when he addressed the woman, he frequently used polite language and almost always used indirectness. For example, he had tried and failed to find a photography store that would make a black-and-white print from a color negative for a brochure they were producing. He let her know that he wanted her to take over the task by stating the situation and allowing her to volunteer to do it. (This is a translation of the Japanese conversation.)

On this matter, that, that, on the leaflet? This photo, I'm thinking of changing it to black-and-white and making it clearer... I went to a photo shop and asked them. They said they didn't do black-and-white. I asked if

Deborah Tannen is University Professor of Linguistics at Georgetown University. This article is adapted from "Talking From 9 to 5," due in October from William Morrow. Copyright © 1994 by Deborah Tannen.

Illustrations by Gary Baseman

46

185 The New York Times Magazine, 1994

A LOOK INTO HELL

A man is cut down between the wooden pews of a parish church; a woman and child are shelved to death in the tall grass. The world may still be averting its gaze, but the continuing carnage cries out for everyone's attention.

PHOTOGRAPHS BY JAMES NACHTWEY

186 Time International, 1994

218

The Fashion Circus

No clowning around. Glamour and whimsy are easy to swallow.

The Fashion Circus

The Fashion Circus

188 Dance Ink, 1995

189 Dance Ink, 1995

220

Short and sleek or long and lean, black stands tall.

Stretch and shine, along with vinyl and velvet, star in a remake of *Attack of the 50 Ft. Woman.*

Bodzilla!

PHOTOGRAPHED BY THIERRY LE GOUÈS

190 Allure, 1995

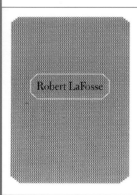

191 Dance Ink, 1995

192 Garden Design, 1995

Has
AIDS
Won?

By Craig Horowitz

193 New York, 1995

194 Texas Monthly, 1995

196 New York Times Magazine, 1995

02/09/95

Independent
Magazine

Can Britain bite back?

197 Independent Magazine, 1995

The SWEET SONG
of JUSTICE

It took the jury less
than three hours to
find Yolanda Saldivar
guilty of murdering Selena.
But for two weeks in
October, all of Texas
followed the most
sensational trial in years.
A behind-the-scenes
look at what happened
inside the courtroom.
by Joe Nick Patoski

198 Texas Monthly, 1995

228

HORROR

GOTHIC

AMERICAN

In the snapshot, they looked like a family picture in 1950s America — three blond children, crew-cut dad and mother in a plaid shirtdress.

Just three years later, in 1968, Pam Walton's mother was dead of lung cancer, her father had remarried — Please see Page E-4, WALTONS

But appearances, as the saying goes, can be so misleading.

They stood together, backs to the camera, gazing up at the Lincoln Memorial.

Filmmaker's family portrait

darker than TV's Waltons

GAYS CAN ROCK
Pansy Division plays queercore/homocore
4

OLD ART FORM
Native dancers star in museum series
4

JUST DON'T ASSUME
Stallone says 'Dredd' isn't just a bloodfest
4

199 Anchorage Daily News/Impulse, 1995

200 Anchorage Daily News/Impulse, 1995

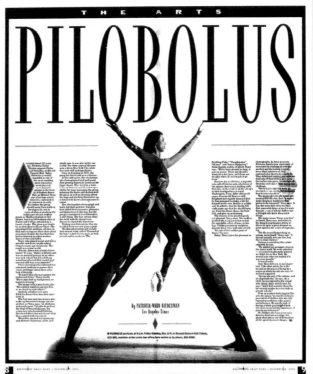

201 Rolling Stone, 1995

202 Rolling Stone, 1995

ASIAN ELEPHANT

"Calcutta," photographed at the Ringling Bros. and Barnum & Bailey Circus, Rochester, N.Y. Fewer than 40,000 Asian elephants remain; the species is on the International Union for the Conservation of Nature's "red list" of animals in danger of extinction.

WEDDING PREPARATION

In keeping with Bedouin tradition, a woman on Egypt's Giza Plateau covers her hands with henna dye in preparation for her wedding. The people and their customs, older than the pyramids, are under increasing pressure from growing urban populations.

ATLANTIC GREEN SEA TURTLE

"Jerry," photographed in Sea Turtles Inc., South Padre Island, Texas. Since the European conquest of the New World, this turtle has been overexploited for its meat, eggs, oil and skin. Its population has been eradicated or reduced throughout most of its range.

THE GANGES

A Hindu man performs yoga at sunrise in the Ganges River in India. The Ganges, sacred to Hindus, is now among the planet's most polluted rivers.

GRIZZLY BEAR

"Bailey," photographed at Dave Richman's Bears Etc., Grand Prairie, Texas. The grizzly has been eradicated from all of the United States except Alaska and the region around Yellowstone National Park.

GREVY'S ZEBRA

Photographed at La Coma Ranch Red Gate, Edinburg, Texas. In Africa, people have slaughtered hundreds of thousands of zebra; and the southward advance of the Sahara has dried up much of the animal's habitat.

GIANT PANDA

"Wen Wen," photographed at the Shanghai Acrobatic Theatre, Shanghai, China. The human population explosion in China has greatly reduced the panda's habitat, and only about 1,000 pandas are believed to remain in the wild.

DRILL

"Cholita," photographed at the Ringling Bros. and Barnum & Bailey Circus, Rochester, N.Y. Drills are on the verge of extinction in the wild, as their native habitat in Cameroon and Nigeria has been leveled for timber and farming.

BODY DESIGN

These villagers from the Chimbu area of New Guinea wear traditional tribal headdress "Bugan" and painted stripes during a celebratory gathering of New Guinea tribes. The indigenous peoples of New Guinea speak more than 800 languages, but the linguistic diversity is vanishing with the disappearance of local cultures.

232

204 New York, 1996

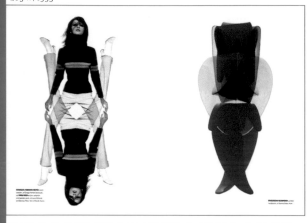

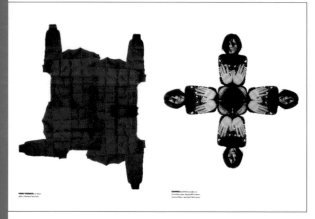

It's no illusion—streamlined, graphic looks and high-tech fabrics are making a major impact.

PHOTOGRAPHED BY RAYMOND MEIER

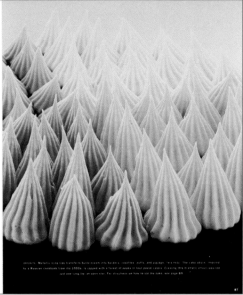

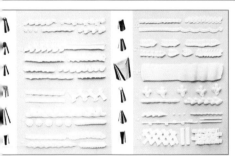

206 Martha Stewart Living, 1995

235

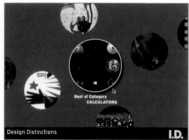

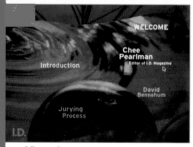

207 I.D., 1996

208 Rolling Stone, 1996

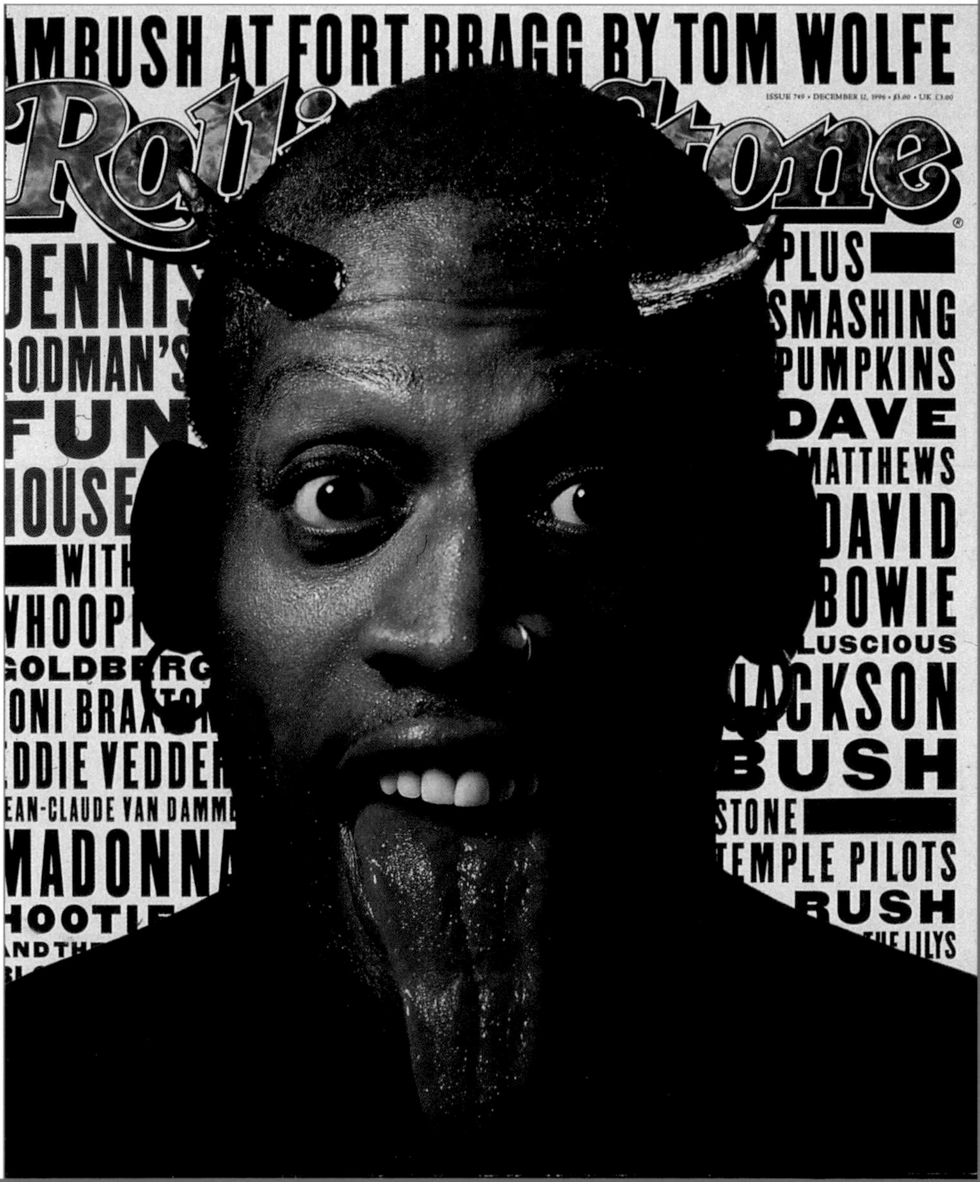

209 GVO Brochure, 1996

BE GREAT PRODUCTS
AREN'T ABOUT
BEAUTIFUL DESIGN

YOU COULD PLAY THE ODDS.
BUT GREAT PRODUCTS
DON'T HAVE TO BE
A GAMBLE.

MAYBE GOOD DESIGN
ISN'T PRETTY

QUATRE HISTOIRES
D'AMOUR

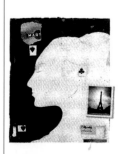

It's an old story:
a guy takes his
wife to Paris for
their anniversary,
without finding out
what she wants.
The next year he
does. She falls
in love with him
all over again.

240

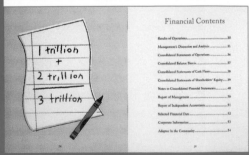

Die Zeilen, die Sie hier lesen, sind eigentlich nichts anderes als sechs bunte Streifen. Kein Wandel, schließlich ist die ganze Welt gestreift. Beweise? Gehen Sie mit uns auf Streife

Endlich mal ein
paar neue Gesichter

Wollen Sie Ihren
Bekanntenkreis um
ein paar
Charakterköpfe
erweitern?
Dann sehen Sie sich
doch mal
zu Hause um.

PHOTOS
FRANÇOIS UND JEAN ROBERT

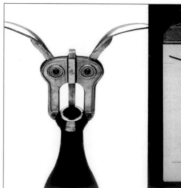

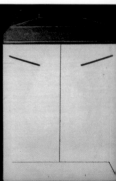

212 Sueddeutsche Zeitung Magazin, 1996

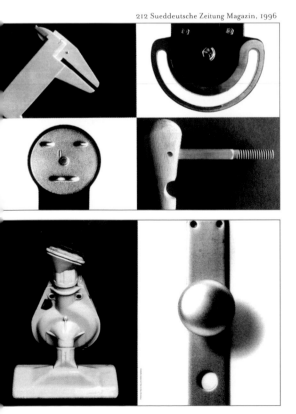

Brooklyn "Before my eyes, what started as fun has become an intense, hazardous competition.

The boy remarkably is nipping off a bare box spring. The body flies, the face is still. He is determined to be the best."

213 BravoRichards, 1996

245

214 La Revista, 1996

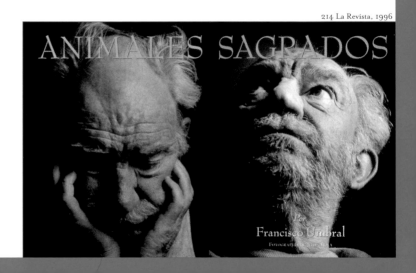

ANÍMALES SAGRADOS

Por
Francisco Umbral

246

BECORDINGSTHEPLEASUREPRINCIPI
BY DON McLEESE

★ ★ ★ ★
I FEEL ALRIGHT
Steve Earle
E-Squared/Warner Bros.

T SEEMS LIKE A COUPLE OF LIFE-
times ago that Steve Earle appeared destined to become the
Bruce Springsteen of country music. Introducing himself with
1986's *Guitar Town*, Earle arrived
on a wave of "new traditionalism"
that extended from the terse con-
servatism of Randy Travis to the
hillbilly flash of Dwight Yoakam.
While others in the class of '86 found
popular acceptance more quickly, Earle
showed the most potential. His Southern populism and unbridled rebel-
liousness offered a bridge between the
hard twang of rural country music and
the harder dynamics of rock, reinforcing
the strengths of both camps rather than
settling for a dilution more typical of
the Eagles.

After continuing down the same road
with 1987's *Exit 0*, an album almost as
strong as *Guitar Town*, Earle took a metal-
lic detour. Both *Copperhead Road* (1988)
and *The Hard Way* (1991) buried some inspired material beneath too many guitars,
undermining the country side of his
music. As Earle began to attain greater
notoriety for his drug use, divorces and
tattoos than for his music, his once-
promising career looked more like a high-
way wreck and was viewed with ap-
prehension by those who slowed down to
gape at the carnage. It was said that Earle
couldn't even get arrested in Nashville –

Show People

217 I.D., 1997

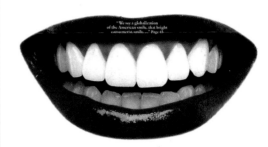

classic
layer cakes
growing euphorbias
arranging pictures
collecting linens
water gardens
sushi 101

MAY 1997
$3.95 USA (CAN. $4.95)

pink

219 Martha Stewart Living, 1997

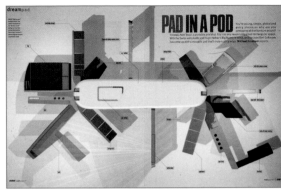

220 Wallpaper*, 1997

Times Square has long represented New York's teeming amusements, the spirited crossroads of memory and desire. Here is where the lights are hallucinatory, where nostalgia and fantasy pay the rent and where any street corner might be a setting for an oppressive don't-they-look-strange standing together?

The surreal photograph makes meaning of the oddest juxtaposition, creates meaning from the barely-visible and half-remembered, then meaning with a swipe of soft focus. The photographs here hint the odd, the irrational, the fantastic Times Square as urban dreamscape.

March 1997. Members of the United States Armed Forces recruiting station, plus one.
Photographs by Lyle Ashton Harris

Beneath the glitz and the greasepaint is a Times Square of hard work and hard knocks. A hit show means eight performances in six days, and that, as veteran actors and actresses will tell you, builds character. Raising golden takes strength and skill. Performing in a wet club is not for the thin-skinned. And there is no place lonelier than a 42d Street corner at 2 A.M. Realism is a photographer aesthetic, and the photographers who employ it take their subjects straight on. The pictures here are by no means all gritty or bleak. But all are faithful to the truths experienced daily by the denizens of Times Square.

April 1997. Christopher Plummer, a resident in "Barrymore," takes a walk. Scenes Wednesdays and Saturdays.
Photographs by Chuck Close

Assignment: Times Square

By Michael Kimmelman

The most famous photograph of Times Square is surely Alfred Eisenstaedt's chestnut of the kissing couple, which summed up the national mood in 1945 because it combined all the right elements: the returning soldier, the woman who welcomed him back and Times Square, the crossroads that symbolized home.

Some people were upset to learn later that Eisenstaedt may have staged the kiss, as if this somehow invalidated the image. The picture had first been published in *Life*, which meant that it was assumed to document what happened serendipitously at the instant the shutter clicked. Of course, all photographs are contrived to one degree or another than the photographer chooses the image, framing what is to be in and out of it, and Eisenstaedt, to insure he'd get the effect he wanted, simply recreated for the camera what was taking place around him anyway. But, if so, he still broke the pact between photojournalist and viewer, creating something that tended toward fiction or theater. In a strange way it was true at least to the spirit of Times Square, the epicenter of Broadway.

That was then. If you want to see where photography is now, take a look in this issue at Philip-Lorca diCorcia's own version of a man and woman embracing in the square. DiCorcia lights his

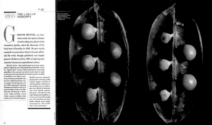

223 Life, 1997

NORBERT ROSING

Natur pur

*Norbert Rosing gilt derzeit als einer der besten Naturfotografen.
Ein soeben erschienener opulenter Bildband über deutsche Nationalparks
handelt die Arbeit des vergangenen Jahres.*

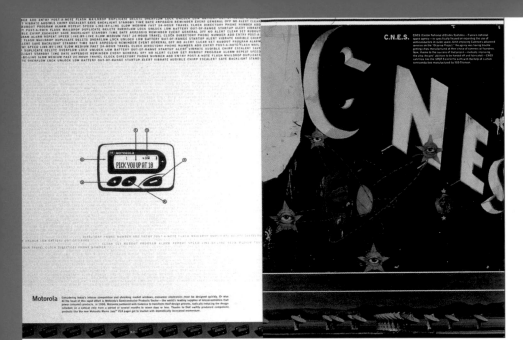

225 Cadence 1996 Annual Report, 1997

VANITY FAIR

$3.50 U.S. / $4.00 CANADA

JUNE 1997

ARNOLD

THE MAN, THE MOVIES, AND THE HUMMER
BY ANNIE LEIBOVITZ

227 Rolling Stone, 1997

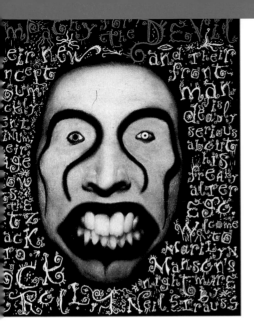

ALMIGHTY GOD THE DEVIL

their new concept album cleverly isn't immune their rage blows out the track rock n roll

and their front man is deadly serious about his freaky alter ego. Welcome to Marilyn Manson's nightmare by Neil Strauss

THE LAST RIDE OF THE POLO SHIRT BANDIT

WILLIAM GUESS WAS HIS NAME—AND IT WAS PROPHETIC. WHEN HE SHOT HIMSELF WHILE SURROUNDED BY THE POLICE, HE LEFT UNANSWERED THE QUESTION THAT HAD STUMPED HIS PURSUERS: WHY DID AN ORDINARY MIDDLE-CLASS TEXAN TURN INTO THE MOST PROLIFIC BANK ROBBER IN THE STATE'S HISTORY? BY HELEN THORPE

TEXAS MONTHLY XXX March 1997

228 Texas Monthly, 1997

259

Afghanistan 1987

Zaire 1994

Mongolska 1996

229 Mizerie, 1997

231 Bloomberg Personal Finance, 1997

COR
THERAPEUTICS, INC.

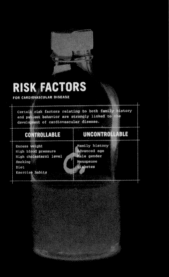

RISK FACTORS
FOR CARDIOVASCULAR DISEASE

Certain risk factors relating to both family history
and patient behavior are strongly linked to the
development of cardiovascular disease.

CONTROLLABLE	UNCONTROLLABLE
Excess weight	Family history
High blood pressure	Advanced age
High cholesterol level	Male gender
Smoking	Menopause
Diet	Diabetes
Exercise habits	

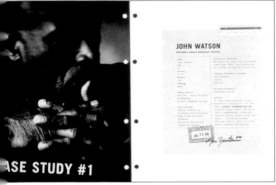

JOHN WATSON

ASE STUDY #1

230 COR Therapeutics 1996 Annual Report, 1997

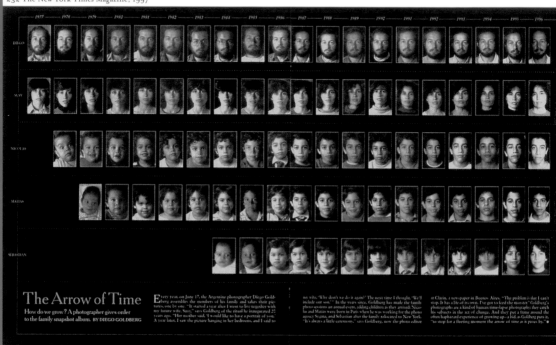

The Arrow of Time

How do we grow? A photographer gives order
to the family snapshot album. BY DIEGO GOLDBERG

Every year, on June 17, the Argentine photographer Diego Goldberg assembles the members of his family and takes their pictures, one by one. "It started a year after I went to live together with my future wife, Susy," says Goldberg of the ritual he inaugurated 22 years ago. "Her mother said, 'I would like to have a portrait of you.' A year later, I saw the picture hanging in her bedroom, and I said to no wife, 'Why don't we do it again?' The next time I thought, 'We'll include our son.'" In the years since, Goldberg has made the family photo sessions an annual event, adding children as they arrived: Nicolas and Matias were born in Paris when he was working for the photo agency Sygma, and Sebastian after the family relocated to New York. "It's always a little ceremony," says Goldberg, now the photo editor at Clarín, a newspaper in Buenos Aires. "The problem is that I can't stop. It has a life of its own. I've got to feed the monster." Goldberg's photographs are a kind of human time-lapse photograph: they catch his subjects in the act of change. And they put a frame around the often haphazard experience of growing up—a bid, as Goldberg puts it, "to stop for a fleeting moment the arrow of time as it passes by." ◼

Abelardo Morell
CAMERA LOOK AT TIMES

"I want a sort of historical record of what a vision sees," says Abelardo Morell, a 48-year-old Cuban immigrant who lives in Brookline, Mass. Thus his product for the ancient technique of the camera obscura, in this case constructed by using the room itself as a camera. Blacking out all but a half-inch notch of a window — the aperture — in Room 1321 at the Marriott in Times Square, Morell shot out a curtain on a tripod over the aperture, directing a lens the room to record the optical effect overnight. Making a single exposure over two days, he captured a series of meditative calm — the issues — superimposed with the onrush of Broadway. "Think about how many people go through this one in two days — millions — and no one stood still long enough to get into," he says. "It's an empty, almost a-person picture."

March 20-21, 1997. Broadway all at once from a room at the Marriott.

234 I.D. Magazine Online, 1997

235 The New York Times, 1997

236 The New York Times, 1997

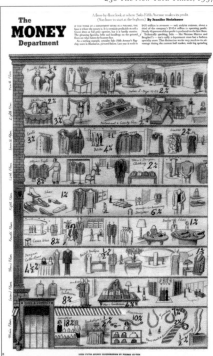

30TH ANNIVERSARY SPECIAL

Rolling Stone

WE'RE OFF...

Seinfeld
Hits the
Road!

237 Rolling Stone, 1998

The End

The 180th and final episode of "Seinfeld," to be broadcast on May 14th, was scheduled to be filmed over nine days, from March 31st to April 8th. ROLLING STONE was there the whole time – for more than 100 hours on set – watching. Hiding in corners. Being nosy. All Jerry Seinfeld asked in return was that the ensuing story not reveal anything. This is that story. BY CHRIS HEATH

RS 787

" I want a life that is a little bit less ordinary. "

JESSICA RIDENOUR, PAGE 93

---

one. My close friends are also involved in resistance.

Returning to formal education at fifteen – Jessica at the College of the Atlantic in Bar Harbor, Maine, Audrey at the University of Maine at Orono – they continued to pursue their own agenda of feminism, psychology, ecology and the history of nonviolence. Under the influence of books of New-Age anti-hierarchical thought such as *Chalice and the Blade*, by Riarle Eisler, and *Dreaming the Dark*, by Starhawk, they turned eighteen and discovered that, as adults, getting arrested for civil disobedience entails less hassle than it used to – because as minors they could only be released to the custody of parents or guardians. So they dropped out and got arrested eight times in less than a year. Their crimes have ranged from dumping baby bottles of their own blood on an Aegis destroyer in Bath to sitting in at the U.S. Army School of the Americas, in Fort Benning, Georgia, an institution known on the left as the School of the Assassins for its training of death squads and torturers all over the Third World.

"It's not always a pleasant thing to be involved with the legal system," says Audrey, who has a habit of defying judges. "You can't go to the bathroom in any privacy; you get strip-searched. The rituals are endless and pointless, except to demonstrate that the guard is the boss and you aren't. The structures of domination that are normally mashed in society become really, really visible in jail, so it's a consciousness-raising experience."

"You realize the prison system is bigger than any-body who's involved," says Jessica, "and it's out of everybody's control. It's not designed to help anyone. It's just victims. There's always a punishment they can inflict and a reward they earn dangle. Society operates the same way, only more subtly, so people from the white middle class don't know."

In one memorable episode last December, they were arrested for praying in front of the White House. On the day of their status hearing in Washington in the middle of January, Jessica got caught in

the worst ice storm in Maine history. When the weather warmed up, the federal marshals hauled her off in manacles and, in a two-week period, flew her first to a prison in Rhode Island, then to a federal transfer center in Oklahoma City, back to Maine, then to Washington again, where a federal judge sentenced her to six weeks in a halfway house.

"While you're getting on and off the plane, they point machine guns at you," Jessica says with a giggle. "It's quite interesting. They do call it Con Air, like the movie. It's these decrepit old airplanes that look like they're going to fall apart. And fifteen men six and a half feet tall guarding me, in chains. Just your tax dollars at work. If there are fifty ways to do something, the legal system will choose the most inefficient."

"I think they would do all fifty and then settle on the slowest," says Audrey.

Jessica is currently living in Maine on "self reliance," meaning she is waiting for a phone call telling her to report in two days to a halfway house, which may or may not be in Maine. Last December, Audrey moved to Jonah House, a resistance community in Baltimore associated with the Plowshares, a pacifist organization whose daring acts of civil disobedience have inspired both legend and long prison sentences. Neither Stewart makes enough money from the occasional odd job to be taxed, and neither would pay if she did. Apart from a few countries by Ani DiFranco and Sweet Honey in the Rock,

they abuse popular culture. They view sex as overrated and have no plans to start families or traditional careers.

"It seems like the government is coming down on people with greater severity," says Audrey. "All these new priorities they're building. Even what happened to my sister, getting a month and a half for a White House vigil, is unheard of. At the School of the Americas demonstration, 600 people got arrested. Twenty-eight of them had been arrested for trespass before, and they got six months. I saw children getting Maced at a demonstration in Plymouth, Massachusetts. Where I live, in the inner city of Baltimore, the DEA [Drug Enforcement Administration] flies black helicopters over the projects all

the time. It's bizarre, and it's frightening. But it's also a sign that something is working. We must be doing something right, or the government wouldn't bother."

"I would like to start a self-sustaining, nonviolent resistance community like Jonah House here in Maine," says Jessica. "It's really difficult to do this work unless you have a support group to take care of things while you're locked up. The prospect of prison doesn't excite me, but it will probably happen." I ask Jessica whether her activism is motivated by some sort of patriotism. "No, I can't use that word in any sense," she says. "I don't believe in national boundaries. I reject every aspect of the American dream. The goal is nonviolent revolution."

SERGE OBOLENSKY | 21 | Writer | Los Angeles

" I was struck by a sense of inspiration just watching him do things we all take for granted. "

PHOTOGRAPH BY DAN WINTERS

TWO YEARS AGO, AT AGE nineteen, Serge Obolensky was grievously injured when he and his brother were playing with firecrackers. It was an adolescent game, the kind of boredom-busting activity that many boys engage in and get away with.

Serge's life basically froze from that point on. He is learning to live without hands, and he is able to find beauty in his daily existence. "Once a day," he says, "I walk through a memory with beautiful fruit trees. They give me a tingly feeling in my brain. I always think that if I could make the rest of the day as high-quality as that walk, I could have perfection in my life."

Serge is clear about his aspirations. "As long as I'm on earth living like this," he says,

"I want to do what's right, to show God I love him. I also have a dream to sing. When I'm alone, I can sing, and it makes me so silly happy. Oh, and I would also like to get married." He reads books on astronautical sciences, loves "trance" music – "It's like an electronic paradise" – and frequently gets its tunes.

Serge feels that he can cause cathartic responses when he encounters strangers who are curious about how he accomplishes simply daily tasks. I met him in a Hollywood diner or so one of those strangers. I was immediately struck by a sense of hope and inspiration just watching Serge do the things we all take for granted. We have since formed a bond and a friendship.

Serge, unable to pursue his passion for drawing, told me he plans to write a book. If his written word has the same effect on people as his physical presence, it could be one powerful piece of work. —DW

239 Ray Gun, 1998

My Dinner with Santa

How often do the giants—the true giants, the All-Timers, the icons, the *capi di tutti capi*—get together? Not often. Not nearly often enough.
In these days of manufactured stardom and celebrity du jour, hardly ever.
That's why Esquire asked these two guys—these two monsters—to get together, mano a Santa, for a little Noel nosh and Yuletide yammer.
The place: Bistro Latino, 1711 Broadway, New York, New York. Santa had the paella. Murray had a salad. Brandy was served.

BY BILL MURRAY

Claus: Have you been a good boy?
Murray: As good as I've ever been.
Claus: I'm not imposing my own standard of goodness. I can't do that. By *your* standards, have you been good?
Murray: I say yes. But this good or bad thing—do you know when I've been sleeping? Do you know when I'm awake?
Claus: I'm a saint. I have, like, second sight. I see you.
Murray: I can't believe I'm sitting here with Santa. I mean, you're a god.
Claus: Oh, right. Don't even start with that. Like I'd even *be here* if it weren't for Jesus. Give me a break. I'm just following in the footsteps, baby. Ever hear of a fella by the name of Jesus Christ of Nazareth? Yeah. He makes Santa Claus of the North Pole look like a pygmy. I'm a pygmy.
Murray: But how do you do it? I mean, the whole enchilada, year in and year out? How do you keep it fresh? For yourself?
Claus: I have a practice that I've developed over the centuries. Look, I can't *force* myself to get into the Christmas spirit. I can't just walk out there and—*bong*—feel all Christmassy somehow. So I start buying things for myself. Something nice. Something a little expensive—just a little bit of blink on it. The one that really works is to walk into Tiffany's on Fifth Avenue. If you can walk in there and find something, as a man—A, you had to walk up to the second floor, so you're already moving, and B, it's gotta cost you a little money.
This year, I bought myself a nice flask.
Murray: I've been sneaking to do this for one friend of mine—I want to

PHOTOGRAPHS BY DAN WINTERS

240 Esquire, 1998

PHOTOGRAPH BY GEOF KERN: 638,000 CIGARETTES

LONG LIVE THE CAREER SMOKER

MY FATHER was in futures trading. He was a lawyer who dealt exclusively with commodities—oranges, pork bellies, gold—representing, from a paper-choked office on Chicago's Wacker Drive, people who had been beguiled by brokers out of their money. It was simple stuff for him; he knew the applicable laws inside and out, it was fairly easy to prove who was at fault, and he was, particularly when he started in the sixties, one of a handful of lawyers in the country practicing such law. Thus, without ever really having to go to court, he never lost.

As children, the three of us (and, much later, four of us) would, in most cases to fulfill this or that homework assignment, ask him to explain his work; we were yearning for details with which to piece something together, to get an idea of what he did with his days. *What was a future? How could you make one?* We knew of some of his clients. There was the Widow, who stoated on being met in Miami. There was the Widow, who had been bilked for half a million or so by her young broker, the Weasel. But we were hungry for more detail, a better understanding. Did he pace back and forth before juries, full of righteous indignation? We had seen TV, movies—*Inherit the Wind, To Kill a Mockingbird.* Was it like that? Did he pound his fist, make impassioned demands of the jurors? *Look at this wretched man, this ruined man! I urge you to look deep into your heart and find a verdict of not guilty!* We knew nothing except what he said, vaguely and occasionally, about his legal successes. He would come home after a case had wrapped and, after changing into his khakis and claiming his spot on the couch, would, with a flourish, clasp his hands together behind his head and say, cocky smile spread wide. "All right, every-

SMOKERS DON'T NEED OUR PITY, AS THE LEGIONS OF LAWYERS LINING UP TO SUE BIG TOBACCO ASSERT. THEY   DON'T NEED THE LAWSUITS, EITHER. IN FACT, THEY DESERVE OUR PRAISE. AN ARGUMENT

BY DAVID EGGERS

241 Esquire, 1998

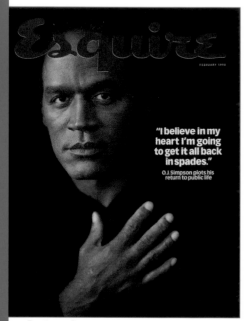

242 Esquire, 1998

243 ESPN, 1998

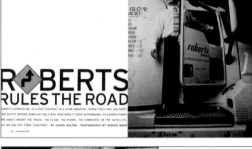

244 Fast Company, 1998

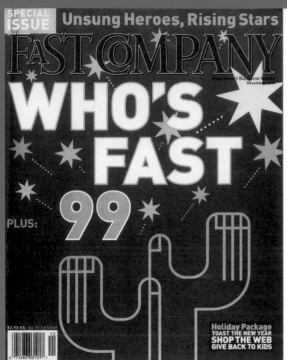

245 Fast Company, 1998

The Real Scandal in Washington Is Newt Gingrich

The Stink at the Other End of Pennsylvania Avenue

BY WILLIAM GREIDER

ILLUSTRATION BY MATT MAHURIN

Cocaine, the CIA, and a Good Man Destroyed

Esquire

SEPTEMBER 1998

Nic Cage Slept Here

America's Actor Goes Home
By Scott Raab

84 Things a Man Should Know

FALL FASHION
The Suits You Need
The Perfect Shirt and Tie
All About Cashmere

A Beautiful Story About an Old Man
By Mike Sager

Terrell Davis's Five Keys to Success
Jeff George's One Way to Fall

RICHARD JEWELL IS ON THE WAY

BY SARA CORBETT

PHOTOGRAPHS BY HARRY BENSON

Rule 1
Don't Panic

Rule 2
Panic First

Esquire **Nic, Cage's Suburban Night-mare** BY SCOTT RAAB

Ol

BY MIKE SAGER

248 Esquire, 1998

272

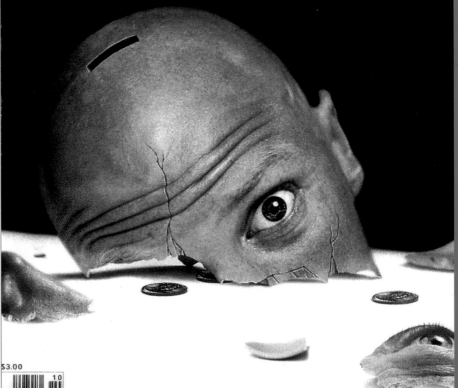

The Coming Economic Collapse
THE FATE OF YOUR MONEY, YOUR JOB, YOUR FAMILY, YOUR FUTURE

Esquire

OCTOBER 1998

DANGEROUS KNOWLEDGE

What Did You Do
After the Crash, Daddy?

$3.00

10

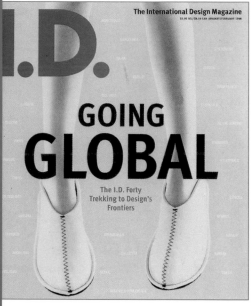

The International Design Magazine
$5.95 US/$8.50 CAN JANUARY/FEBRUARY 1998

I.D.

GOING
GLOBAL

The I.D. Forty
Trekking to Design's
Frontiers

The International Design Magazine

I.D.

John Huckenberry reports
from within the Mouse

Inside
Disney

Inside
Disney

BY JOHN HUCKENBERRY

The International Design Magazine
$5.95 US/$8.50 CAN MAY 1998

I.D.

PETER SAVILLE: **Prince of Print**
WINNING WHEELS: **Slicing Through Air**
PILLS: **Designing Drugs**
ROBOTS: **Coming to Life**

Wonder Woman
*Biomechanical design and an unstoppable spirit
enable Aimee Mullins to triumph on the track*

spaghetti science

Designing pasta: the art and engineering of complex carbohydrates.

BY PAOLA ANTONELLI
PHOTOGRAPHY BY MIKAKO KOYAMA

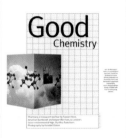

Good
Chemistry

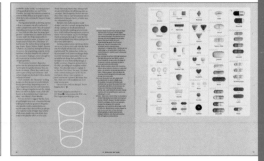

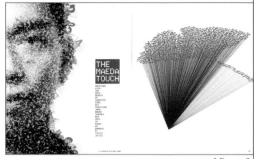

251 Rolling Stone, 1998

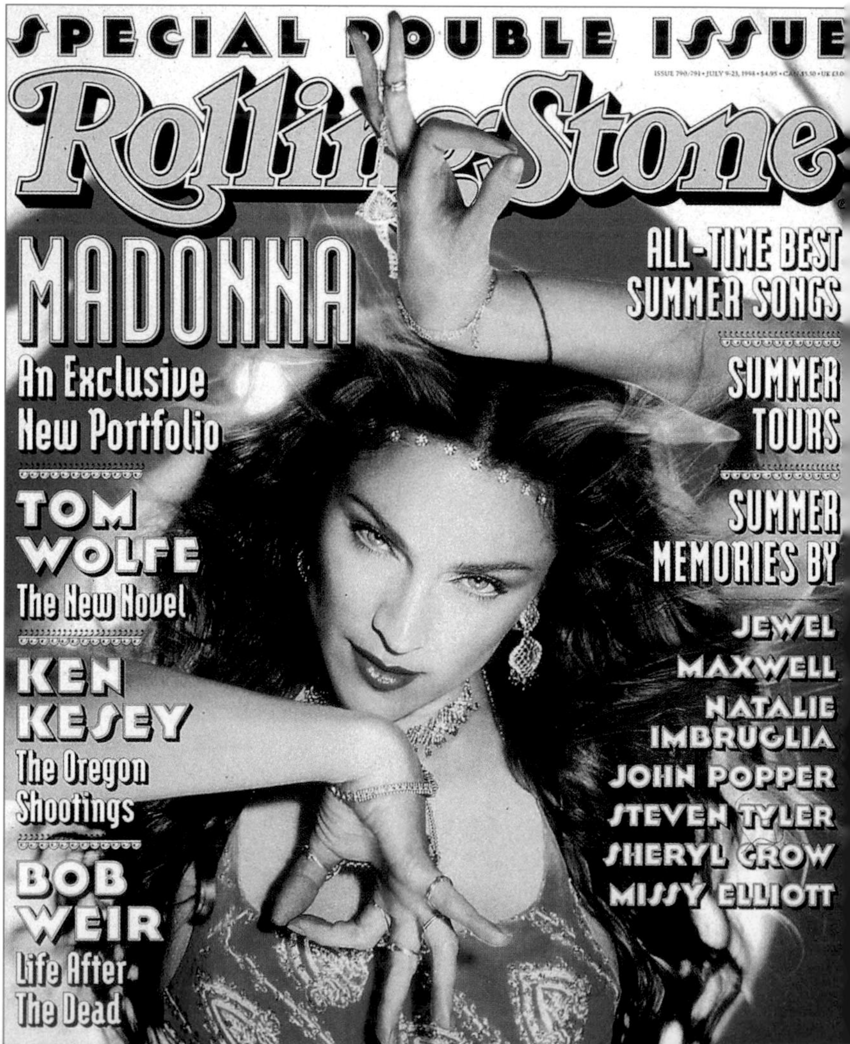

SPECIAL DOUBLE ISSUE

Rolling Stone

ISSUE 790/791 • JULY 9-23, 1998 • $4.95 • CAN. $5.50 • UK £3.00

MADONNA
An Exclusive
New Portfolio

TOM
WOLFE
The New Novel

KEN
KESEY
The Oregon
Shootings

BOB
WEIR
Life After
The Dead

ALL-TIME BEST
SUMMER SONGS

SUMMER
TOURS

SUMMER
MEMORIES BY

JEWEL
MAXWELL
NATALIE
IMBRUGLIA
JOHN POPPER
STEVEN TYLER
SHERYL CROW
MISSY ELLIOTT

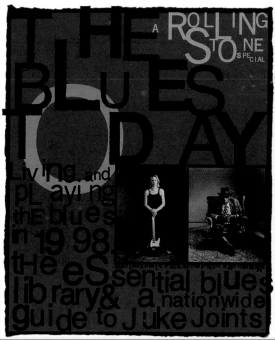

A ROLLING STONE SPECIAL

THE BLUES TODAY

Living and Playing the blues in 1998: the eSsential blues library & a nationwide guide to Juke Joints

THE STAR OF "FEAR AND LOATHING IN LAS VEGAS" GOES GONZO INTO THE PSYCHE OF HUNTER S. THOMPSON AND LIVES TO TELL ABOUT IT

JOHNNY DEPP's SAVAGE JOURNEY

BY CHRIS HEATH

PHOTOGRAPHS BY DAN WINTERS

ATHLETE

Vince Carter delivers the best three seconds in sports—and a whole lot more

BY TIM KEOWN   PHOTOGRAPHS BY ISABEL SNYDER

LONE **WOLF**

The ball goes to Kevin Garnett now. He just has to grab it.

by Ric Bucher

FOOTBALL FEVER > HOT JAGS
COOL 'NOLES

VINCE CARTER

254 Rolling Stone, 1999

The Best
Ideas, Stories and Inventions of the Last Thousand Years

ELMORE LEONARD ON 'EVERYMAN'

Richard Powers On the telltale eye

Wole Soyinka
ON TYRANNY'S FATE

OLIVER SACKS
On the periodic table

A.S. Byatt
ON THE GREATEST
STORY
EVER TOLD

UMBERTO ECO ON LEGUMES

Plus: Lorrie Moore on the best love song, Paul Auster on the best game, Penelope Fitzgerald on the best nuisance, and other judgments by R.W. Apple Jr., Margaret Atwood, Russell Baker, Ron Chernow, Jared Diamond, Charles Johnson, Alison Lurie, David Macaulay, Joyce Carol Oates, Frank Rich, Bernhard Schlink, Teller, Pramoedya Ananta Toer, Marina Warner and many more. Contents, page 18.

A Special Issue

The New York Times Magazine
APRIL 18, 1999 / SECTION 6

Narrate
Or
Die
Why Scheherazade keeps on talking

By A.S. Byatt

255 The New York Times Magazine, 1999

Ss Hh OoWw Aa Nn Dd TtEe Ll Ll

It's never too early for kids to start questioning the meaning of fashion. The ABC's of spring children's wear.

Photographs by Robert Trachtenberg | Styled by Elizabeth Stewart

256 The New York Times Magazine, 1999

257 ESPN, 1999

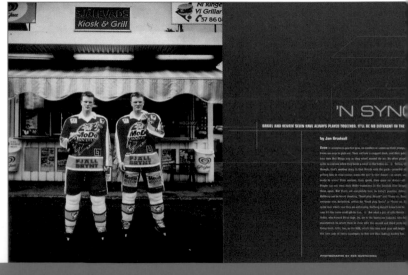

'N SYNC

DANIEL AND HENRIK SEDIN HAVE ALWAYS PLAYED TOGETHER. IT'LL BE NO DIFFERENT IN THE

by Jan Gradvall

The New York Times Magazine

JANUARY 17, 1999 / SECTION 6

**Bill Clinton's
Legacy
(First Draft)**
By Jacob Weisberg

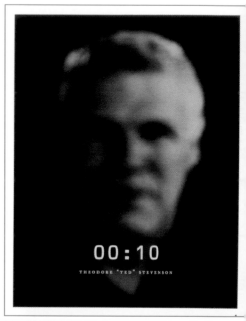

00:10

THEODORE "TED" STEVENSON

00:01

SAMUEL G. WASHINGTON

00:00

DOLORES L. GREENFIELD

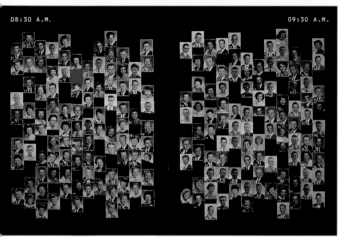

$19,500,000 $19,500,000
$19,500,000 $19,500,000
$19,500,000 $19,500,000
$19,500,000 $19,500,000
$19,500,000 $19,500,000
$19,500,000 $19,500,000
$19,500,000 $19,500,000
$19,500,000 $19,500,000
$19,500,000 $19,500,000
$19,500,000 $19,500,000
$19,500,000 $19,500,000
$19,500,000 $19,500,000

$468,000,000

12:00 A.M.   12:00 P.M.
01:00 A.M.   01:00 P.M.
02:00 A.M.   02:00 P.M.
03:00 A.M.   03:00 P.M.
04:00 A.M.   04:00 P.M.
05:00 A.M.   05:00 P.M.
06:00 A.M.   06:00 P.M.
07:00 A.M.   07:00 P.M.
08:00 A.M.   08:00 P.M.
09:00 A.M.   09:00 P.M.
10:00 A.M.   10:00 P.M.
11:00 A.M.   11:00 P.M.

24 HOURS

08:30 A.M.   09:30 A.M.

259 Collateral Therapeutics 1998 Annual Report, 1999

Photograph by **MARK SELIGER**

Photograph by **DAVID LACHAPELLE**

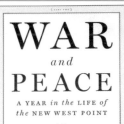

[PART TWO]

WAR
and
PEACE

A YEAR *in the* LIFE *of*
the NEW WEST POINT

. . .

By DAVID LIPSKY
PHOTOGRAPHS *by* MARK SELIGER

260 Rolling Stone, 1999

261 Nickelodeon Website, 1999

hedgechic

At a time when even hedge funds need hedging, a fund of funds can tailor your search for a way to reduce risk and to diversify.

By Jeanette Bronyck • Photographs by Hugh Kretschmer

Hedge funds have always been an intriguing investment category

Liquidity is sometimes a problem

SHINORAMA 1

photographs by Kishin Shinoyama

Eight years back, when I saw Kishin Shinoyama shooting Tokyo, it upset his idealized view. Tokyo is a photograph "Up until this, photography had exploited hints in reality. Shinoyama has been to realize that photography is in the audience like overwatching. Shinoyama. And of this same hints, the city of Tokyo is exhausting over some societal, verbal periodically in only a landmark on "Tokyo" in photographs as in the ever-looking idea into look at his. His of protestors of something set based on day. Boy, and all of a kind of "ambar Harnessed into particular in Tokyo. Shinoyama, standing an endless scenes of photographs of 20th-century art, standing all the aforementioned proof of his single ideas at who welcome "Shinoyama" "When topsy-turvy Shinoyama and his core presented the "Tokyo" and this kind has to the photography. And the audience institutation of "Tokyo". I have of our theater, approached of Tokyo in Kishin Shinoyama. Into it and has been over its experimentation and trivia has every time, Simulation is framed the measured was more as we.

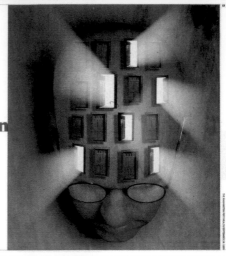

PEOPLE USED TO THINK THE BRAIN
WAS STATIC AND INEVITABLY
DECLINED WITH AGE. ACTUALLY,
THE BRAIN NEVER STOPS
CHANGING—AND WE NEVER STOP
LEARNING. BY DON COLBURN

ILLUSTRATION BY WILLIAM DUKE

The Infinite Brain

It's about three pounds
of wrinkled, pinkish-gray matter with the consistency of jello—and yet, in Emily Dickinson's words, "wider than the sky."

The human brain's nearly infinite reach comes from the elaborate circuitry of its billions of neurons—a marvel that has led some to call it the world's most complex computer.

But scientists are zeroing in on another quality of the brain that distinguishes it from even the most powerful PC: its adaptability.

It turns out the brain is plastic.

Not that it's made of vinyl. Plastic in the sense of *flexible* and *dynamic.*

The brain is not a cerebral black box, wired forever by age 2 or 3, as once thought. It remodels itself *See* BRAIN, *Page 11*

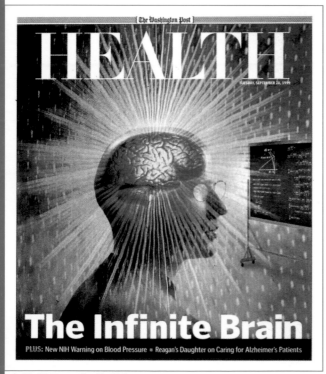

264 The Washington Post/Health Section, 1999

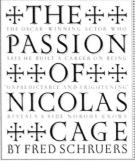

⛭THE⛭⛭
THE OSCAR-WINNING ACTOR WHO
PASSION
SAYS HE BUILT A CAREER ON BEING
⛭⛭OF⛭⛭
"UNPREDICTABLE AND FRIGHTENING"
NICOLAS
REVEALS A SIDE NOBODY KNOWS
⛭⛭CAGE
BY FRED SCHRUERS

Your ad here

What's wrong with a little self-promotion?

PHOTOGRAPHY BY STEPHANE SEDNAOUI

So you've got the billboard, now it's time to work on your slogan: Ralph Lauren Swimwear crocheted bikini top, $234 (with bottoms); Ralph by Ralph Lauren corduroy short shorts, $45.

DECEMBER 1999 JANE 111

You Had to Be There

Fresh from the runway of history, the
actress Salma Hayek is the height of fashion.

Photographs by Matthew Rolston • Styled by Elizabeth Stewart

LIKE A VIRGIN Women of the architocracy in the mid-
16th century didn't seem to mind the stiff look
completed by Queen Elizabeth. Today ruffs, epaulets
(period wig, plucked forehead and brows [translated text]
rib-crushing corset and the infamous farthingale, a hoop
Alexandra Byrne, nominated for an Academy Award in
costume design for the 1998 film "Elizabeth," has replicated
the look in this exposure from the movie. Gold and pearl
jewelry by Cynthia Bach As Newton-Marcus.

THE 1999
HALL OF FAME

THE SOPRANOS

Because, despite getting rocked at the Emmys by West Coast voters suffering from too much sunshine and chopped salad, the cast of the HBO series has the deepest bench strength and scariest laudprints of any television ensemble, not to mention the coolest character names (Uncle Junior, Big Pussy Bonpensiero). Because there hasn't been such a viper-mother as Nancy Marchand's Livia since I, Claudius, a more put-upon son than James Gandolfini's Tony Soprano, who shuffles into his midlife crisis like a bibeating bear, his eyelids at half-mast from the weight of all the greenbacks he has to whack, or a more milked daughter-in-law than Edie Falco's Carmela, whose clipped delivery could slice foreskins (her recurring cry: "What am I, an idiot?"). Because, brilliantly devised and co-written by David Chase, this mass minisseries cruises the Jersey suburbs like a stolen hearse, eyeing the American Dream through dark tinted glass.

From left: David Chase (creator and co-writer of the series), Jamie Lynn Sigler (Meadow Soprano), Robert Iler (Anthony Soprano Jr.), Dominic Chianese (Uncle Junior), Nancy Marchand (Livia Soprano), Edie Falco (Carmela Soprano), James Gandolfini (Tony Soprano), Lorraine Bracco (Dr. Jennifer Melfi), Michael Imperioli (Christopher Moltisanti), Steve Van Zandt (Silvio Dante), Tony Sirico (Paulie Walnuts), Jerry Adler (Hesh Rabkin), and Vincent Pastore (Big Pussy Bonpensiero).

Photographed by ANNIE LEIBOVITZ in New York City on September 7, 1999

294

270 Esquire, 1999

2000–

John Jerde: Neon Urbanist

B

By Gini Alhadeff
PHOTOGRAPHS BY ADAM BARTOS

FABLES OF THE RECONSTRUCTION

For ancient and crumbling Lancias, Bugattis, and Alfa Romeos, salvation comes in a small town outside Turin, at the hands of the master restorers at Carrozzeria Officina Meccanica.

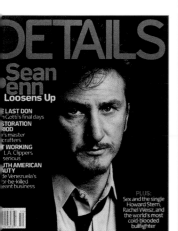

DETAILS

Sean Penn
Loosens Up

THE LAST DON
In Gotti's final days

RESTORATION
PERIOD
's master
crafters

T WORKING
L.A. Clippers
serious

UTH AMERICAN
UTY
de Venezuela's
or-be-killed
eant business

PLUS:
Sex and the single
Howard Stern,
Rachel Weisz, and
the world's most
cold-blooded
bullfighter

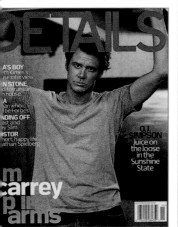

DETAILS

A'S BOY
th Kimes's
se interview

N STONE
terranean
house

an who
be Forbes

NDING OFF
ast and
y Slim

STOR
ort, happy life
than Spielberg

O.J.
SIMPSON
Juice on
the loose
in the
Sunshine
State

m
carrey
p in
arms

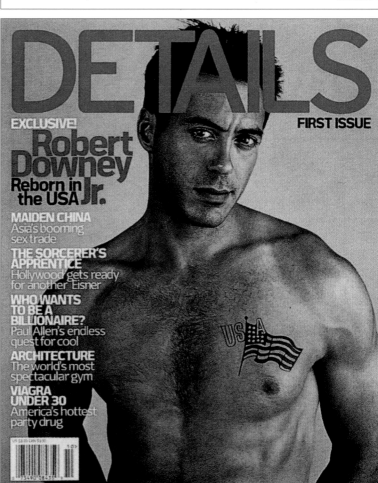

DETAILS
FIRST ISSUE

EXCLUSIVE!
Robert Downey
Reborn in the USA Jr.

MAIDEN CHINA
Asia's booming
sex trade

THE SORCERER'S APPRENTICE
Hollywood gets ready
for another Eisner

WHO WANTS TO BE A BILLIONAIRE?
Paul Allen's endless
quest for cool

ARCHITECTURE
The world's most
spectacular gym

VIAGRA UNDER 30
America's hottest
party drug

USA

298

273 Fast Company, 2000

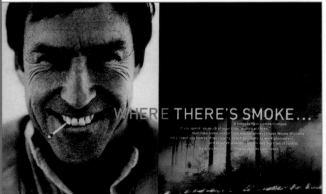

From heroin to heroine

FIVE YEARS AGO ELASTICA FRONT WOMAN JUSTINE FRISCHMANN SEEMED
TO HAVE IT ALL: A NUMBER-ONE ALBUM, AN ADORING PUBLIC, AND A
ROCK STAR BOYFRIEND. THEN JUST AS FAST AS IT CAME, IT CRUMBLED.
THE BAND SPLIT, HER BOYFRIEND LEFT, AND THE PRESS REVILED
HER FOR BEING A MIDDLE-CLASS JUNKIE. NOW SHE'S BACK FOR MORE.
CARMEL ALLEN GETS HER SIDE OF THE STORY
PHOTOGRAPHED BY TANY

NYLON

anna
paquin's
leap year

my
generation

jakob dylan   jared leto   marla sokoloff

WHEN THE GOING GETS TOUGH...

FAST COMPANY

...THE
TOUGH
GET
REAL

A 100-Page Special Report
ON THE NEW REALITIES
OF THE NEW ECONOMY—
and HOW TO KEEP BUILDING YOUR COMPANY,
INSPIRING YOUR COLLEAGUES,
ADVANCING YOUR CAREER,
and MAKING A DIFFERENCE

PLUS

> TO HELL WITH BORING WORK
THE END OF BORING POLITICS
> THE GREAT TALENT CAPER
> (REALLY) RISKY BUSINESS
> "I SURVIVED THE DOTCOM CRASH"

Süddeutsche Zeitung

MAGAZIN

No.52 ———— 29.12.2000

Deutschland 2010

Eine Gesellschaft auf der Suche

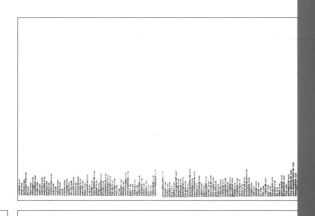

301

sex 1.164.888

yahoo 1.011.053
porno 566.125
erotik 504.088
chat 391.656
lycos 300.429
sms 273.506

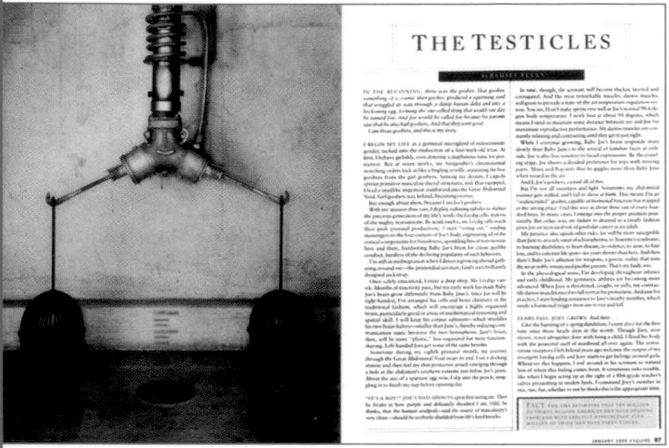

THE TESTICLES

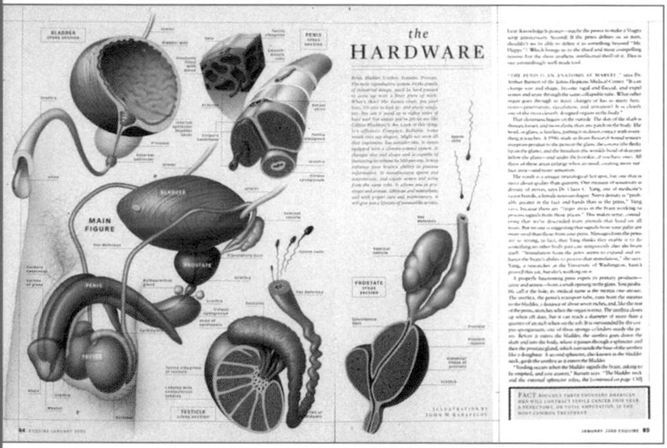

the HARDWARE

ILLUSTRATION BY JOHN W. KARAPELOU

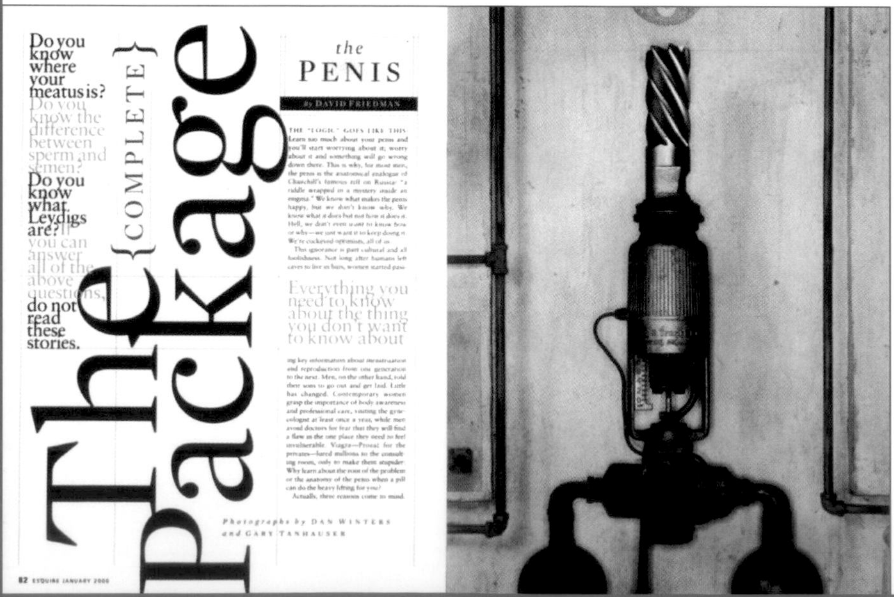

Do you know where your meatus is? Do you know the difference between sperm and semen? Do you know what Leydigs are? If you can answer all of the above questions, do not read these stories.

The {COMPLETE} Package

the PENIS

By DAVID FRIEDMAN

THE "LOGIC" GOES LIKE THIS: Learn too much about your penis and you'll start worrying about it, worry about it and something will go wrong down there. This is why, for most men, the penis is the anatomical analogue of Churchill's famous tell on Russia: "a riddle wrapped in a mystery inside an enigma." We know what makes the penis happy, but we don't know why. We know what it does but not how it does it. Hell, we don't even want to know how or why—we just want it to keep doing it. We're cockeyed optimists, all of us.

This ignorance is part cultural and all foolishness. Not long after humans left caves to live in huts, women started pass-

Everything you need to know about the thing you don't want to know about

ing key information about menstruation and reproduction from one generation to the next. Men, on the other hand, told their sons to go out and get laid. Little has changed. Contemporary women grasp the importance of body awareness and professional care, visiting the gynecologist at least once a year, while men avoid doctors for fear that they will find a flaw in the one place they need to feel invulnerable. Viagra—Prozac for the privates—lured millions to the consulting room, only to make them stupider. Why learn about the root of the problem or the anatomy of the penis when a pill can do the heavy lifting for you?

Actually, three reasons come to mind.

Photographs by DAN WINTERS and GARY TANHAUSER

277 Esquire, 2000

278 Rolling Stone, 2000

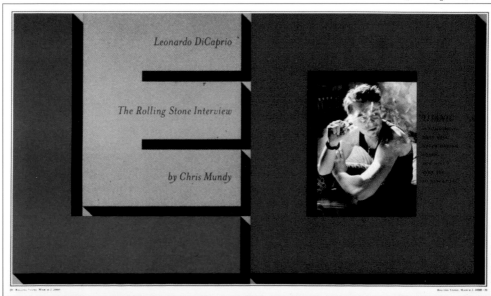

Leonardo DiCaprio

The Rolling Stone Interview

by Chris Mundy

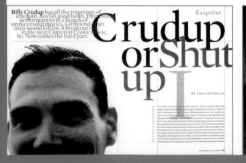

&

David Crosby, Stephen Stills, Graham Nash & Neil Young
sit shoulder to shoulder on wooden stools around a forest of
microphones. On the far left, Stills plays a gentle riff on a
snow-white, wide-body electric guitar. Across from him,
Young, wearing a red flannel shirt and a black baseball cap,
strums an acoustic guitar and sings "Old Man," from his 1972
album, *Harvest*.

Young's shivery tenor sounds fragile in the cold, dark
space of the Convocation Center in Cleveland. But when the
other three enter the chorus with swan-diving harmonies –
"Old man, look at my life/I'm a lot like you" – the song blooms
with fresh meaning. Crosby, Stills, Nash and Young are no
longer the four young bucks who overwhelmed rock in 1969
with pedigree and promise. They are in their fifties, and they
sing "Old Man," a reflection on passing youth and lost opportunity, with electrifying honesty. Unfinished business runs
deep in those bruised gold voices.

There is no applause at the end – because there is no audience. CSNY are in final rehearsals for their first concert tour
since 1974. Opening night, in Detroit, is four days away. But to
hear this band in a big, empty room is to experience magic in
its native state. Everything that makes CSNY one of rock's
premier melodramas – drugs, feuds, Crosby's 1994 liver transplant and new celebrity as a sperm donor for lesbian moms
Melissa Etheridge and Julie Cypher; Nash's boating accident
BY DAVID FRICKE >>> PHOTOGRAPHS BY MARK SELIGER >

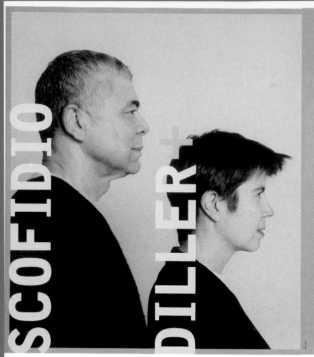

SCOFIDIO

DILLER +

Elizabeth Diller and Ricardo Scofidio are architects. It just happens that they haven't designed much (but that their colleagues would recognize as buildings. To appreciate their approach to architecture, you have to understand two things: it moves beyond traditional conceptions of what buildings should be, but it is the purest form of modernism we have today.

Their collaboration began in 1979, when Scofidio abandoned his 10-person practice to join Diller, who had just graduated from Cooper Union in New York City. To survive in the grim economic climate of the late 1970s, they worked on small, ephemeral projects such as stage sets and art installations. More importantly, they chose this path, and have stuck with it, because of their desire to be "provocateurs," as Scofidio puts it.

As such, they are less concerned with traditional architecture and construction than with analyzing the way social conventions dictate the way people use spaces, objects, and events. Diller + , as they see it, is to reveal those rules, and, where it makes sense, free us from them.

Diller + Scofidio tell stories with space and form about what what. Their buildings and artworks reveal patterns of use always accepted (like dinner-table etiquette), but that actually roles on us. These architects display the instruments, such cameras, that hold our actions. They make us aware that they used and enclose us, but force us to move and behave in specific w

UNDER SURVEILLANCE

Elizabeth Diller and Ricardo Scofidio have always made architecture. Now they're making buildings. By Aaron Betsky

Diller + Scofidio: A P
Diller + Scofidio recent
their first two major buil
the Brasserie
in New York City's Seag
and a low-income house
in Gifu, Japan. Both also
complex, unconventiona
to architecture to be co
more traditionally archit
terms. We present these
chronologically on the fo
pages, in the context o
future projects.

Photograph: Steve Pyke

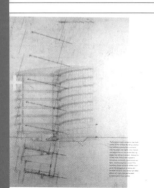

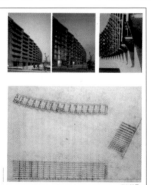

The Brasserie exaggerates the exhibitionist act of seeing and being seen, heightening our awareness of both the absurdity and beauty of social rituals.

281 Architecture, 2000

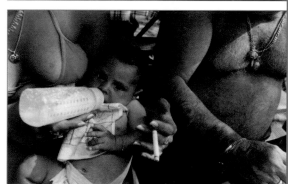

In Search of Dylan McDermott

THE MAN YOUR GIRLFRIEND THINKS ABOUT WHEN YOUR GIRLFRIEND THINKS ABOUT MEN

Three days changed Dylan McDermott's life unalterably. Today is not one of them, but it is a very good day. ¶ Right now, he is sitting alone in the living room of his recently purchased Brentwood house, a 1920s Spanish mansion just off a coral-tree-shaded jogging lane. The move here late last year, to the house previously owned by Melanie Griffith and Antonio Banderas, confirmed that McDermott has finally found his place in Hollywood. He is in his fourth season as the star of the legal drama *The Practice*, and in the spring he will star in a movie he's very proud of, *Texas Rangers*, a gritty western in which he plays a Confederate soldier turned lawman. ¶ Yet at this excellent moment in his life, he looks a little grave. In part, that's because of his strong, dark features—a face brooding enough for a long career in cigarette ads. But it's also because he is pondering a different time. "I came out here," he says, looking back fifteen years to when he first moved to Los Angeles, "went to a party, and Jack Nicholson is there. You see the guy who's made it, and it's like, Oh, shit, this is gonna take a while. Certain actors, they just show up and—boom!—they've arrived. But I was never that guy." He turns quiet and seems slightly ill at ease. ¶ Then the women enter the room. There is a flash of golden hair, wild and curly, as his three-year-old daughter, Coco, bounds awkwardly around the couch, a tiny hand up at her face, the other tightly clutching a piece of construction paper. "She's got something in her eye," says his wife, Shiva, rushing in after her daughter. Shiva is thirty, eventually beautiful in a half-Persian, half-Irish way. "She won't let me see." ¶ "Lemme see your eye, baby," McDermott says, gently pulling away the little fingers. "I know. . . . I know . . . We have to, baby. . . ." he says, looking to find the source of his daughter's pain. "I know. . . ." Suddenly Coco sits up straight, blinks three

5

283 Esquire, 2000

The deadly virus isn't just killing its victims. It's annihilating the way Africa mourns its dead.

Ebola's Shadow

Photograph by Jodi Bieber

Grief in Africa is often alleged to be a belief in the good that the newly dead can do for the living. In traditions that endure among Christians and Muslims alike the recently deceased, if properly buried, are believed to be able to watch out for their kinfolk and guard them from catastrophe.

Outbreaks of Ebola hemorrhagic fever in Africa lay waste not just to human life, but also to the scant comforts of death.

The highly infectious virus — an outbreak of which has killed more than 150 people in Uganda in recent months — causes vomiting, diarrhea and massive bleeding. There is no cure. Treatment is a frantic attempt to replace body fluids. Ebola kills about half the people it attacks. Whoever it does not kill it terrifies.

Where there is Ebola, the traditional ceremonies of death in Africa become insanely risky. Bodies cannot be lovingly washed and dressed for their journey to a spirit world. Coffins cannot be the centerpiece of a grave-village feast. Poor often capitalists mourning, as neighbors turn against the relatives of the dead. In Uganda, neighbors have burned the homes of families that lost kin to the virus.

The World Health Organization has strict rules for disposing of the Ebola dead. There are instated like a viral time bomb — defused by masked technicians with goggles, gowns, boots and gloves. Bodies are dressed with bleach, packed into wooden coffins and buried in fields set away from the living. When there are empty burials are over, technicians spray themselves with bleach.

The rules of epidemic isolation have helped contain Ebola outbreaks in Congo, Gabon, Sudan and the Ivory Coast. Once the dying and the dead are sealed away from the rest of the world, outbreaks of Ebola tend to burn themselves out.

In Uganda, civil war and poverty have complicated the discovery and isolation of the infected. It is slow and often risky for health workers to travel in search of sick people. Roads have to be cleared by the army to reduce the chance of rebel attack, but history suggests that over the next few months the brave technicians in the weird outfits will triumph over the virus—at least in Uganda, at least for a while.

When Ebola is gone, though, its survivors will be dutifully grieved. Loved ones will be dead. And the traditions of Africa will have done nothing to mitigate the finality of their dying. — **Blaine Harden**

Untouchable in Africa: Guns like Gulu, Uganda, Ebola corpses must be buried in quarantined fields.

284 The New York Times Magazine, 2000

experience the

real

thing

A COKE BOTTLE, ONE OF THE MOST RECOGNIZABLE SHAPES IN THE WORLD,
GIVES SHAPE TO THE COCA-COLA BRANDING EXPERIENCE IN LAS VEGAS,
WHERE NOSTALGIA, STORYTELLING, AND TECHNOLOGY CREATE A MAGIC FORMULA.
By Jill Rosenfeld   Photography by Stan Kennedy

EWIGER
SCHLAF
HINTER GLAS

PERFECT FORM

The bodies that fit their sport.

Before considering "world-class athlete" as a career choice, you might want to do a quick inventory. Long thighs? Try rowing. Big feet? Swimmer. Small and stocky? Weight lifting. Tiny and slim? Jockey or gymnast. Unremarkable in any way? There's still hope. You may have a large heart (Tour de France) or one with a previously unsuspected capacity to switch from maximum output to resting rate in seconds (biathlon, in which you ski for miles, then flop on your belly and target-shoot, pulling the trigger during the calm between heartbeats). But perhaps the best advice of all comes from Per-Olof Åstrand, the Swedish sage of exercise physiology, who counsels, "To become an Olympic athlete, choose your parents well."

This plan is not foolproof. Even the genetically superior can end up in the wrong place: the Siberian marlin, the Sudbasese ski jumper, the Amish race-car driver, and so on. But, thanks to the smorgasbord of sports played and regularly televised in the United States, potential athletes have a tremendous advantage here, and perfect specimens of every kind can find the one sporting contest that most purely expresses their genius. This coincidence of talent and opportunity would be wasted without dedication, and the athletes on the following pages have reached the peak of their pursuits through a combination of all three. The five-time Olympic gold medalist Jenny Thompson, for example, set a world record in the hundred-metre freestyle in 1992, and seven years later, long after most of her similarly gifted contemporaries had travelled off for good, she set another, in the hundred-metre butterfly.

Some initially resist their calling. Lisa Leslie, of the W.N.B.A.'s Los Angeles Sparks (at right), who was six feet tall in sixth grade, hated it when people told her she was going to be a basketball player—until the most popular girl in seventh grade asked her to join the team. "We went seven-and-oh, and I've been playing ever since," Leslie says. "I think basketball was just my destiny. It found me."

—Kevin Conley

Lisa Leslie, at home with her cousin Ashley and her niece Brianna. Opposite: Tracy O'Hara, the top college pole-vaulter.

287 The New Yorker, 2000

288 Max, 2000

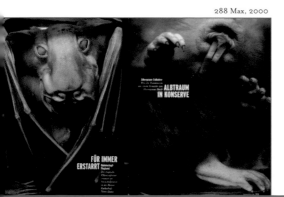

289 Vanity Fair, 2000

290 Rolling Stone, 2000

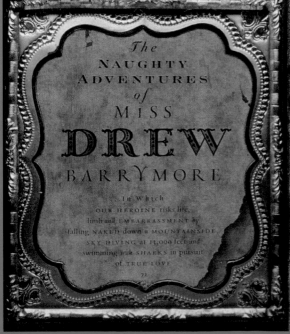

PERSONAL BEST

INSIDE
416 GNARLY DUDE
422 ENEMY OF THE
432 DR. SOUTH

GQ's GUIDE TO HEALTH, FITNESS & GROOMING

So You Think You've Got Problems Now...

That's not pain you're feeling—it's your body telling you where it needs some prevention.
Pay attention, act now, and avoid a future of agony.

The Eyes Have It

ILLUSTRATIONS BY BRIAN CRONIN

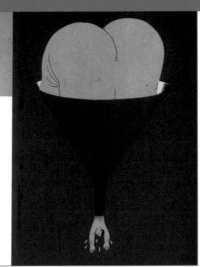

Gnarly, Dude

Six Ways to Avoid Brain Drain

—JOHN HODGMAN

The Spine Who Loved Me

Light at the End of the Tunnel

—ZARE—
—EL ZARE—GILBERT

The Battle of Wounded Knee

293 GQ, 2000

The New York Times Magazine

SEPTEMBER 23, 2001 / SECTION 6

Remains of the Day By Richard Ford Colson Whitehead Richard Powers Robert Stone James Traub Stephen King Jennifer Egan
Roger Lowenstein Judith Shulevitz Randy Cohen William Safire Andrew Sullivan Jonathan Lethem Michael Lewis Margaret Talbot Charles McGrath
Walter Kirn Deborah Sontag Allan Gurganus Michael Ignatieff Kurt Andersen Jim Dwyer Michael Tolkin Matthew Klam Sandeep Jauhar Lauren Slater
Richard Rhodes Caleb Carr Fred R. Conrad Joju Yasuhide Angel Franco Joel Sternfeld Katie Murray Steve McCurry Carolina Salguero Lisa Kereszi
Jeff Mermelstein William Wendt Andres Serrano Richard Burbridge Paul Myoda Julian LaVerdiere Taryn Simon Kristine Larsen

295 Time, 2001

296 Esquire, 2001

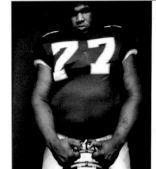

TheEnlightenedMan

FIXING KOREA

The Seo
governme
has made ta
progress to
economic re

297 Global, 2001

com

Restoring the Laws of Year

Wired
for
Growth
Spain's
Telefonica
reinvents itself
as a global
ecommunications
leader.

Q

A
Question
of
Degree

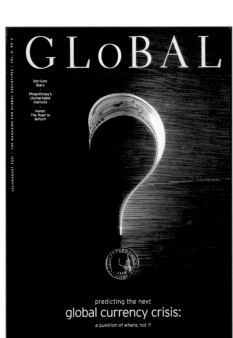

GLoBAL

Dot-Com
Diary

Philanthropy's
Uncharitable
Instincts

Korea:
The Road to
Reform

JULY/AUGUST 2001 | THE MAGAZINE FOR GLOBAL EXECUTIVES | VOL. 4, NO. 2

?

predicting the next
global currency crisis:
a question of where, not if

319

spring nursery

298 Martha Stewart Baby, 2001

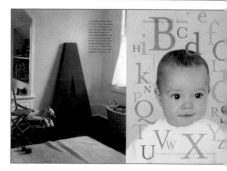

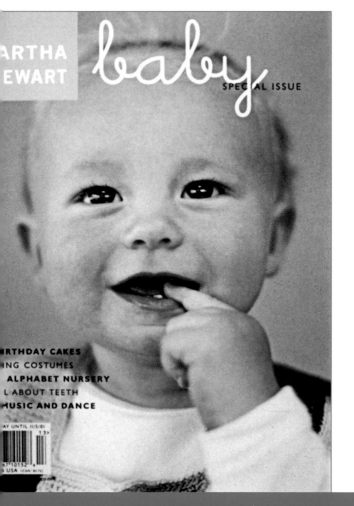

MARTHA
STEWART

baby

SPECIAL ISSUE

BIRTHDAY CAKES
NG COSTUMES
ALPHABET NURSERY
L ABOUT TEETH
MUSIC AND DANCE

AY UNTIL JUS/01

321

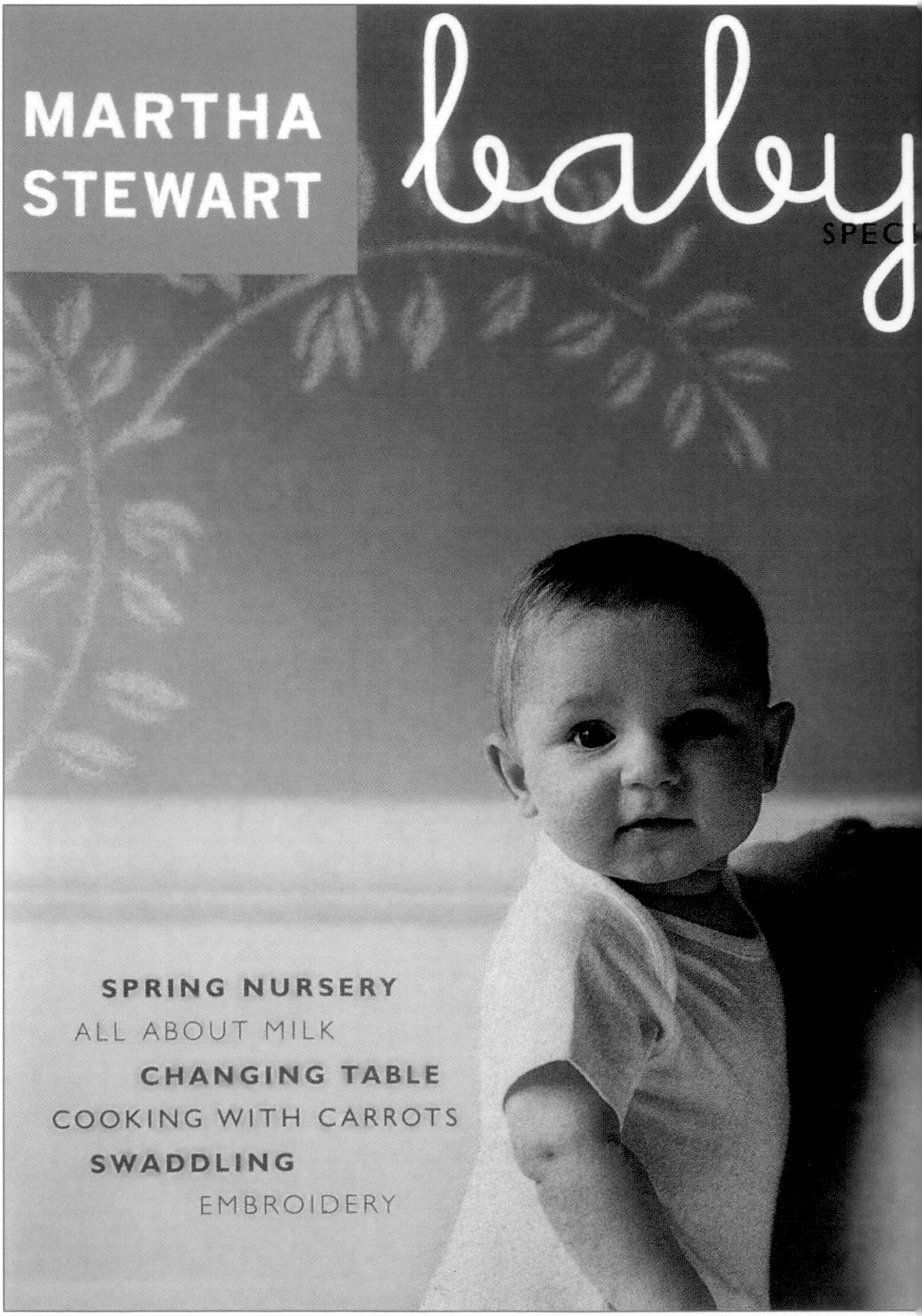

MARTHA STEWART baby SPEC

SPRING NURSERY
ALL ABOUT MILK
CHANGING TABLE
COOKING WITH CARROTS
SWADDLING
EMBROIDERY

299 Martha Stewart Baby, 2001

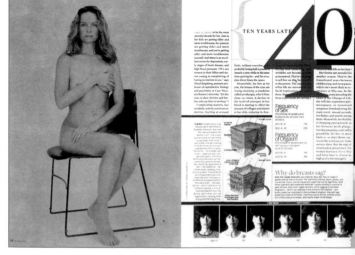

324

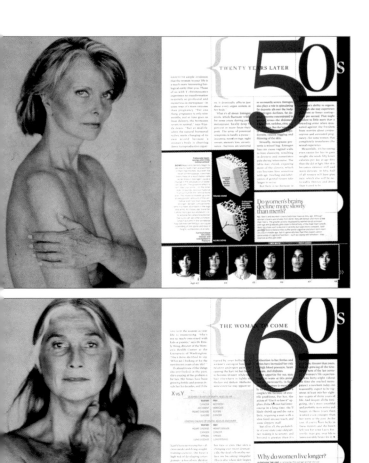

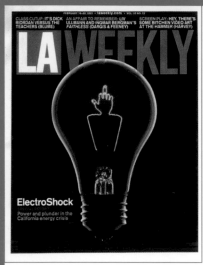

301 LA Weekly, 2001

3 short short stories

[a] Russell Banks
[b] T. R. Pearson
[c] Archer Bradford

Photographs by Tom Sobolik

303 Esquire, 2001

LASE QUINT
PAUL McCARTHY

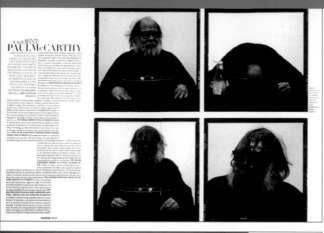

LASE QUINT
DAMIEN HIRST

LASE QUINT
ORLAN

MAGAZIN

ÉL ES

SE LLAMA   Y EN SUS OBRAS UTILIZA EL "KETCHUP" PARA DENUNCIAR LA VIOLE
EL CONSUMO. LA FRANCESA   SE HACE IMPLANTES DE SILICONA FRENTE A LA ESTÉTICA IM
TA, Y   DISECA ANIMALES PARA MOSTRAR LA PASIÓN POR LA VIDA. ¿SON LOS GENI
ARTE CONTEMPORÁNEO O UNA PANDILLA DE LOCOS? SUS COTIZACIONES MILLONARIAS LES DAN LA

306 Utah Carol.com, 2001

The Next
Wonders

Trophy buildings are luring
the traveling masses as never
before. RAYMOND MEIER
captures the year's most exciting
structures—from New Caledonia
to New York. We also deliver
the lowdown on what to do
in the surrounding area.
It's all over but the ogling

SENDAI, JAPAN
SENDAI MEDIATHEQUE PROJECT

Like a Tokyo apartment, where
one room functions as living,
dining, and sleeping quarters,
Toyo Ito's partition-free design
is two-hour bullet train up the
coast from the capital) packs a
multitude of functions into a
single space. When it opens
this year, the conglomeration of
concrete slabs and steel plates
held aloft by helical columns
will host art installations, visiting library collections, film series, and lectures spilling over
from the local university. Within
its two-ply glass membrane,
light and air flow as freely as
the exchange of ideas. Rays hit-
ting the roof travel down
through the structure with the
aid of strategically placed optic
devices, and the pillars function as vents, keeping temper-
ature temperate no matter the
season (2-1 Kasuga-machi,
Aoba-Ku; www.smt.city.sendai.
jp/en/index.html).

Places & Prices
Walk, jog, or hop
your design to meet
where can you eat
and sleep? See
"The Wonderland
Series," page 108.

The
Swimmer

Like Burt Lancaster
before him, David Hasselhoff
plays the part of the
charming and winsome Neddy
Merrill, who pool-hops
his way home as a cast of
backstabbing neighbors
lounge around in the season's
hottest resort clothes.

Credits on Page 96

He was a pilgrim, an explorer,
a man with a destiny, and
he knew that he would find friends
all along the way.

The Hallorans did not wear
bathing suits. . . . Their nakedness
was a detail in their uncompromising
zeal for reform, and he stepped
politely out of his trunks.

The Biswangers did not belong
to Neddy's set. . . . They were
the sort of people who discussed the
price of things at cocktails.

308 The New York Times Magazine, 2001

309 Martha Stewart Living, 2001

310 The New York Times Magazine, 2001

How to Please Elise

An easy-to-follow 68-step guide to mastering the piano. | By Christoph Niemann

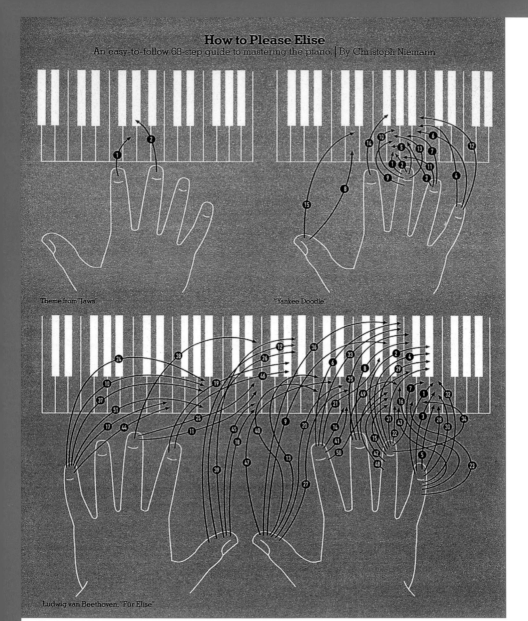

Theme from "Jaws"

"Yankee Doodle"

Ludwig van Beethoven, "Für Elise"

311 The New York Times Magazine, 2001

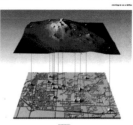

justice without borders

Justice Without Borders Some crimes are so heinous, say legal experts, that they transcend jurisdictional boundaries. People accused of them should be prosecuted anywhere in the world, regardless of where the incident occurred — and regardless of the nationality of anyone involved. But which crimes should fall under the umbrella of international justice? War crimes? Apartheid? Terrorism? Drug trafficking? There's no good answer: international justice can be a dismally ad hoc affair. So this year, 30 scholars and jurists had the bright idea of meeting to try and standardize this new realm of law.

The conference was held at Princeton University in January. The resulting manifesto, "The Princeton Principles on Universal Jurisdiction," represents a coming of age for the idea of international justice. The document aims to settle procedure about when and how a court in one country can try a foreign national for crimes committed in another. Among its conclusions: war crimes, genocide, crimes against humanity, piracy, slavery, crimes against peace and torture are the seven deadly sins that automatically qualify for universal jurisdiction. But wherever it takes place, the trial must conform to international norms of due process and human rights. No one can be tried in absentia. The accused can't stand trial twice for the same crime. No one can claim immunity from prosecution for crimes of this magnitude — not former heads of state, not those suspected of crimes committed many years in the past, not even, in some cases, those who have been granted amnesty by the government of the country where they committed the crime.

Must a state extradite war-crimes suspects who seek refuge on their own soil? Yes, says the Princeton group — unless the prosecuting state employs the death penalty, torture or cruel and degrading punishment. Osama bin Laden, if indicted for crimes against humanity, could be prosecuted anywhere in the world — but if the prosecuting state employed the death penalty, no country would be obligated to extradite him there. American courts automatically have jurisdiction over terrorists acts committed on United States soil. But if a third country proposed, as the Bush administration has, to try bin Laden before a military tribunal, states could refuse to extradite him there too.

Universal jurisdiction was the principle behind the Nuremberg trials for Nazi leaders at the end of World War II, as well as today's war-crimes tribunals for the former Yugoslavia and Rwanda. The jurisdictional scope and procedural standards of those courts were determined by international agreement. The Princeton Principles aim to bring similar clarity to the process of trying war-crimes suspects in national courts far from the scene of the crime.

How far can the international justice regime be extended? Stephen Macedo, a Princeton political-science professor who helped organize the conference where the principles were devised, is careful to keep his claims for universal jurisdiction on this side of modesty. "Should bin Laden really be brought to justice before a court?" Macedo asks. "Do we have enough proof for that? I don't think these categories of universal jurisdiction are adequate to deal with every military threat and strategy we face." But if judicial action can't replace political action, it can hopefully replace some other things we wouldn't be sorry to do without. Collective blame, for instance. Or revenge. LAURA SECOR

Kustom In the beginning, there was mass production and there was made-to-measure, and those were the only two kinds of fashion that anyone who cares about such things was ever seen wearing. Now there's something in between: kustom. Customization of vintage clothes — "kustom," to its hip practitioners — has become an inescapable force in the market. Like ready-to-wear and couture, kustom comes in high fashion and low; it can range from a Kiss concert T-shirt

KUSTOM
Photographs by Erika Aoshima

Women's U.P.S. uniform
redone by the designer Magda Berliner

cut into a halter to the corseted-and-altered U.P.S. uniform at left to a Chanel original refashioned for a new era.

Some credit the Spanish designer Miguel Adrover with starting the trend. Adrover made a name for himself by sending a refashioned Burberry trench coat out on the runway. Some credit stores like Ron Herman in Los Angeles, where rock T-shirts and used Levi's and Armani pants are studded and bedazzled and then sold for hundreds of dollars a pair. Kustom collections like the New York-based Imitation of Christ and the Paris house E.2 have developed a celebrity following. E.2's customized dresses, rescued from thrift-store bins and refashioned by E.2's designers, have been worn by Madonna and Gwyneth Paltrow to many parties.

Crusty Lucken, a Los Angeles designer, calls herself a couturier, costumer and customizer. "Customizing works in two ways," she says. "It makes a vintage piece more modernized in style, but it also makes the fit more custom to the individual. And it also allows you to work with the amazing fabrics and detailing of major labels that, frankly, you couldn't afford to manufacture on your own." Customizing is to fashion what rap is to music: by sampling and remixing the styles of the past, it takes the elitism, and the startup costs, out of the art form. For practiced customizers, the original label in the garment is part of its pedigree. They add their own label to the one already there. So a Tom Ford for Gucci, inspired by Pucci, becomes a Crusty Lucken for Tom Ford for Gucci. AMY M. SPINDLER

Laptop Composing A few years ago, people were talking about the virtual office, which allowed workers to stay home and connect to the workplace via computers. The trend was short-lived (it turns out that most people like having a nonvirtual office). But these days, musicians are embracing the idea of a virtual recording studio. No episode of the MTV program "Cribs," which takes viewers inside the mansions of pop-music stars, is complete until we've seen the artist's home studio, where he can lay down tracks wherever inspiration hits. And now, using laptop computers and simple keyboards, people can create music wherever they roam.

The Icelandic singer Bjork has called "Vespertine," her latest album, "a love affair in the laptop." She used one to put together sounds while traveling between Reykjavik, London and Manhattan. For her recent tour, she took along the computercentric duo Matmos, who provided laptop accompaniment. The Neptunes, the Virginia-based production team that has crafted hits for Britney Spears and Jay-Z, are also virtual-studio partisans. Chad Hugo, one of the Neptunes, says he often travels with a miniature keyboard and sampler so he can sketch out new songs on the road. And Herbie Hancock has added an iBook to the arsenal of instruments in his touring ensemble. In the electronica underground, the familiar image of a musician hunkered over a laptop has become something of a running joke: at a recent electronic music festival, a bunch of virtual producers performed together as Fleetwood Macintosh.

The leading software for editing and recording on a laptop is called Pro Tools, which has been adopted by both do-it-yourself dabblers and big-money producers. Radiohead used it to create its recent cut-and-paste symphonies. Ensaj Krasniz used it to record his slick new album "Lenny." Before technology like Pro Tools, low-budget recordings were instantly recognizable: there was tape hiss, distortion, muddiness. Now it's a lot harder to tell the professionals from the amateurs.

If there's one thing the Internet has taught us, it's that new technology rarely destroys old ways of doing business. Similarly, the

hallelujah

it's collection time again. sunday fashions, how great thou art. photographed by marcelo krasilcic

313 Nylon, 2001

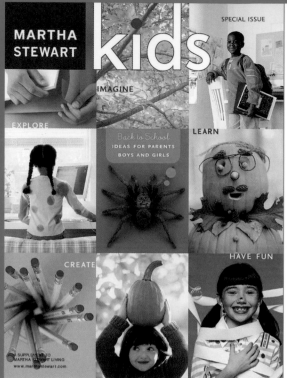

315 Martha Stewart Kids, 2002

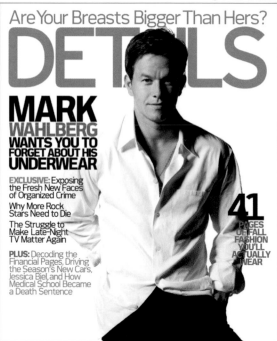

Are Your Breasts Bigger Than Hers?

DETAILS

MARK
WAHLBERG
WANTS YOU TO
FORGET ABOUT HIS
UNDERWEAR

EXCLUSIVE: Exposing
the Fresh New Faces
of Organized Crime

Why More Rock
Stars Need to Die

The Struggle to
Make Late-Night
TV Matter Again

PLUS: Decoding the
Financial Pages, Driving
the Season's New Cars,
Jessica Biel, and How
Medical School Became
a Death Sentence

41
PAGES
OF FALL
FASHION
YOU'LL
ACTUALLY
WEAR

340

317 Real Simple, 2002

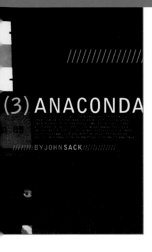

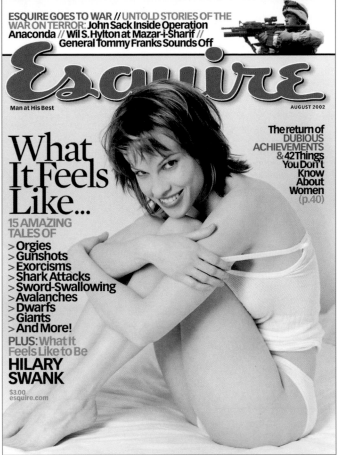

ESQUIRE GOES TO WAR // UNTOLD STORIES OF THE
WAR ON TERROR: **John Sack Inside Operation
Anaconda** // **Wil S. Hylton at Mazar-i-Sharif** //
General Tommy Franks Sounds Off

Esquire

Man at His Best

AUGUST 2002

The return of
**DUBIOUS
ACHIEVEMENTS
& 42 Things
You Don't
Know
About
Women**
(p. 40)

What
It Feels
Like...

**15 AMAZING
TALES OF**
> Orgies
> Gunshots
> Exorcisms
> Shark Attacks
> Sword-Swallowing
> Avalanches
> Dwarfs
> Giants
> And More!

PLUS: What It
Feels Like to Be
**HILARY
SWANK**

$3.00
esquire.com

318 Esquire, 2002

Instant Carnage

Food Styling
Victoria Granof

Photography
Kenji Toma

Pain de moutarde à Charleston

Asperges blanches, sauce béarnaise

Truite fumée au citron

319 Beople, 2002

Moules marinière

Cuisses de grenouille

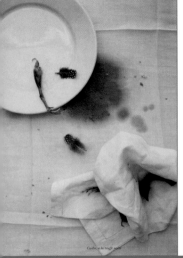

Caille, et la truffe noire

Mousse au chocolat

320 Copy, 2002

GQ
GENTLEMEN'S QUARTERLY

NICK TOSCHES
Living Forever

ALAN RICHMAN
Cloning Elvis

PETER RICHMOND
Secrets of Aging Well

ELIZABETH GILBERT
The Indomitable Jim MacLaren

CHRIS RAYMOND
Building the Perfect Athlete

ANONYMOUS
Lust

DREW HIEFORENT
Losing 125 Pounds

TIEN-LON HO
The Hedonist's Guide to Health

the Male species

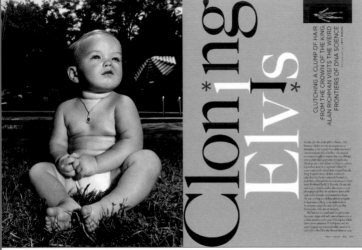

Cloning *Elvis*

CLUTCHING A CLUMP OF HAIR FROM THE CROWN OF THE KING, ALAN RICHMAN VISITS THE WEIRD FRONTIERS OF DNA SCIENCE

Photographs by JEFF RIEDEL

WHEN THE AUTHOR'S BODY STOPPED PRODUCING TESTOSTERONE, HE LOST EVERYTHING: HIS DRIVE, HIS WILL, HIS SOUL. DOCTORS HAD TO INJECT HIM WITH THE GOOD STUFF. AND, BOY, WAS IT GOOD. ONCE THE JUICE FLOWED THROUGH HIM AGAIN, HIS LIBIDO ROSE LIKE A PHOENIX. THAT'S WHEN THINGS GOT DIRTY BY ANONYMOUS

Photographs by MATT MAHURIN

the beast in M

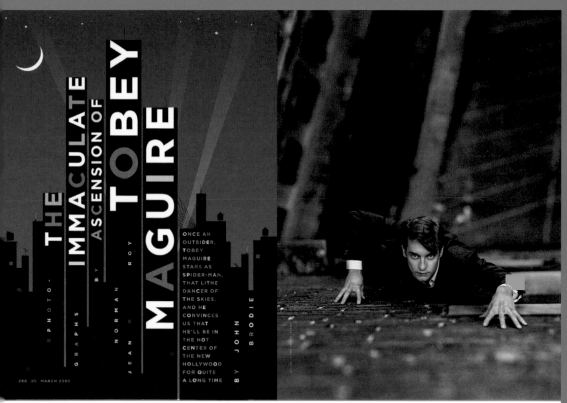

THE IMMACULATE ASCENSION OF TOBEY MAGUIRE

PHOTOGRAPHS BY NORMAN JEAN ROY

BY JOHN BRODIE

ONCE AN OUTSIDER, TOBEY MAGUIRE STARS AS SPIDER-MAN, THAT LITHE DANCER OF THE SKIES. AND HE CONVINCES US THAT HE'LL BE IN THE HOT CENTER OF THE NEW HOLLYWOOD FOR QUITE A LONG TIME

286 GQ MARCH 2002

THE RULE OF LAW

ACCORDING TO HOLLYWOOD'S RELUCTANT GOLDEN BOY JUDE LAW, THE TRICK IS TO:
1. MARRY A STRONG, SEXY WOMAN & HAVE A PASSEL OF KIDS
2. EMBRACE YOUR INNER MISCREANT—AS HE DOES THIS MONTH IN "ROAD TO PERDITION," OPPOSITE NEWMAN & HANKS

PHOTOGRAPHS BY MARK SELIGER

GENTLEMEN'S QUARTERLY 120   121   BY LUCY KAYLIN

348

Editorial and Op-Ed pages, 14-15
Education Advertising
Careers in Education and
Health Care Employment

The New York Times

Week in Review

UNSEEN: A SPECIAL SECTION ON INTELLIGENCE

Marko Illic

Not Much Has Changed in a System That Failed

By JAMES RISEN and DAVID JOHNSTON

WASHINGTON

EVEN though American intelligence agencies were harshly criticized after the terrorist attacks on New York and Washington for having missed signs that attacks were planned, there has been surprisingly little fundamental restructuring in the year since. Certainly there has been less change than was predicted in the weeks after Sept. 11, 2001.

A broad debate has begun over how to reorganize domestic and foreign intelligence in the face of a supple, unfamiliar and suicidal new form of threat. Still, the Central Intelligence Agency and the Federal Bureau of Investigation have proven remarkably resilient in defense of their own turf.

Even as Congress argues over the shape of a new

The F.B.I. and C.I.A. missed signals a year ago. Now they do well in capital turf wars.

Homeland Security Department, for example, it is clear that the department will not get broad espionage or law enforcement powers that could challenge the current status of either the C.I.A. or F.B.I.

To be sure, the security agencies have been busy changing some procedures and reinforcing some abilities. Some legal and regulatory restrictions that had hampered coordination between the C.I.A. and the F.B.I.

have been eased. Under the new USA Patriot Act, for example, the C.I.A. can have access to secret grand jury material and wiretap information obtained under the Foreign Intelligence Surveillance Act.

And senior officials now can work more closely together: Attorney General John Ashcroft and the F.B.I. director, Robert S. Mueller III, are included with the director of central intelligence, George J. Tenet, in a daily meeting with President Bush on terrorist threats.

The F.B.I. has also begun a reorganization designed to bolster its analytical ability and to break down attitudes at the bureau that kept it oriented toward the prosecution of criminal cases rather than the early detection of terrorist plots. But the effort is far from complete, and the basic arrangement in which the bureau controls domestic intelligence is intact.

At the same time, the C.I.A. has greatly enlarged its counterterrorism center and has started a crash drive

to hire more analysts, case officers and translators. Its covert action abilities, which withered in the 1990's after the cold war ended, are gradually being revived, as is the agency's paramilitary arm, the Special Activities Division, which sent C.I.A. officers to work with Special Operations forces in Afghanistan.

Despite the chorus of critics who charged that the Sept. 11 attacks represented an intelligence failure on the scale of Pearl Harbor, the C.I.A. and F.B.I. have not been broken up or subsumed into any new terror-fighting organization. Indeed, both agencies got big budget increases after Sept. 11 — Congressional decisions that confirmed the agencies' clout even as they responded to the public's yearning for safety.

At the same time Congress was approving the money, though, lawmakers complained that intelligence

Continued on Page 7

Sharing Information

Learning to Spy With Allies

By DOUGLAS FRANTZ

WHAT will Al Qaeda do next? One big problem in figuring it out has been that, in important ways, the terrorist network is more effectively globalized than the modern intelligence organizations that try to penetrate it.

The spy agencies are a throwback to the days when nations fought each other, rather than an amorphous international web of nihilists with no national interests or political program to slow them down.

So even as Al Qaeda moves its people and money around the globe as if national boundaries no longer exist, the spy agencies keep checking their backs to make sure none of their traditional rivals (or allies) are stealing trade secrets or otherwise turning cooperation to its own advantage.

The year since Sept. 11 has made intelligence officials think about this, though, and they are trying, with some success, to change.

"The way we think of Al Qaeda today is the day-before-yesterday's version," said Magnus Ranstorp, deputy director of the Center for the Study of Terrorism and Political Violence at the University of St. Andrews in Scotland. "We are dealing with human beings united in commitment. The organization mutates and transforms itself according to operational requirements."

Al Qaeda's foes do not share information as well or adapt as quickly. Their mentality erects barriers to sharing sensitive information with domestic sister agencies, let alone foreign governments. Secrecy is a hallowed right, and breaking down that tradition is proving

difficult.

But interviews with terrorism experts and intelligence and counterterrorism authorities across Europe in recent weeks found unanimous recognition of the problem.

"These (terrorist) groups communicate and support each other in logistics, such as falsification of identification and finances and weapons procurement," said Klaus Ulrich Kersten, head of Germany's criminal investigations agency, the Bundeskriminalamt. "This means that the intelligence work of secret services requires an exchange of information between countries. To intensify cooperation with many countries, including in North Africa and the Middle East."

Across Europe, intelligence officials say that since American bombs began falling in Afghanistan last October, radicals who learned their skills at camps there have dispersed to their home countries and other places, changing the nature of the threat. For example, the suicide bombing that killed 21 outside a Tunisian synagogue in April appears to have been the work of a Qaeda operative trained in Afghanistan. The German police said he appeared to be working on orders from a network leader hiding in Pakistan.

To face such threats, Mr. Kersten and others envi-

Continued on Page 7

WHAT WOULD JESUS DO?

BUT MORE IMPORTANT, WHAT WERE JESUS' FITNESS SECRETS? IF YOU WERE ONE OF THE GROWING MILLIONS OF AMERICANS LIVING IN THE MULTIMILLION-DOLLAR CHRISTIAN ALTERNACULTURE—IN WHICH EVERYTHING IN MAINSTREAM CULTURE GETS CLONED AND THEN LEACHED OF "SINFUL" CONTENT—YOU'D KNOW. WALTER KIRN SPENDS SEVEN STRANGE DAYS WALKING IN THE SHOES OF THE FAITHFUL

THE SEX GODDESSES

RALPH LAUREN IN THE PURPLE

WE RAISE OUR GLASSES TO TOAST THE INCOMPARABLE MR. LAUREN AS HE CELEBRATES HIS THIRTY-FIFTH ANNIVERSARY AS THE PREEMINENT U.S. DESIGNER OF STYLISH MEN'S CLOTHING BY GLENN O'BRIEN

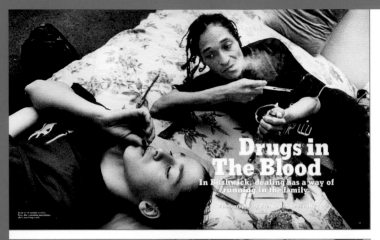

Drugs in The Blood

In Bushwick, dealing has a way of running in the family

Photographs by Brenda Ann Kenneally

329 Sports Illustrated, 2002

330 The New York Times Magazine, 2002

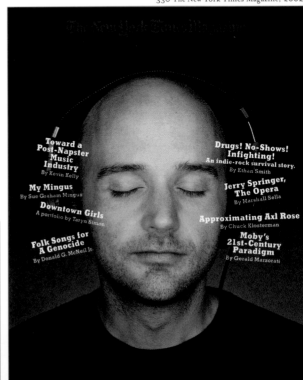

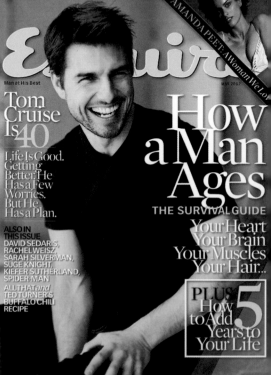

TRUNK SHOW

IN 1961, AUB LAIDLAW—THE PANICKSTRICKEN INSPECTOR FOR SYDNEY'S BONDI BEACH, WHO WAS KNOWN TO CARRY A RULER TO ENSURE that the sides of women's bikinis conformed to the regulations. Bondi inhabitants received a gotten token for holding a custom-made swimming garment called the Speedo. Invented earlier that year by Sydney designer Peter Travis, the revolutionary budding trunk was the subject of one of the country's most notorious court cases. Although the Speedo eventually received eventually acceptable for public display because they smuggled on public hair, to this day there are those who associate fashioned differences. 6. While to many men have no trouble showing their embarrassing strips of nylon and Lycra—in my youth, those guys were pejoratively known as Guidos in Speedos—most Americans would rather hit the beach in surf-style suck as knee-mobile tents to an Esquire town swears bon-labrel. Also known as "boomerockers," "dickstickers," and "banana hammocks," Speedos are dismissed by many middle men as too floozy and gay—the sartorial equivalent of sporting a rainbow-flag tattoo. "Even I wouldn't wear Speedos," says a self-proclaimed open-minded menswear executive at Polo Ralph Lauren. "They're like mustaches—hilarious but so campy." 6. "They're camp," says artist Stacey Moffatt, whose voyeuristic 1991 beach-culture documentary, Heaven, is floored as elegant

BY HORACIO SILVA
Photographs by Lisa Kereszi

333 Salon News, 2002

334 Print, 2002

335 Time, 2003

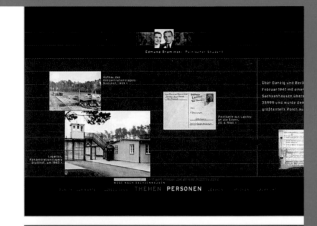

336 C-D Rom: Lest We Forget, 2003

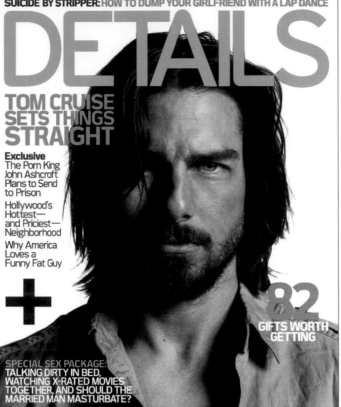

SUICIDE BY STRIPPER: HOW TO DUMP YOUR GIRLFRIEND WITH A LAP DANCE

DETAILS

TOM CRUISE SETS THINGS STRAIGHT

Exclusive
The Porn King John Ashcroft Plans to Send to Prison

Hollywood's Hottest— and Priciest— Neighborhood

Why America Loves a Funny Fat Guy

82
GIFTS WORTH GETTING

SPECIAL SEX PACKAGE:
TALKING DIRTY IN BED, WATCHING X-RATED MOVIES TOGETHER, AND SHOULD THE MARRIED MAN MASTURBATE?

337 Details, 2003

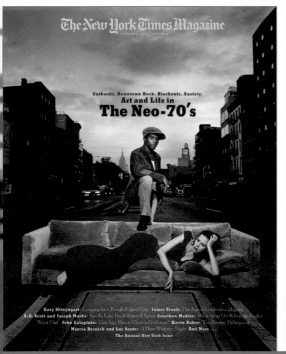

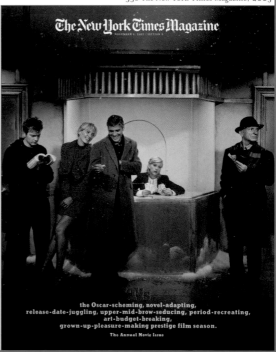

339 GQ, 2003

340 W, 2003

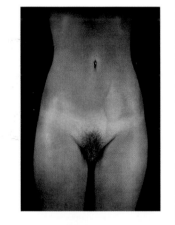

Chuck Close

kate moss portfolio

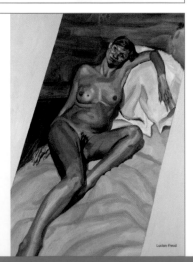

Lucian Freud

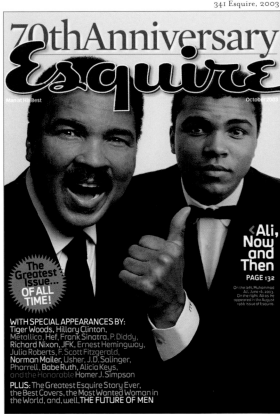

70thAnniversary

Esquire

Man at His Best

October 2003

< Ali,
Now
and
Then
PAGE 132

On the left, Muhammad
Ali, June 16, 2003.
On the right, Ali as he
appeared in the August
1966 issue of Esquire.

The
Greatest
Issue...
OF ALL
TIME!

WITH SPECIAL APPEARANCES BY:
Tiger Woods, Hillary Clinton,
Metallica, Hef, Frank Sinatra, P. Diddy,
Richard Nixon, JFK, Ernest Hemingway,
Julia Roberts, F. Scott Fitzgerald,
Norman Mailer, Usher, J.D. Salinger,
Pharrell, Babe Ruth, Alicia Keys,
and the Honorable Homer J. Simpson

PLUS: The Greatest Esquire Story Ever,
the Best Covers, the Most Wanted Woman in
the World, and, well, THE FUTURE OF MEN

"Sing a Song of Ray Romano"
(It's more of a dirge, actually)

THE FUTURE
OF WOMEN

70

By ROBERT KURSON
ILLUSTRATION BY C.F. PAYNE

Hillary's
Last
Chance

AND, AS LIFE AND LUCK WOULD HAVE
IT, ALSO HER FIRST CHANCE.
BEHOLD THE LIBERATION OF HRC.

Donatella Versace is wearing David Webb's 18k gold, platinum, diamond, ruby and emerald necklace, $44,200, at David Webb, New York. $44,600. Dress by Versace.

guys & dolls

The models—pop culture icons re-created by stylist Jane How and photographer Mario Sorrenti in deli meats, candy and Band-Aids—are fake. but the jewelry they're wearing is oh so real.

Photographs By Mario Sorrenti
Styled By Jane How

342 W Jewelry, 2003

VISUAL AND PERFORMING ARTS   VOL 7 : NO 1

2wice

animal

CLOVEN
KINGDOM

BROKEN
MAN

GQ GOES IN SEARCH OF THE NEXT BIG THING

Photographs by Fred Woodward
Interviews by Michael Hainey

CASTING CALL

WE'RE LOOKING TO DISCOVER THE NEXT BIG STAR. Wanted: Female Actors 18-25 to play strong, sultry, uninhibited lead. Open call Nov. 7 & 8. Don't miss out on this incredible casting opportunity. Please call 310-314-4403 or 212-286-7835 for details.

SPEND MORE THAN FIVE MINUTES IN LOS ANGELES AND YOU SEE THEM. The hopefuls. The believers. The would-be, could-be starlets. They are the soul of the town, the obsession of the business. They come from everywhere and nowhere, driven by the dream that they are just a break away from being discovered, a day away from stardom.

WE WANTED TO KNOW THEIR STORIES. To find them, we placed the ad above in an L.A. paper. These are the women we discovered. Keep an eye out. Maybe you'll see them. Maybe you won't.

STORY START — JENNIFER GARNER

DARLING — SWEETHEART

DESIGN GETS PERSONAL

BETAVILLE

profilin'

For the past decade, *Vibe* photography has married the form of high art with the function of serving the streets. As a result, these pictures represent a wide spectrum of subjects and genres, from a venerated Latino adult star to a notorious white rapper. The sequence of these portraits—from the upcoming book *Vib 10 Years of Vibe Photography*—tells a provocative story about our history, our sensuality, and our rage.

V gallery

> **UNBREAKABLE**

> **UNSTOPPABLE**

346 Vibe, 2003

345 eDesign, 2003

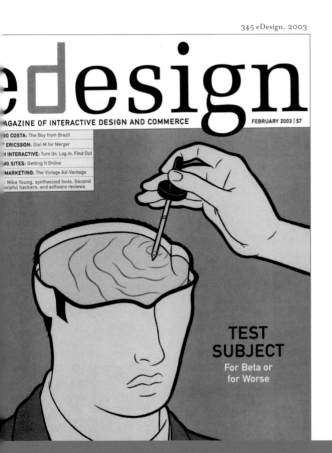

edesign

MAGAZINE OF INTERACTIVE DESIGN AND COMMERCE   **FEBRUARY 2003 | $7**

O COSTA: The Boy from Brazil

ERICSSON: Dial M for Merger

INTERACTIVE: Turn On, Log In, Find Out

G SITES: Getting It Online

MARKETING: The Vintage Ad-Vantage

Mike Young, synthesized fonts. Second helpful hackers. and software reviews

TEST SUBJECT

For Beta or for Worse

THE WAR
COMES HOME
After Marine Corporal
Evan Jones died in
Iraq, the people in
his hometown of
Lamoni, IF, say,
1, 1891, decorated
the town square with
American flags to
welcome him home.
The 21-year-old
returned with the
82nd Airborne
Support Battalion
invasion March 24
as he and three
other Marines tried
to secure the
Saddam Canal in
southeastern Iran.
According to a
reconstruction of the
incident in the Des
Moines Register,
Jones and fellow
Bradley crewmen of
town flagged as they
swept from the south
bank to the north—
roughly 150 yards—
while hauling 20 to
40 lbs. of gear.
Their combat teams
became waterlogged
and probably got
stuck in the mud at
the bottom of the
canal.
Photograph for
TIME by
Anthony Suau

THIS IS WORSHIP
Bereaved, covered Shi'ite women prayed
before a statue in Karbala, Iraq, in April.
Hundreds of thousands took part in the
pilgrimage, each gathering had been
militarized for years by Saddam Hussein.
Photograph for TIME
by James Nachtwey—VII

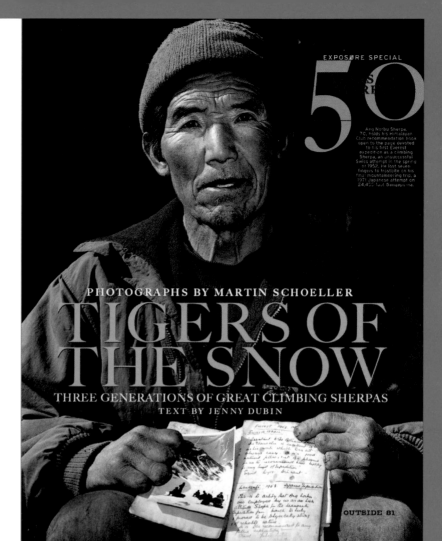

Ang Norbu Sherpa, 70, holds his Himalayan Club recommendation book open to the page devoted to his first Everest expedition as a climbing Sherpa, an unsuccessful Swiss attempt in the spring of 1952. He lost seven fingers to frostbite on his final mountaineering trip, a 1971 Japanese attempt on 24,400-foot Bengapunie.

PHOTOGRAPHS BY MARTIN SCHOELLER

TIGERS OF THE SNOW

THREE GENERATIONS OF GREAT CLIMBING SHERPAS
TEXT BY JENNY DUBIN

OUTSIDE 81

349 The New York Times Magazine, 2003

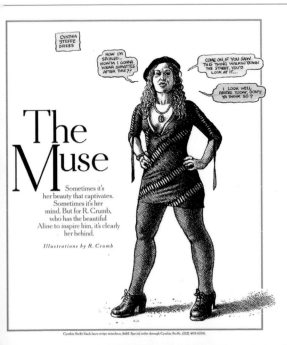

The Muse

Sometimes it's her beauty that captivates. Sometimes it's her mind. But for R. Crumb, who has the beautiful Aline to inspire him, it's clearly her behind.

Illustrations by R. Crumb

351 Vanity Fair, 2003

352 The Guardian, 2003

353 El Mundo Metropoli, 2003

354 Martha Stewart Kids, 2003

355 Interior Design, 2003

356 Comcast High-Speed Internet, 2003

357 Rawls Exchange, 2003

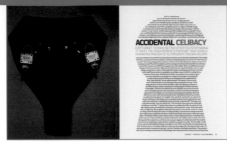

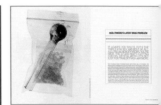

358 Details, 2004

374

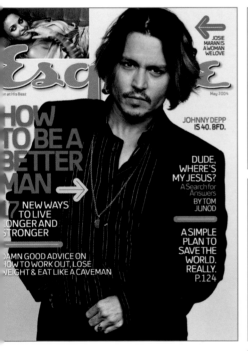

ARM CANDY

Lou Bohème

Graphic Design

MODERN BAROQUE

The Originals

The New York Times Style Magazine

DESIGN FALL 2004

360 The New York Times Style Magazine, 2004

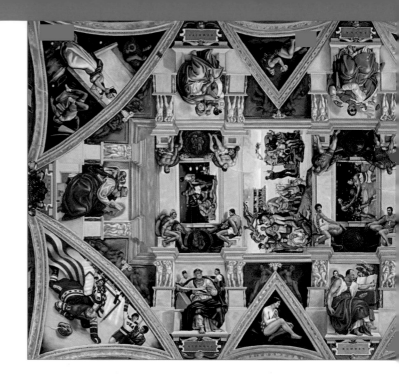

361 GQ, 2004

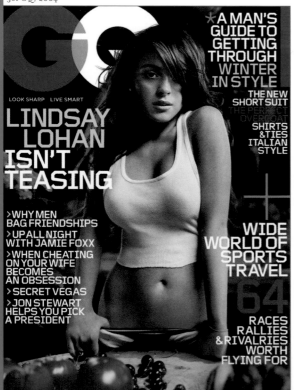

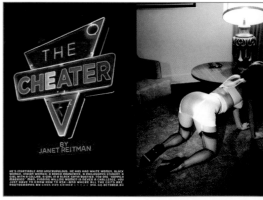

362 Sports Illustrated, 2004

wĕn´ty~fîrst
ĕn´tu~ry fŏx(x).

1. By now you've heard a lot about what a talented actor JAMIE FOXX is— with career-making erformances in *Collateral* and *Ray*. . But where the 36-year-old actor *eally* makes it happen is right here home, where the barbecue is red up, everyone is bringing bottle, and the man of the house is orking the phones, rounding up e ladies. **3.** CHRIS HEATH invites imself in for some time with ctober's biggest surprise.
Photographs by MARK SELIGER)

379

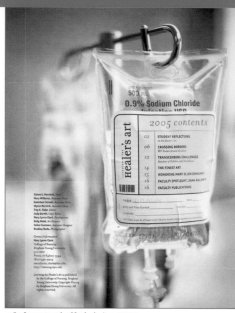

363 The New York Times Magazine, 2004

364 Learning the Healer's Art, 2004

365 Dialogue, 2004

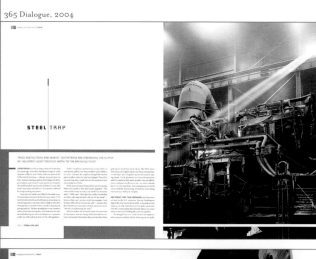

STEEL TRAP

366 The New Yorker, 2004

367 SEE: The Potential of Place, 2004

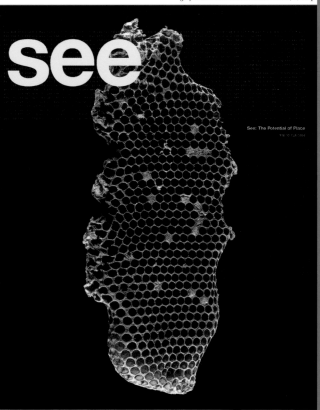

Photographer Michael Wolf's daunting images of Hong Kong offer a glimpse of humanity's uncanny ability to adapt to even the most overwhelming and surreal of landscapes.

The City Revealed

In his *Aesthetics of Density*, Vittorio Magnago Lampugnani writes of Hong Kong, "The imploding city with a vast unintended beauty is also the city of a new, unreal urban idyll. It is a city in which the vast number of people living in extremely close proximity offers a breathtaking spectacle, at once fascinating and distressing."

March 2004 **Dwell 23**

"IT WORKS TO APPROACH IT AS IF WHAT I'M DOING HERE IS A REAL THING. THIS OUTFIT I'M WEARING—I'M NOT TRYING TO BE FUNNY."

In 1947, six years after becoming a British province, Hong Kong had a population of 21,900. Today, six years after the return to Chinese control, 6.8 million people call the 80-square-kilometer island and surrounding areas home. Opposite page: Block Five of the Kwai Shing government housing complex. This page: The Pinnacle Estate in the Tseung Kwan O district.

369 dwell, 2004

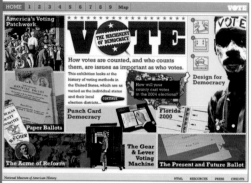

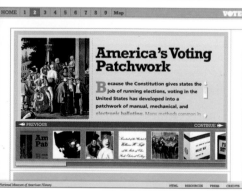

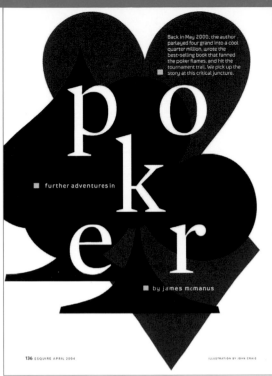

poker

■ further adventures in

■ by james mcmanus

136 ESQUIRE APRIL 2004

ILLUSTRATION BY JOHN CRAIG

373 Esquire, 2004

374 Vanity Fair, 2004

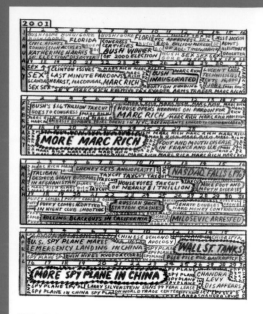

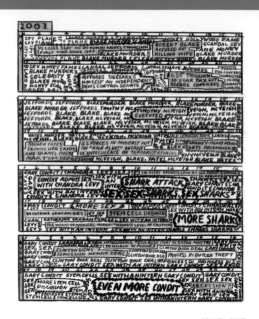

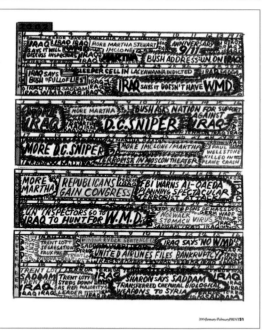

375 Print, 2004

Index-

1973-79
SPD Gold
Winners

1973

001
The New York Times Magazine
Art Director: Stan Mack
Designer: Stan Mack
Artist: Richard Hess

002
The New York Times Magazine
Art Director: Stan Mack
Designer: Stan Mack
Photographer: Fred Burrell

003
McCall's
Art Director: Alvin Grossman
Designer: Alvin Grossman
Photographer: Irwin Horowitz

004
The New York Times
"The Week in Review"
Art Director: Eric Seidman
Designer: Eric Seidman
Artist: Eric Seidman

005
The New York Times Magazine
Art Director: Stan Mack
Designers: Stan Mack,
Louis Silverstein

006
The Atlantic
Art Director: Jacques Buens
Designer: Dianne Penny
Photographer: Sam Hall

007
The New York Times Magazine
Art Director: Stan Mack
Designer: Stan Mack
Photographer: Peter Simon

008
Folio
Art Director: Steve Phillips
Designer: Steve Phillips
Artist: Ed Soyka

009
Popular Photography
Art Director: Shinichiro Tora
Photographer: Ansel Adams

010
Mineral Digest
Art Director: Robert Sadler
Designer: Robert Sadler
Artist: James Spanfeller

011
Oui
Art Director: Don Menell
Designer: Michael Brock
Photographer: Hiro

012
Horizon
Art Director: Ken Munowitz
Designer: Ken Munowitz
Photographer: Herbert Migdoll

013
Oui
Art Director: Don Menell
Designer: Michael Brock
Artist: Roy Carruthers

1974

014
Life
Art Director:
Elton Robinson

015
The 5 Minute Hour
Art Director: Bob Paganucci
Designer: Bob Paganucci
Artist: Alan Cober

016
Avant Garde
Art Directors: Herb Lubalin
& Tom Bodkin
Designer: Herb Lubalin
Artist: Roy Carruthers

017
U & lc
Art Director: Herb Lubalin
Designer: Herb Lubalin

018
Art in Virginia
Art Director: Raymond Geary
Designer: Raymond Geary
Photographer: Dean Brown

019
Minneapolis Tribune
Thursday Section
Design Director: Michael Carroll
Designer: Bruce Bjerva
Photographer: Kent Kobersteen

020
McCall's
Art Directors: Alvin Grossman,
Carveth Kramer
Designer: Kit Hinrichs
Artists: Kit Hinrichs, Nancy Stahl,
Margaret Cuzak, Marlowe Goodson

021
National Geographic World
Art Director: Charles O. Hyman
Designer: Charles O. Hyman
Artist: Graphicsgroup Inc.
Photographer: Michael Pfleger

022
Oui
Art Director: Don Menell
Designer: Don Menell
Artist: Christian Piper

023
Distillers Corp. – Seagram's Ltd.
Art Director: Arnold Saks
Designers: Arnold Saks,
Tomas Nittner

Photographers: Phil Marco,
Arthur Schatz

024
New York
Art Directors: Milton Glaser,
Walter Bernard
Designer: Milton Glaser
Artist: Richard Hess

1975

025
Rolling Stone
Art Director: Tony Lane
Designer: Roger Black
Artist: Bruce Wolfe

026
Printing Salesman's Herald
Art Director: R.O. Blechman
Designer: Miho
Artist: R.O. Blechman

027
Champion International Corp.
– 1974 Annual Report
Art Director: Richard Hess
Designer: Richard Hess
Photographer: Richard Hess

028
Audubon
Art Director: Daniel J. McClain
Designers: Daniel J. McClain,
Les Line
Photographer: Jim Bones

029
Oui
Art Director: Don Menell
Designer: Jean-Pierre Holley
Artist: Alex Ebel

030
U & lc
Art Director: Herb Lubalin
Designer: Herb Lubalin

031
Pastimes
Art Director:
B. Martin Pedersen
Designer: B. Martin Pedersen

1976

032
Playboy
Art Director: Arthur Paul
Designer: Len Willis
Illustrator: Kunio Hagio

033
Hoof Beats
Art Director: Jan V. White
Designer: Jan V. White
Photographer: George Smallsreed

034
Kodak International
Photography
Art Directors: Kenn Jacobs,
Erwin Ritenis
Designer: Erwin Ritenis
Photographers: Various

035
Quest 77
Art Director: Noel Werrett
Designer: Noel Werrett

036
The Arthur Young Journal
Art Director: David Starwood
Designer: Will Martin
Photographers: Don Jim,
Lee Boltin, Beverly Peterson

037
U & lc
Art Director: Herb Lubalin
Designer: Herb Lubalin
Illustrator: Jerome Snyder

038
California Business
Art Director: Bob Kinkead
Designer: Bob Kinkead

039
Emergency Medicine
Art Directors: Ira Silberlicht,
Tom Lennon
Designers: Tom Lennon,
Irving J. Cohen
Photographer: Shig Ikeda

040
American Ephemera
Art Director: Stuart Silver
Designer: Al Grossman
Illustrator: Museum Collections
Photographer:
Museum Studios

1977

041
Rolling Stone
Art Director: Roger Black
Designer: Bea Feitler
Photographer: Annie Leibovitz

042
Psychology Today
Art Director: Neil Shakery
Designer: Neil Shakery
Photographer: Bill Longcore

043
People
Art Director: Robert N. Essman
Designer: Sanae Yamazaki
Photographer: George Long

044
People
Art Director: Robert N. Essman
Designer: Robert N. Essman
Photographer:
Jay Leviton/Atlanta

045
Field & Stream
Art Director: Victor J. Closi
Designer: Victor J. Closi
Illustrator: Roy Doty

046
Rolling Stone
Art Director: Roger Black
Designer: Carla Barr

Illustrators: Milton Glaser,
John Cage, Ray Johnson,
Victor Kotowitz

047
The New York Times
Art Director: Ruth Ansel
Illustrator: Stan Shaffer
Photographer: Stan Shaffer

048
American Preservation
Art Director: Peter Bradford
Designer: Peter Bradford
Illustrator: Peter Bradford
Photographers: Ave Bonar,
John Carney, Bob Bragg,
Terry Cooper, Marion E.
Warren, Morley Baer

049
Quest 77
Art Director: Noel Werrett
Designers: Noel Werrett,
Bary Drury, Eberhard
Luethke, Peter Morance

1978

050
The New York Times
Art Director: Jerelle Kraus
Category Design: Cover

051
Metropolitan Museum
Art Director: Stuart Silver
Category Design:
Single Issue

052
Rolling Stone
Art Director: Roger Black
Designer: Mary Shanahan
Photographer: Hiro
Category Photography:
Single Spread

053
Playboy
Art Director: Arthur Paul
Designer: Kerig Pope
Illustrator: Frank Gallo
Category Illustration:
Single Spread

1979

054
Life
Art Director: Bob Ciano
Category Design: Story

055
Playboy
Art Directors: Arthur Paul,
Tom Staebler
Designer: Len Willis
Illustrator: Marshall Arisman
Category Illustration: Story

056
Nautical Quarterly
Art Director: B. Martin Pedersen
Designer: B. Martin Pedersen
Category Design: Entire Issue

057
Life
Art Director: Bob Ciano
Category Photography:
Entire Story

1980-89 SPD Gold Winners

1980

058
Nautical Quarterly
Art Director: B. Martin Pedersen
Designer: B. Martin Pedersen
Photographer: Allen Weitz
Publisher: Nautical Quarterly

059
U & lc
Art Director: Herb Lubalin
Illustrator: Cover art Wally Neibart;
Inside: various artists
Publisher: International
Typeface Corp.

060
U & lc
Art Director: Herb Lubalin
Illustrator Cover art Wally Neibart;
inside art various artists
Publisher: International Typeface Corp.

061
Nautical Quarterly
Art Director: B. Martin Pedersen
Designer: B. Martin Pedersen
Photographer: Sam Abell
Publisher: Nautical Quarterly

1981

062
Esquire
Art Director: Robert Priest
Designer: Stephen Doyle
Illustrator: Gotfried Helnwein
Publisher: Esquire Publishing

063
Nautical Quarterly
Art Director: B. Martin Pedersen
Designer: B. Martin Pedersen
Illustrator: Daniel Maffia
Publisher: Jonson Pedersen
Hinrichs & Shakery, Inc.

064
Nautical Quarterly
Art Director: B. Martin Pedersen
Designer: B. Martin Pedersen
Illustrator: Daniel Maffia
Publisher: Jonson Pedersen
Hinrichs & Shakery, Inc.

065
Postgraduate Medicine
Art Director: Tina Adamek
Designer: Tina Adamek
Illustrator: John Jude Palencar
Publisher: McGraw-Hill, Inc.

066
The Plain Dealer Magazine
Art Director: Greg Paul
Illustrator: Brad Holland
Publisher: The Plain Dealer
Publishing Company

067
Penthouse
Art Director: Joe Brooks
Designer: Claire Victor
Illustrator: Marvin Mattelson
Publisher: Penthouse
International

068
Foremost-McKesson
Annual Report
Art Director: Neil Shakery
Designer: Neil Shakery,
Barbara Vick
Illustrator: Jean Michel Folon
Publisher: Foremost-McKesson

069
Foremost-McKesson
Annual Report
Art Director: Neil Shakery
Designers: Neil Shakery,
Barbara Vick
Illustrator: Jean Michel Folon
Publisher: Foremost-McKesson

070
Cal Today
Art Director: Howard Shintaku
Designer: Howard Shintaku
Illustrator: Mitchell H. Anthony
Publisher: San Jose Mercury News

071
Life
Art Director: Bob Ciano
Designer: Bob Ciano
Illustrator: Brad Holland
Publisher: Time Inc.

072
Life
Art Director: Bob Ciano
Designer: Bob Ciano
Illustrator: Brad Holland
Publisher: Time Inc.

073
Life
Art Director: Bob Ciano
Designer: Bob Ciano
Illustrator: Brad Holland
Publisher: Time Inc.

1984

074
Arts & Architecture
Art Director: Rip Georges
Publisher: Arts &
Architecture Incorporated
Category Design: Entire Issue

075
The Boston Globe
Art Director: Lucy Bartholomay
Designer: Lucy Bartholomay
Illustrator: Debroah Perugi-MAP
Photographer: Stan Grossfeld

Publisher: Globe Newspaper Co.
Category Design: Single
Special Issue

076
Arts & Architecture
Art Director: Rip Georges
Designer: Rip Georges
Publisher: Arts & Architecture, Inc.
Category Design:
Story Presentation

077
The New York Times Magazine
Art Director: Ken Kendrick
Designer: Ken Kendrick
Illustrator: Matt Mahurin
Publisher: The New York Times
Category Design: Cover

078
Industrial Design
Art Director: Karen Krieger
Designer: Annlee Polus
Photographer: Steve Cooper
Publisher: Design Publications, Inc.
Category Design: Cover

079
Fortune
Art Director: Margery Peters
Illustrator: Gary Hallgren
Publisher: Fortune Magazine
Category Illustration: Cover

080
The Boston Globe Magazine
Art Director: Ronn Campisi
Designer: Ronn Campisi
Illustrator: Gene Grief
Publisher: Globe Newspaper Co.
Category Design: Tabloid Cover

081
Texas Monthly
Art Director: Fred Woodward
Designers: Fred Woodward,
David Kampa
Illustrators: Various
Publisher: Texas Montly, Inc.
Category Illustration: Story

082
New York
Art Director: Robert Best
Designer: Patricia Von Brachel
Photographers: David Walters,
Tony McGee
Publisher: Murdoch Magazines
Category Design: Story

083
Mother Jones
Art Director: Louise Kollenbaum
Designer: Dian-Aziza Ooka
Illustrators: Marshall Arisman,
Matt Mahurin, Brad Holland,
John Collier, Sue Coe
Publisher: Foundation for
National Progress
Category Illustration: Story

084
Mother Jones
Art Director: Louise Kollenbaum
Designer: Dian-Aziza Ooka

Illustrators: Marshall Arisman,
Matt Mahurin, Brad Holland,
John Collier, Sue Coe
Publisher: Foundation for
National Progress
Category Illustration: Story

1985

085
Texas Monthly
Art Director: Fred Woodward
Designer: Fred Woodward
Photographer: Helmut Newton
Publisher: Texas Monthly, Inc.
Category Design: Story

086
New York
Art Director: Robert Best
Designer: Robert Best
Publisher: Murdoch Magazines
Category Design:
Single Special Issue

087
Sports Illustrated
Art Director: Michael Grossman
Publisher: Time Inc.
Category Design: Story

088
The New York Times Magazine
Art Director: Ken Kendrick
Designer: Ken Kendrick
Illustrator: Anita Kunz
Publisher: The New York Times
Category Illustration: Story

089
Rolling Stone
Art Director: Derek W. Ungless
Designer: Angelo Savaides
Photographer: Chris Callis
Publisher: Straight Arrow
Publications
Category Photography:
Single Page/Spread

090
Rolling Stone
Art Director: Derek W. Ungless
Designer: Derek W. Ungless
Photographer: Albert Watson
Photo Editor: Laurie Kratchovil
Publisher: Straight Arrow
Publications
Category Photography:
Single Page/Spread

091
Manhattan, Inc.
Art Director: Nancy Butkus
Designer: Nancy Butkus
Photographer: George Lange
Publisher: Metrocorp
Category Photography: Story

1986

092
Life
Art Director: Charles W. Pates
Designers: Jean Foos, Keith Davis
Photographers: Various
Publisher: Time, Inc.

Category Design:
Single Special Issue

093
The New York Times Magazine
Art Directors: Ken Kendrick,
Diana LaGuardia
Designer: Ken Kendrick
Photographer: Peter Lindbergh
Publisher: The New York Times
Category Design: Story

094
Connoisseur
Art Director: Carla Barr
Designer: Carla Barr
Photographer: Sandi Fellman
Publisher:
The Hearst Corporation
Category Design: Cover

095
Metropolis
Art Director: Helene Silverman
Designer: Helene Silverman
Illustrator: Helene Silverman
Publisher: Belerophone
Publishing, Inc.
Category Design: Cover

096
New York
Art Director: Robert Best
Designers: Josh Gosfield, David
Walters, Rhonda Rubinstein
Illustrators: Various
Publisher:
Murdoch Magazines, Inc.
Category Design:
Single Special Issue

097
The New York Times Magazine
Art Director: Diana LaGuardia
Designer: Diana LaGuardia
Photographer: Michael O'Neill
Publisher: The New York Times
Category Design: Story

098
L.A. Style
Art Director: Rip Georges
Publisher: L.A. Style, Inc.
Category Design: Overall

099
The New York Times Magazine
Art Directors: Ken Kendrick,
Diana LaGuardia
Designer: Ken Kendrick
Photographers: Letizia Battaglia,
Franco Zecchin
Publisher: The New York Times
Category Design: Story

1987

100
Premiere
Art Directors: Robert Best,
David Walters
Designers: Robert Best,
David Walters
Publisher: Murdoch/Hachette
Issue: October 1987
Category: New Magazine

101
Photo/Design
Art Director:
Deborah Gallagher Lewis
Photographer: Albert Porter
Publisher:
Billboard Publications, Inc.
Issue: Jan/Feb 1987
Category Photo: Cover

102
Regardie's
Art Directors: Rip Georges,
Pamela Berry
Designers: Rip Georges,
Pamela Berry
Illustrators: J. Wooley, J. Bennett,
S. Pietsch, R. Hess, S. McCray,
D. Maffia, C.F. Payne, A. Kunz,
S. Earley, A. Russo, S. Brodner,
M. Arisman
Publisher: Regardie's
Issue: Nov/Dec 1987
Category: Special Section
& Illustration

103
The New York Times Magazine
Art Director: Diana LaGuardia
Designer: Janet Froelich
Photographer: Sebastião Salgado
Photo Editor: Kathy Ryan
Publisher: The New York Times
Issue: June 7, 1987
Category Photography: Story

104
Art Center Review #2
Art Director: Kit Hinrichs
Designers: Kit Hinrichs,
Lenore Gartz
Illustrators: John Mattos,
Walid Saba
Photographers: Henrik Kam,
Steven Hellor
Client: Art Center College of Design
Agency: Pentagram Design
Issue: October 1, 1987
Category Design: Entire Issue

105
Photo Metro
Art Director: Henry Brimmer
Photographer: Charly Franklin
Publisher: Photo Metro
Issue: September 1987
Category Design: Entire Issue

106
Rolling Stone
Art Director: Fred Woodward
Designers: Joele Cuyler,
Raul Martinez
Photographers: Hiro, Annie
Leibovitz
Photo Editor: Laurie Kratochvil
Publisher: Straight Arrow Publishers
Issues: November 5 –
December 10, 1987
Category Design: Entire Issue

1988

107
Goucher College Annual Report
Art Directors: Kate Berquist,

Anthony Rutka
Designer: Kate Berquist
Illustrator: Gary Kelley
Photographer: Barry Holniker
Client: Goucher College
Agency: Rutka/Weadock Design,
Baltimore, MD
Issue: December 1988
Category Design: Single Issue

108
Spy
Art Director: Alex Isley
Designer:
Cathy Gilmore-Barnes
Publisher: Spy Publishing
Partners
Issue: May 1988
Category Design:
Single Page/Spread

109
Italian Vogue
Art Director: Fabien Baron
Photographer: Satochi
Publisher: Condé Nast
International Inc.
Issue: September 1988
Category Design: Cover

110
Italian Vogue
Art Director: Fabien Baron
Photographer: Satochi
Illustrator: Matts Gustavsonn
Publisher: Condé Nast
International Inc.
Issue: November 1988
Category Design:
Single Page/Spread

111
Italian Vogue
Art Director: Fabien Baron
Publisher: Condé Nast
International Inc.
Category Design:
Single Page/Spread

112
Italian Vogue
Art Director: Fabien Baron
Illustrator: Georgia O'Keefe
Publisher: Condé Nast
International Inc.
Issue: December 1988
Category Design:
Single Page/Spread

113
Fannie Mae–Home Annual Report
Art Directors: Peter Harrison,
Susan Hochbaum
Designer: Susan Hochbaum
Photo Editor: Diane Cook
Client: Fannie Mae
Agency: Pentagram Design, NYC
Issue: April 1988
Category Design: Single Issue

114
Arena
Art Director: Neville Brody
Designer: Neville Brody
Issue: Winter 1988
Category Photography: Story

115
Life
Art Director:
Tom Bentkowski
Designer: Nora Sheehan
Photographer:
Laurie Sparham
Publisher: Time, Inc.
Issue: April 1988
Category Photography:
Single Page/Spread

116
Life
Designer: Robin Brown
Photographer:
Mary Ellen Mark
Photo Editor: Peter Howe
Publisher: Time, Inc.
Issue: June 1988
Category Photography: Story

117
Rolling Stone
Art Director: Fred Woodward
Designer: Joele Cuyler
Photographer:
Richard Avedon
Photo Editor: Jim Franco
Publisher: Straight Arrow
Publishers
Issue: April 7, 1988
Category Photography:
Single Page/Spread

118
Italian Vogue
Art Director: Fabien Baron
Photographer: Herb Ritts
Publisher: Condé Nast
International, Inc.
Issue: October 1988
Category Photography:
Single Page/Spread

119
Life
Designer: Tom Bentkowski
Photographer:
Sebastião Salgado
Photo Editor: Peter Howe
Publisher: Time, Inc.
Issue: August 1988
Category Photography: Story

120
Viewpoint
Design Director:
Barbara Glauber
Art Director: Peter Deutsch
Photographer: Steve Hill
Client: Ernst & Whinney
International
Agency: Deutsch Design,
Inc. NYC
Issue: March 1988
Category Photography: Story

121
Life
Art Director: Tom Bentkowski
Photographer: Donna Ferrato
Photo Editor: Peter Howe
Publisher: Time, Inc.
Issue: October 1988
Category Photography: Story

1989

122
Rolling Stone
Art Director: Fred Woodward
Designer: Fred Woodward
Photographer: Herb Ritts
Photo Editor:
Laurie Kratochvil
Publisher: Straight Arrow
Publishers
Issue: June 15, 1989
Category Design: Story

123
Rolling Stone
Art Director: Fred Woodward
Designer: Fred Woodward
Illustrator: Brian Cronin
Publisher: Straight Arrow
Publishers
Issue: September 7, 1989
Category Illustration:
Single Page/Spread

124
Sports Illustrated
Art Director: Steven Hoffman
Designer: Steven Hoffman
Photographer:
Heinz Kluetmeier
Publisher: Time Warner Inc.
Issue: April 1989
Category Photography:
Single Page/Spread

125
Esquire
Art Director: Rip Georges
Designer: Rip Georges
Photographer: Michael O'Neill
Publisher: Hearst Publications
Issue: November 1989
Category Photography: Cover

126
Mohawk Paper Mills
Art Director: Seymour Chwast
Designers: Seymour Chwast,
Roxanne Slimak
Illustrator: Seymour Chwast
Photographer:
Barbara Dominowski
Client: Mohawk Paper Mills, Inc.
Agency: The Pushpin Group
Issue: January 1989
Category Design: Overall

127
Life
Art Director: Tom Bentkowski
Designer: Dean Abatemarco
Publisher: Time Warner Inc.
Issue: February 1989
Category Photography: Story

128
Condé Nast Traveler
Art Director: Diana LaGuardia
Designer: Audrey Razgaitis
Photographer: Richard Misrach
Photo Editor: Kathleen Klech
Publisher: Condé Nast
Publications, Inc.
Issue: March 1989
Category Photography: Story

1990

129
Rolling Stone
Art Director: Fred Woodward
Designers: Fred Woodward,
Gail Anderson
Illustrator: Josh Gosfield
Publisher: Straight Arrow Publishers
Issue: February 1990
Category Illustration: Story

130
Beach Culture
Art Director: David Carson
Designer: David Carson
Photographer: Geof Kern
Publisher: Surfer Publications
Issue: Aug/Sept 1990
Category Design: Cover

131
Rolling Stone
Art Director: Fred Woodward
Designer: Fred Woodward
Photographer:
Andrew MacPherson
Photo Editor: Laurie Kratochvil
Publisher: Straight Arrow Publishers
Issue: June 14, 1990
Category Design: Story

132
Texas Monthly
Design Director: D.J. Stout
Designer: D.J. Stout
Photographer:
Max Aguilera-Hellweg
Photo Editor: D.J. Stout
Publisher: Texas Monthly
Issue: May 1990
Category Photography: Story

133
Global
Design Director: Gary Koepke
Illustrator: Brian Cronin
Publisher: Redgate Communications
Issue: Spring 1991
Category Design:
Single Page/Spread

134
Life
Art Director: Tom Bentkowski
Designer: Marti Golon
Photographer: Eugene Richards
Photo Editor: Peter Howe
Publisher: Time Warner, Inc.
Issue: June 1990
Category Photography: Story

135
Teaching At Art Center Book
Design Director: Rebeca Mendez
Designers: Rebeca Mendez,
Ellen Eisner
Illustrator: Marjo Wilson

Publisher: Art Center
College of Design
Issue: December 1990
Category Design: Special Issue

136
The Washington Times
Design Director: Joseph Scopin
Art Director: Josh Kascht
Designer: Josh Kascht
Illustrator: Josh Kascht
Publisher: The Washington Times
Issue: February 1990
Category Design: Cover

137
Universal Foods Corporation
Design Director: Pat Samata
Art Director: Greg Samata
Designers: Pat & Greg Samata
Photographers: Sondro Miller,
Marc Norberg
Photo Editor: Pat Samata
Agency Samata Associates
Issue: December 1990
Category Design: Special Issue

138
Associated Press Annual Report
Design Director: Kent Hunter
Designer: Saeri Yoo Park
Photographers: Cheryl Rossom,
Associated Press
Illustrator: Saeri Yoo Park
Publisher: Frankfurt, Kips Balkind
Issue: 1990
Category Design: Special Issue

139
26-A Journal About Type
& Typography
Design Director: Bob Manley
Art Director: Gary Koepke
Designer: Gary Koepke
Photographer: Steve Marsel
Agency: Koepke Design/
Altman & Manley
Issue: August 1990
Category Design: Special Issue

140
The New York Times Magazine
Design Director: Tom Bodkin
Art Director: Janet Froelich
Designer: Kathi Rota
Photographer: James Nachtwey
Photo Editor: Kathy Ryan
Publisher: The New York Times
Issue: June 1990
Category Photography: Story

1991

141
Ads Against AIDS
Design Director: Robert Priest
Art Director: Alejandro Gonzalez
Designers: Adam Smith,
Charlene Benson, Diana Haas
Illustrators: Sue Coe, Paul Davis,
Ken Fischer, Carl Fischer,
Eric Fischl, Jenny Holtzer
Photographers: Nan Golden, Greg
Gorman, Hiro, Annie Leibovitz,
Zoe Lenard, Matt Mahurin, Mary
Ellen Mark, Kurt Markus, Wayne

Maser, Steven Meisel, Sheila
Metzner, Ray Navarro, Herb Ritts,
Michael Roberts, Matthew Rolston,
Sebastião Salgado, Francesco
Scavullo, Deborah Turbeville,
Max Vadukel, William Wegman
Photo Editor: Martha Maristany
Publisher: Condé Nast
Publications, Inc.
Issue: November 1991
Category Design: Special Issue

142
GQ
Design Director: Robert Priest
Art Designer: Alejandro Gonzalez
Designers: Adam Smith,
Charlene Benson
Illustrator: Sue Coe
Publisher: Condé Nast
Publications, Inc.
Issue: October 1991
Category Illustration:
Single Page/Spread

143
Life
Design Director: Tom Bentkowski
Designer: Marti Golon
Photographer: Athur Grace/Sygma
Photo Editor: Peter Howe
Publisher: Time Inc.,
Magazine Co.
Issue: September 1991
Category Photography: Story

144
The New York Times Magazine
Art Director: Janet Froelich
Designer: Janet Froelich
Photographer: Sebastião Salgado
Photo Editor: Kathy Ryan
Publisher: The New York Times
Issue: June 199
Category Photography: Story

145
Rolling Stone
Art Director: Fred Woodward
Designers: Gail Anderson,
Catherine Gilmore-Barnes,
Debra Bishop, Geraldine Hessler,
Angela Skouras
Photo Editor: Laurie Kratochvil
Publisher: Straight Arrow
Publishers
Issue: May 1991
Category Design: Special Issue

146
Rolling Stone
Art Director: Fred Woodward
Illustrator: Philip Burke
Publisher: Straight Arrow Publishers
Issue: October 1991
Category Illustration: Story

147
The New York Times Magazine
Art Director: Janet Froelich
Designer: Janet Froelich
Illustrators: Marshall Arisman,
Michael Bartalos, Brian Cronin,
Blair Drawson, Henrik Drescher,
Amy Guip, Janet Wooley
Publisher: The New York Times

Issue: December 1991
Category Illustration: Story

148
Time
Design Director: Arthur Hochstein
Art Director: Rudolph C. Hoglund
Designer: Mirko Ilic
Publisher: Time Inc., Magazine Co.
Issue: June 1991
Category Design: Cover

149
Interview
Design Director: Tibor Kalman
Designer: Kristin Johnson
Photographer: Kurt Markus
Photo Editor: Suzanne Donaldson
Publisher: Brandt Publications
Agency M & Co.
Issue: January 1991
Category Design:
Single Page/Spread

150
Rolling Stone
Art Director: Fred Woodward
Designer: Fred Woodward
Illustrator: Matt Mahurin
Publisher: Straight Arrow
Publishers, Inc.
Issue: October 1991
Category Illustration:
Single Page/Spread

1992

151
Rolling Stone
Art Director: Fred Woodward
Designers: Fred Woodward, Gail
Anderson, Catherine Gilmore-
Barnes, Debra Bishop, Angela
Skouras, Geraldine Hessler
Photographers: Albert Watson,
Bruce Weber, Mark Seliger,
Annie Leibovitz, Herb Ritts,
Kurt Markus
Photo Editor: Laurie Kratochvil
Publisher: Straight Arrow
Publishers, Inc.
Issue: November 12, 1992
Category Design: Entire Issue

152
Dance Ink
Design Director: J. Abbott Miller
Designers: J. Abbott Miller,
Dina Radeka
Photographer: Josef Astor
Photo Editor: Kate Schlesinger
Publisher: Dance Ink, Inc.
Studio Design Writing Research
Issue: Winter 1992
Category Design: Entire Issue

153
Harper's Bazaar
Creative Director: Fabien Baron
Art Director: Joel Berg
Designer: Johan Svensson
Photographers: Patrick
Demarchelier, Peter Lindbergh
Publisher: The Hearst Corporation
Issue: September 1992
Category Design: Redesign

154
Harper's Bazaar
Creative Director: Fabien Baron
Art Director: Joel Berg
Photographer:
Patrick Demarchelier
Publisher: The Hearst Corporation
Issue: September 1992
Category Design:
Single Page/Spread

155
The Washington Post Magazine
Art Director: Richard Baker
Designer: Richard Baker
Illustrator: Geof Kern
Photo Editor:
Deborah Needleman
Publisher:
The Washington Post Co.
Issue: November 15, 1992
Category Illustration:
Single Page/Spread

156
Parenting
Art Director: Dian-Aziza Ooka
Designer: Allyson Appen
Photographer: Robert Holmgren
Photo Editor: Tripp Mikich
Issue: October 1992
Category Photography:
Photojournalism & Portraits

157
Details
Art Director: B.W. Honeycutt
Designers: B.W. Honeycutt,
Markus Kiersztan
Illustrators: Peter Bagge,
Jonathan Rosen, Gilberto
Hernandez, Kaz, Bob Camp,
Mack White, Dan Cowles,
Drew Friedman, Ivan Velez,
Jr., Maurice Vellekoop, Dean
Rohrer, Kyle Baker
Publisher: Condé Nast
Publications, Inc.
Issue: August 1992
Category Illustration: Story

158
The New York Times Magazine
Art Director: Janet Froelich
Designer: Kathi Rota
Photographer: Sebastião Salgado
Photo Editor: Kathy Ryan
Publisher: The New York Times
Issue: February 2, 1992
Category Photography:
Photojournalism & Portraits

159
The New York Times Magazine
Art Director: Janet Froelich
Designer: Janet Froelich
Photographer: James Nachtwey
Photo Editor: Kathy Ryan
Publisher: The New York Times
Issue: December 6, 1992
Category Photography:
Photojournalism & Portraits

160
Harper's Bazaar
Creative Director: Fabien Baron

Art Director: Joel Berg
Designer: Johan Svensson
Photographer: Peter Lindbergh
Publisher: The Hearst
Corportation
Issue: December 1992
Category Photography:
Fashion & Beauty Story

1993

161
Rolling Stone
Art Director: Fred Woodward
Designer: Fred Woodward
Photographer:
Patrick Demarchelier
Photo Editor: Laurie Kratochvil
Publisher: Wenner Media
Issue: September 16, 1993
Category Design: Cover

162
Rolling Stone
Art Director: Fred Woodward
Designer: Fred Woodward
Photographer:
Andrew MacPherson
Photo Editor: Laurie Kratochvil
Publisher: Wenner Media
Issue: March 1, 1993
Category Design: Cover

163
The New York Times Magazine
Art Director: Janet Froelich
Designer: Nancy Harris
Photographer: Matuschka
Photo Editor: Sarah Harbutt
Publisher: The New York Times
Issue: August 15, 1993
Category Photography:
Photojournalism & Portraits

164
Travel & Leisure
Design Director: Lloyd Ziff
Designer: Lloyd Ziff
Photographer: Philip Quirk
Photo Editor: Hazel Hammond
Publisher: American Express
Publishing
Issue: March 1993
Category Design: Cover

165
Vibe
Design Director: Gary Koepke
Art Director: Richard Baker
Designer: Gary Koepke
Photographer: Dan Winters
Photo Editor: George Pitts
Publisher: Time Inc. Ventures
Issue: October 1993
Category Design: Cover

166
GQ
Creative Director: Robert Priest
Designer: Robert Priest
Illustrator: C.F. Payne
Publisher: Condé Nast
Publications, Inc.
Issue: April 1993
Category Illustration:
Single Page/Spread

167
Travel & Leisure
Design Director: Lloyd Ziff
Designer: Lloyd Ziff
Photographer: Geof Kern
Photo Editor: Hazel Hammond
Publisher: American
Express Publishing
Issue: May 1993
Category Photography:
Still Life, Interiors & Travel

168
W
Design Director:
Dennis Freedman
Art Director: Kirby Rodriguez
Designers: Edward Leida,
Myla Carver
Photographer: Perry Ogden
Photo Editor: Dennis Freedman
Publisher: Fairchild Publications
Issue: November 1, 1993
Category Photography:
Fashion & Beauty Story

169
Men's Journal
Art Director: Matthew Drace
Designer: Matthew Drace
Photographer: Raymond Meeks
Publisher: Wenner Media
Issue: March/April 1993
Category Photography:
Photojournalism & Portraits Story

170
The New York Times Magazine
Art Director: Janet Froelich
Designer: Petra Mercker
Photographer: Kurt Markus
Photo Editor: Kathy Ryan
Publisher: The New York Times
Issue: September 12, 1993
Category Photography:
Fashion & Beauty Story

1994

171
Rolling Stone
Art Director: Fred Woodward
Designers: Fred Woodward,
Gail Anderson, Geraldine
Hessler, Lee Bearson
Photographers: Cheryl Koralik,
Albert Watson, Mark Hanauer,
Dan Borris, Jose Picayo, Steven
White, Mark Seliger, Frank
Ockenfels 3, Matt Mahurin
Photo Editors: Jodi Peckman,
Denise Sfraga, Fiona McDonagh
Publisher: Wenner Media
Issue: November 17, 1994
Category Design: Entire Issue

172
Rolling Stone
Art Director: Fred Woodward
Designers: Fred Woodward,
Gail Anderson
Photographer: Sebastião Salgado
Photo Editors: Jodi Peckman
Publisher: Wenner Media
Issue: September 22, 1994
Category Design: Story

173
EYE
Art Director: Stephen Coates
Designer: Stephen Coates
Client: EMAP Business
Communications
Issue: Autumn 1994
Category Design: Entire issue

174
El Mundo
Design Director: Carmelo Caderot
Art Director: Rodrigo Sanchez
Designers: Rodrigo Sanchez,
Miguel Buckenmeyer
Photographer: Andre Rau
Publisher: Unidad Editorial S.A.
Issue: November 6, 1994
Category Design: Story

175
Martha Stewart Living
Art Director: Gael Towey
Designers: Gael Towey,
Constance Old, Lisa Naftolin
Photographers: Victor Schrager,
Victoria Pearson, Carlton
Davis, Thibault Jeanson, Stewart
Ferebee, Maria Robledo,
O'Hana Enderle, John Dolan
Photo Editor: Heidi Posner
Publisher: Time Inc.
Issue: Weddings 1994
Category Design: Entire Issue

176
Harper's Bazaar
Creative Director: Fabien Baron
Art Director: Joel Berg
Designer: Johan Svensson
Photographers: Richard Avedon,
Patrick Demarchelier,
Raymond Meier
Publisher: The Hearst
Corporation-Magazines Division
Issue: March 1994
Category Design: Entire Issue

177
Rolling Stone
Art Director: Fred Woodward
Designers: Fred Woodward,
Gail Anderson, Geraldine
Hessler, Lee Bearson
Illustrator: Mark Ryden
Publisher: Wenner Media
Issue: November 17, 1994
Category Illustration:
Single Page/Spread

178
Rolling Stone
Art Director: Fred Woodward
Designer: Gail Anderson
Illustrator: Anita Kunz
Publisher: Wenner Media
Issue: December 29, 1994
Category Illustration:
Single Page/Spread

179
Harper's Bazaar
Creative Director: Fabien Baron
Art Director: Joel Berg
Designer: Johan Svensson
Photographer: Raymond Meier

Publisher: The Hearst
Corporation-Magazines Division
Issue: March 1994
Category Design: Spread

180
Colors
Editor in Chief: Tibor Kalman
Design Director: Tibor Kalman
Art Director: Scott Stowell
Designer: Leslie Mello
Photo Editors: Alfredo Albertone,
Ilana Rein, Alice Albert
Publisher: Colors Magazine, SRL
Issue: June 1994
Category Design: Entire Issue

181
The Boston Globe
Art Director: Lucy Bartholomay
Designer: Lucy Bartholomay
Photographer: Stan Grossfeld
Photo Editor: Lucy Bartholomay
Publisher: The Boston Globe
Publishing Co.
Issue: December 29, 1994
Category Photography:
Reportage & Travel Story

182
Rolling Stone
Art Director: Fred Woodward
Designers: Fred Woodward,
Lee Bearson
Photographer: Mark Seliger
Photo Editor: Jodi Peckman
Publisher: Wenner Media
Issue: December 15, 1994
Category Photography: Still Life
& Interiors Single Page/Spread

183
Anchorage Daily News/Impulse
Design Director: Galie Jean-Louis
Art Director: Galie Jean-Louis
Photographer: Scott Schafer
Photo Editor: Galie Jean-Louis
Illustrator: Kevin E. Ellis
Publisher: Anchorage Daily News
Issue: December 24, 1994
Category Design: Front Page

184
Rolling Stone
Art Director: Fred Woodward
Designers: Fred Woodward,
Gail Anderson, Lee Bearson
Illustrator: Ralph Steadman
Publisher: Wenner Media
Issue: December 15, 1994
Category Illustration:
Single Page/Spread

185
The New York Times Magazine
Art Director: Janet Froelich
Designer: Nancy Harris
Illustrator: Gary Baseman
Publisher: The New York Times
Issue: August 28, 1994
Category Illustration:
Single Page/Spread

186
Time International
Art Director: Arthur Hochstein

Publisher: The Hearst
Corporation-Magazines Division
Issue: March 1994
Category Design: Spread

Designer: Jane Frey
Photographer: James Nachtwey
Photo Editors: Michele
Stephenson, Robert Stevens
Publisher: Time Inc.
Issue: July 4, 1994
Category Photo Story:
Reportage & Travel

187
W
Creative Director:
Dennis Freedman
Design Directors:
Edward Leida, Jean Griffin
Art Director: Kirby Rodriguez
Designers: Edward Leida,
Rosalba Sierra
Photographer: Raymond Meier
Publisher: Fairchild Publications
Issue: December 1994
Category Photography:
Fashion & Beauty

1995

188
Dance Ink
Art Director: J. Abbott Miller
Designers: J. Abbott Miller,
Paul Carlos, Luke Hayman
Photographers: Josef Astor,
Marcia Lippman, David Michalek,
Stewart Shining
Photo Editor:
Katherine Schlesinger
Studio: Design/Writing/
Research, New York
Publisher: Dance Ink, Inc.
Issue: June 1995
Category Design: Entire Issue

189
Dance Ink
Art Director: J. Abbott Miller
Designers: J. Abbott Miller,
Paul Carlos, Luke Hayman
Photographers: K.C. Bailey,
Andrew Eccles, Jeff Jacobson,
Anthony Saint James,
Joel Meyerowitz
Photo Editor:
Katherine Schlesinger
Publisher: Dance Ink, Inc.
Issue: September 1995
Category Design: Entire Issue

190
Allure
Design Director: Shawn Young
Designer: Shawn Young
Photographer: Thierry Le Gowes
Photo Editor: Claudia Lebenthal
Publisher: Condé Nast
Publications, Inc.
Issue: July 1995
Category Design: Story

191
Dance Ink
Art Director: J. Abbott Miller
Designers: J. Abbott Miller,
Paul Carlos, Luke Hayman
Photographers: Josef Astor,
K.C. Bailey, Andrew Eccles,

Timothy Greenfield Sanders,
Duane Michals
Photo Editor:
Katherine Schlesinger
Studio: Design/Writing/
Research, New York
Publisher: Dance Ink, Inc.
Issue: December 1995
Category Design: Entire Issue

192
Garden Design
Creative Director:
Michael Grossman
Art Director: Paul Roelofs
Photo Editor: Susan Goldberger
Illustrator: Ross MacDonald
Publisher: Meigher Communications
Issue: February/March 1995
Category Design: Story

193
New York
Design Director: Robert Best
Art Director: Syndi Becker
Designer: Robert Best
Photographers: Chris Bobin,
Paul Manangan
Photo Editor: Margery Goldberg
Publisher: K-III Publications
Issue: February 20, 1995
Category Design: Spread

194
Texas Monthly
Creative Director: D.J. Stout
Designers: D.J. Stout,
Nancy McMillen
Photo Editor: D.J. Stout
Illustrator: David Cowles
Publisher: Texas Monthly
Issue: February 1995
Category Design: Spread

195
Guitar World
Design Director: Peter Yates
Designers: Sandra Monteparo,
Peter Yates
Photographers: Danny Clinch,
Sue Schaffner, Charles Peterson,
Catherine McGann, Marty Temme,
Lorinda Sullivan, Kwaku Alston
Illustrators: Matt Cambell,
Jay Lincoln, Mark Marek
Publisher: Harris Publications
Issue: December 1995
Category Design: Entire Issue

196
The New York Times Magazine
Art Director: Janet Froelich
Designer: Lisa Naftolin
Photographer: Richard Burbridge
Photo Editor: Kathy Ryan
Publisher: The New York Times
Issue: June 25, 1995
Category Design: Cover

197
Independent Magazine
Creative Director: Vince Frost
Designer: Vince Frost
Photographer: Giles Revell
Studio Frost Design
Publisher: Mirror Group

Issue: September 2, 1995
Category Design: Cover

198
Texas Monthly
Creative Director: D.J. Stout
Designers: D.J. Stout,
Nancy McMillen
Illustrator: Owen Smith
Publisher: Texas Monthly
Issue: February 1995
Category Design: Spread

199
Anchorage Daily News/Impulse
Creative Director:
Galie Jean-Louis
Designer: Galie Jean-Louis
Photo Editor: Galie Jean-Louis
Illustrator: Amy Guip
Publisher: Anchorage Daily News
Issue: July 17, 1995
Category Design: Front Page

200
Anchorage Daily News/Impulse
Creative Director: Galie Jean-Louis
Designers: Kevin Ellis, Lance
Lekander, Mike Bain
Photo Editor: Galie Jean-Louis
Illustrators: Lance Lekander,
Kevin Ellis
Publisher: Anchorage Daily News
Issue: October 6, 1995
Category Design: Redesign

201
Rolling Stone
Art Director: Fred Woodward
Illustrator: Jonathan Rosen
Publisher: Wenner Media
Issue: October 5, 1995
Category Illustration:
Single Page/Spread

202
Rolling Stone
Art Director: Fred Woodward
Designers: Fred Woodward,
Gail Anderson
Photographer: Sebastião Salgado
Photo Editor: Jodi Peckman
Publisher: Wenner Media
Issue: February 23, 1995
Category Photography:
Reportage & Travel Story

203
Philadelphia Inquirer Magazine
Design Director: Christine Dunleavy
Art Director: Bert Fox
Designer: Christine Dunleavy
Photographers:
James Balog, Chris Rainier
Photo Editor: Bert Fox
Publisher: Philadelphia Inquirer
Issue: April 6, 1995
Category Photography: Reportage
& Travel Story

204
New York
Design Directors: Robert Best,
Syndi Becker
Designers: Robert Best,
Syndi Becker, Deanna Lowe

Photographer: Christian Witkin
Photo Editor: Margery Goldberg
Publisher: K-III Publications
Issue: December 25, 1995-
January 1, 1996
Category Photography:
Portraits Story

205
W
Creative Director: Dennis Freedman
Design Director: Edward Leida
Designer: Edward Leida
Photographer: Raymond Meier
Publisher: Fairchild Publications
Issue: December 1995
Category Photo: Illustration

206
Martha Stewart Living
Creative Director: Gael Towey
Art Director: Anne Johnson
Designer: Anne Johnson
Photographer: Carlton Davis
Photo Editor: Heidi Posner
Publisher: Time Inc.
Issue: May 1995
Category Photography:
Still Life & Interiors Story

1996

207
I.D.
Art Directors: Steve Simula,
A. Arefin, Andrea Fella
Designers: Sherie Bauer, Steve
Simula, Tony Ramos, Andrea Fella,
Colette Moti, Floris Keizer
Photographer: Chris Gallo
Studio: Fitch Inc.
Publisher: I.D. Magazine
Issue: July 1996
Category Design: Entire Issue

208
Rolling Stone
Creative Director: Fred Woodward
Designer: Fred Woodward
Photographer: Albert Watson
Photo Editor: Jodi Peckman
Publisher: Wenner Media
Issue: December 12, 1996
Category Design: Cover

209
GVO Brochure
Creative Director: Bill Cahan
Designers: Bob Dinetz,
Kevin Roberson
Photographers: Geof Kern,
Holly Stewart
Illustrators: Nick Dewar,
Doug Aitken
Studio: Cahan & Associates
Issue: August 1996
Category Design: Overall Design

210
Adaptec 1996 Annual Report
Art Director: Bill Cahan
Designer: Kevin Roberson
Illustrator: Richard McGuire
Studio: Cahan & Associates
Issue: June 1996
Category Design: Entire Issue

211
Sueddeutsche Zeitung Magazin
Art Director: Markus Rasp
Designers: Anne Blaschke, Otto
Dzemla, Wilhelm Raffelsberger
Photographers: Julias Shulman,
Herb Ritts, Henriette Grindat,
Bernd & Hilla Becher, Ettore
Sottsass, James Nachtwey, William
Klein, Arino Eimu, Christoph
Valentien, Julian Germain
Photo Editors: Eva Ernst,
Claudia Mueller
Publisher: Magazin Verlagsges
Issue: April 4, 1996
Category Design: Feature

212
Sueddeutsche Zeitung Magazin
Art Director: Markus Rasp
Designers: Anne Blaschke, Otto
Dzemla, Wilhelm Raffelsberger
Photographers: Francois Robert,
Jean Robert
Photo Editors: Eva Ernst,
Claudia Mueller
Publisher: Magazin Verlagsges
Issue: November 29, 1996
Category Photography: Still Life
& Interiors Story

213
Bravo Richards
Creative Director: Jurek Wajdowicz
Designers: Lisas LaRochelle,
Jurek Wajdowicz
Photographer: Eugene Richards
Studio: Emerson, Wajdowics Studios
Client: Island Paper Mills/E.B. Eddy
Forest Products, Ltd.
Issue: September 1996
Category: Photo Illustration

214
La Revista
Design Director: Carmelo Caderot
Art Director: Rodrigo Sanchez
Designers: Rodrigo Sanchez,
Miguel Buckenmeyer, Maria
Gonzalez, Amparo Redondo
Photographer: Jose Ayma
Photo Editor: Chema Conesa
Publisher: Unidad Editorial S.A.
Category Photography:
Portrait Story
Issue: March 3, 1996

215
Rolling Stone
Art Director: Fred Woodward
Illustrator: Brian Cronin
Publisher: Wenner Media
Issue: March 7, 1996
Category Illustration:
Single Page/Spread

216
W
Creative Director: Dennis Freedman
Design Director: Edward Leida
Art Director: Kirby Rodriguez
Designers: Kirby Rodriguez,
Marcella Bove
Illustrator: Larry Fink
Publisher: Fairchild Publications

Category Photography:
Reportage & Travel Story

1997

217
I.D.
Creative Directors: Luke
Hayman, Tony Arefin
Art Director: Andrea Fella
Designer: Miranda Dempster
Photographer: James Wojcik
Publisher: I.D. Magazine
Issues: March/April 1997,
May 1997, September/
October 1997
Category: Magazine of the
Year Finalist

218
The New York Times Magazine
Art Director: Janet Froelich
Designer:
Catherine Gilmore-Barnes
Photo Editor: Kathy Ryan
Publisher: The New York Times
Issues: May 18, 1997, September
28, 1997, November 16, 1997
Category: Magazine of the
Year Finalist

219
Martha Stewart Living
Design Director: Eric A. Pike
Art Directors: James Dunlinson,
Scot Schy, Claudia Bruno,
Agnethe Glatved
Designer: Robert Fisher
Photographers: Antonine Bootz,
Amy Neunsinger, James Merrel,
Reed Davis, Maria Robledo,
Henry Bourne, Gentl + Hyers,
Evan Sklar, Ferando Bengoechea
Photo Editor: Heidi Posner
Illustrator: Harry Bates
Publisher: Martha Stewart Living
Omnimedia
Issues: February 1997, May
1997, November 1997
Category: Magazine of the
Year Finalist

220
Wallpaper*
Creative Director:
Martin Jacobs
Art Director: Herbert Winkler
Designer: Jonnie Vigar
Photo Editor: Ariel Childs
Illustrator: Walter Chin
Publisher: Time Inc.
Issues: July/August 1997,
September/October 1997,
November/December 1997
Category: Magazine of the
Year Finalist

221
I.D.
Design Director: Luke Hayman
Art Director: Andrea Fella
Designer: Miranda Dempster
Photographer: James Wojcik
Publisher: I.D. Magazine
Issue: September/October 1997
Category Design: Entire Issue

222
The New York Times Magazine
Art Director: Janet Froelich
Designer: Catherine Gilmore-Barnes
Photo Editor: Kathy Ryan
Publisher: The New York Times
Issue: May 18, 1997
Category Design: Feature

223
Life
Design Director: Tom Bentkowski
Art Director: Sharon Okamoto
Designers: Tom Bentkowski, Sharon
Okamoto, Melanie DeForest,
Sam Serbin, Sarah Garcea
Photographers: Gregory Heisler,
Sylvia Plachy, David Newman,
Seiji Fukasawa
Publisher: Time Inc.
Issue: Fall 1997
Category Design: Entire Issue

224
Leica World
Creative Director: Horst Moser
Designers: Carin Drexler,
Horst Moser
Photographer: Norbert Rosing
Studio: Independent
Medien Design
Publisher: Leica Camera AG
Issue: September 1997
Category Design: Feature Story

225
Cadence 1996 Annual Report
Creative Director: Bill Cahan
Designer: Bill Dinetz
Photographers: Amy Guip,
Tony Stromberg
Illustrators: Bob Dinetz,
Jason Holley, Riccardo Vecchio,
Mark Todd
Studio: Cahan & Associates
Issue: March 1997
Category Design: Entire Issue

226
Vanity Fair
Creative Director: David Harris
Designers: Gregory Mastrianni,
David Harris
Photographer: Annie Leibovitz
Photo Editors: Susan White,
Lisa Berman
Publisher: Condé Nast
Publications, Inc.
Issue: June 1997
Category Design: Cover

227
Rolling Stone
Art Director: Fred Woodward
Designers: Fred Woodward,
Gail Anderson
Photographer: Matt Mahurin
Photo Editor: Jodi Peckman
Publisher: Wenner Media
Issue: January 23, 1997
Category Design:
Single Page/Spread

228
Texas Monthly
Creative Director: D.J. Stout

Designer: D.J. Stout
Photo Editor: D.J. Stout
Illustrator: Melinda Beck
Publisher: Texas Monthly
Issue: March 1997
Category Design:
Single Page/Spread

229
Mizerie
Designer: Jan Zacharias
Photographer: Antonin Kratochvil
Photo Editor: Galerie Pecka
Studio: Atelier Puda
Publisher: Galerie Pecka
Issue: April 1997
Category Photography:
Reportage & Travel Story

230
COR Therapeutics
1996 Annual Report
Creative Director: Bill Cahan
Art Director: Bill Cahan
Designer: Kevin Roberson
Photographers: Keith Bardin,
John Kolesa, Tony Stromberg
Illustrator: Kevin Roberson
Studio: Cahan & Associates
Issue: April 1997
Category Design: Entire Issue

231
Bloomberg Personal Finance
Art Director: Carol Layton
Designer: Carol Layton
Photographer: Rodney Smith
Photo Editor: Mary Shea
Publisher: Bloomberg L.P.
Issue: July/August 1997
Category: Photo Illustration

232
The New York Times Magazine
Art Director: Janet Froelich
Photographer: Diego Goldberg
Photo Editor: Kathy Ryan
Publisher: The New York Times
Issue: February 2, 1997
Category Photography:
Portrait Single Page/Spread

233
The New York Times Magazine
Art Director: Janet Froelich
Designer:
Catherine Gilmore-Barnes
Photographer: Abelardo Morell
Photo Editor: Kathy Ryan
Publisher: The New York Times
Category Photography:
Reportage & Travel Story

234
I.D. Magazine Online
Creative Director: Tony Arefin
Art Director: Peter Girardi
Designer: Andrea Fella
Photographer: James Wojcik
Studio: Funny Garbage
Publisher: I.D. Magazine
Category New Media:
Overall Design
Issues: March/April 1997,
May 1997, September/
October 1997

235
The New York Times
Art Director: Nicholas Blechman
Illustrator: Howard Horowitz
Publisher: The New York Times
Issue: August 30, 1997
Category Illustration: Spread

236
The New York Times Magazine
Art Director: Janet Froelich
Designer: Nancy Harris
Illustrator: Pierre Le-Tan
Publisher: The New York Times
Category: Information Graphics

1998

237
Rolling Stone
Art Director: Fred Woodward
Designer: Fred Woodward
Photographer: Mark Seliger
Photo Editor: Rachel Knepfer
Publisher: Straight Arrow Publishers
Issue: May 28, 1998
Category Design: Cover

238
Rolling Stone
Art Director: Fred Woodward
Designers: Fred Woodward,
Gail Anderson, Siung Tjia,
Eric Siry, Hannah McCaughey
Photographers: Mark Seliger,
Dan Winters
Photo Editors: Rachel Knepfer,
Fiona McDonagh
Publisher: Straight Arrow Publishers
Issue: May 28, 1998
Category Design: Entire Issue

239
Ray Gun
Art Directors: Barry Deck,
Robyn Forest
Designer: Barry Deck
Photographer: Andrea Giacobbe
Photo Editor: Robyn Forest
Issue: November 1998
Category Photography: Fashion &
Beauty, Still Life & Interiors Story

240
Esquire
Design Director: Robert Priest
Art Director: Rockwell Harwood
Designer: Joshua Liberson
Photographer: Dan Winters
Photo Editor: Patti Wilson
Publisher: The Hearst Corporation-
Magazines Division
Issue: December 1998
Category Photography:
Reportage, Travel, Portraits
Single Page/Spread

241
Esquire
Design Director: Robert Priest
Art Director: Rockwell Harwood
Designer: Joshua Liberson
Photographer: Geof Kern
Photo Editor: Patti Wilson
Publisher: The Hearst Corporation-
Magazines Division

Issue: April 1998
Category Photography:
Reportage, Travel, Portraits
Single Page/Spread

242
Esquire
Design Director: Robert Priest
Art Director: Rockwell Harwood
Designer: Joshua Liberson
Photographer: Gregory Heisler
Photo Editor: Patti Wilson
Publisher: The Hearst Corporation-
Magazines Division
Issue: February 1998
Category Design: Cover

243
ESPN
Design Director: F. Darrin Perry
Art Director: Peter Yates
Photographer: Fergus Greer
Photo Editor: John Toolan
Publisher: Disney
Issue: December 14, 1998
Category Design:
Single Page/Spread

244
Fast Company
Art Director: Patrick Mitchell
Designers: Gretchen Smelter,
Emily Crawford, Rebecca Rees,
Patrick Mitchell
Photographers: Mary Ellen Mark,
Scogin Mayo
Publisher: Fast Company
Issue: September 1998
Category Design: Entire Issue

245
Fast Company
Art Director: Patrick Mitchell
Designers: Gretchen Smelter,
Emily Crawford, Rebecca Rees,
Patrick Mitchell
Photographers: Chris Buck,
David Barry
Illustrators: Barry Blitt,
Douglas Fraser, Art Spiegelman
Publisher: Fast Company
Issue: October, November,
December 1998
Category: Magazine of the
Year Finalist

246
ABCNews.com
Creative Director:
Kate L. Thompson
Art Director: Betsy Vardell
Designer: Betsy Vardell
Photographer: AP
Photo Editor: Alizabeth Fritz
Illustrator: Mark Bloch
Online Address:
http://abcnews.go.com/sections/
world/balkans/index.html
Publisher: ABCNews
Issue: August 1998
Category New Media: Feature

247
Rolling Stone
Art Director: Fred Woodward
Illustrator: Matt Mahurin

Publisher: Straight Arrow Publishers
Issue: November 12, 1998
Category Illustration: Spread

248
Esquire
Design Director: Robert Priest
Art Director: Rockwell Harwood
Designer: Joshua Liberson
Photographers: Dan Winters, Matt
Mahurin, Brian Velenchenko,
Anton Corbijn, Harry Benson
Photo Editor: Patti Wilson
Publisher: The Hearst Corporation-
Magazines Division
Issue: September, October,
November 1998
Category: Magazine of the
Year Finalist

249
Esquire
Design Director: Robert Priest
Art Director: Rockwell Harwood
Designer: Joshua Liberson
Photographer: Matt Mahurin
Photo Editor: Patti Wilson
Publisher: The Hearst Corporation-
Magazines Division
Issue: October 1998
Category Design: Cover

250
I.D.
Design Director: Luke Hayman
Designers: Miranda Dempster,
Darren Ching
Photographers: Annabel Elston,
Graham MacIndoe, James Wojcik,
Nick Knight, Mikako Koyama,
Davies & Starr, Jay Zuckerkorn,
Steve Richter, John Holderer
Illustrators: Antoine Bordier,
Lex Curtiss, J.J. Gifford
Publisher: F&W Publications
Issue March/April,
September/October 1998
Category: Magazine of the
Year Finalist

251
Rolling Stone
Art Director: Fred Woodward
Designers: Fred Woodward,
Gail Anderson, Siung Tjia,
Eric Siry, Hannah McCaughey
Photographers: Dan Winters,
David LaChapelle, Mark Seliger,
Mary Ellen Mark
Photo Editors: Rachel Knepfer,
Fiona McDonagh
Publisher: Straight Arrow Publishers
Issue: May 28, June 11,
July 9, 1998
Category: Magazine of the
Year Finalist

1999

252
Big
Creative Director: Marcelo Jünemann
Art Directors:
Markus Kiersztan, Lee Swillingham,
Stuart Spalding, Rico Lins
Designers: Garland Lyn,

David Lee, Solve Sundsbo,
Alex Rutterfold, Dagmar Rizzolo,
Keren Ora Admoni, Thais Lima,
Mariama Guimaraes
Photographers: Kishin
Shinoyama, Solve Sundsbo
Publisher: Big Magazine, Inc.
Issue: June 1999, #22; October
1999, #23; December 1999, #26
Category: Magazine of the
Year Finalist

253
ESPN
Creative Director: Peter Yates
Art Directors: Henry Lee,
Yvette L. Francis
Designers: Peter Yates, Reyes
Melendez, Jeanine Melnick,
Yvette L. Francis, Gage Kuo
Photographers: Isabel Snyder, Mary
Ellen Mark, Pam Len, Gregory
Heisler, Nitin Vadukul, Eric Tucker
Photo Editor: Nik Kleinberg
Illustrators: Silverkid New York,
Todd McFarlane
Publisher: Disney Publishing
Worldwide
Issue: November 15, 1999; November
29, 1999; December 27, 1999
Category: Magazine of the
Year Finalist

254
Rolling Stone
Art Director: Fred Woodward
Designers: Fred Woodward,
Gail Anderson, Siung Tjia,
Ken DeLago, Andy Omel,
Lee Berresford
Photographers: Mark Seliger,
David LaChapelle, Kurt Markus,
Peter Lindbergh
Photo Editors: Rachel Knepfer,
Fiona McDonagh, Audrey Landreth
Illustrator: Steve Brodner
Publisher: Straight Arrow Publishers
Issues: November 11, 1999; December
16, 1999; December 30, 1999
Category: Magazine of the
Year Finalist

255
The New York Times Magazine
Art Directors: Janet Froelich,
Joele Cuyler
Designers: Joele Cuyler,
Ignacio Rodriguez
Photographers: Tom Schierlitz,
Dan Winters, Catherine
Chalmers, Joel Peter Witkin,
David LaChapelle
Photo Editors: Kathy Ryan,
Sarah Harbutt
Publisher: The New York Times
Issue: April 18, 1999; September
19, 1999; December 5, 1999
Category: Magazine of the
Year Finalist

256
The New York Times Magazine
Art Director: Janet Froelich
Designer: Claude Martel
Photographer: Robert Trachtenberg
Stylist: Elizabeth Stewart

Publisher: The New York Times
Issue: February 28, 1999
Category Design: Feature

257
ESPN
Creative Director: Peter Yates
Designer: Reyes Melendez
Photographer: Per Gustavson
Photo Editor: Nik Kleinberg
Publisher: Disney Publishing
Worldwide
Issue: October 4, 1999
Category Design: Spread/
Single Page

258
The New York Times Magazine
Art Director: Janet Froelich
Designer: Jennifer Gilman
Publisher: The New York Times
Issue: January 17, 1999
Category Design: Cover

259
Collateral Therapeutics
1998 Annual Report
Creative Director: Bill Cahan
Designer: Kevin Roberson
Photographers: Christine Alicino,
Bill Phelps, Robert Schlatter,
Ken Probst
Studio: Cahan & Associates
Issue: April 1999
Category Design: Entire Issue

260
Rolling Stone
Art Director: Fred Woodward
Designers: Fred Woodward,
Gail Anderson, Siung Tjia,
Ken DeLago, Andy Omel,
Lee Berresford
Photographers: Mark Seliger,
Linda McCartney, Jim Marshall
Photo Editors: Rachel Knepfer,
Audrey Landreth
Illustrator: Steve Brodner
Publisher: Straight Arrow Publishers
Issue: December 16, 1999
Category Design: Entire Issue

261
Nickelodeon Website
Creative Director: David L. Vogler
Design Director: David L. Vogler
Art Director: Michael Redding
Designers: Michael Beeler,
Colm Fox, Jason Arena,
Patrick Dorey, Chiaki Watanabe-
Darcy, Jenny Nordeman,
Kevin Laughran, Michele Dauchtry,
Dave Maro, Melani Larson,
Andrea Koronkiewicz,
Beegee Tolpa
Publisher: Nickelodeon Online
Online Address: www.Nick.com
Issue: December 1, 1999
Category New Media: Website

262
Bloomberg Wealth Manager
Art Director: Laura Zavetz
Designer: Laura Zavetz
Photographer: Hugh Kretschmer
Publisher: Bloomberg L.P.

Issue: September/October 1999
Category: Photo Illustration

263
Big
Creative Director:
Marcelo Jünemann
Art Director: Markus Kiersztan
Designers: Garland Lyn, David Lee
Photographer: Kishin Shinoyama
Publisher: Big Magazine, Inc.
Issue: December 1999, #26
Category Photography:
Portrait Story

264
The Washington Post
Health Section
Art Director:
Stacie Harrison Reistetter
Illustrator: William Duke
Issue: September 28, 1999
Category: Photo Illustration

265
Rolling Stone
Art Director: Fred Woodward
Designers: Fred Woodward,
Gail Anderson
Photographer: Peter Lindbergh
Photo Editor: Rachel Knepfer
Publisher: Straight Arrow Publishers
Issues: November 11, 1999
Category Photography: Portrait
Single Page/Spread

266
Los Angeles
Creative Director: David Armario
Designers: David Armario,
Myla Sorensen
Illustrator: Brian Cronin
Issue: December 1999
Category Illustration:
Single Page/Spread

267
Jane
Art Director: Johan Svensson
Designer: Amy Demas
Photographer: Stephane Sednaoui
Photo Editor: Cary Estes Leitzes
Publisher: Fairchild Publications
Issue: December 1999
Category Photography: Fashion
& Beauty Story

268
The New York Times Magazine
Art Director: Janet Froelich,
Joele Cuyler
Designers: Joele Cuyler,
Ignacio Rodriguez
Photographer: Matthew Rolston
Photo Stylist: Elizabeth Stewart
Publisher: The New York Times
Issue: May 16, 1999
Category Photography: Fashion
& Beauty Story

269
Vanity Fair
Design Director: David Harris
Art Director: Gregory Mastrianni
Photographer: Annie Leibovitz
Photo Editors: Susan White,

Lisa Berman, SunHee Grinnell,
Kathryn MacLeod
Publisher: Condé Nast
Publications, Inc.
Issue: December 1999
Category Photography: Portrait
Single Page/Spread

270
Esquire
Design Director: John Korpics
Photographer: Matthew Welch
Photo Editor: Simon Barnett
Publisher: The Hearst Corpora-
tion—Magazines Division
Issue: December 1999
Category Photography:
Portrait Story

2000–04
SPD Gold
Winners

2000

271
Architecture
Art Director: Lisa Naftolin
Designers: Lisa Naftolin,
Claudia Brandenburg, Lynn Yeo
Photo Editor: Alexandra Brez
Photographers: Richard Johnson,
Jussi Tiainen, Christian Richters,
Peter Aaron, Heinrich Helfenstein,
Inigo Manglano-Ovalle, Timothy
Hursley, Robert Polidori, Gail
Albert Halaban, Richard Barnes
Publisher: VNU
Issues: July 2000, August 2000,
December 2000
Category: Magazine of the
Year Finalist

272
Details
Creative Director:
Dennis Freedman
Design Director: Edward Leida
Art Director: Rockwell Harwood
Illustrator: Jason Holley
Photo Editor: Alice Rose George
Photographers: Adam Bartos,
Juergen Teller, Carter Smith,
Steven Klein, Bruce Weber
Publisher: Fairchild Publications
Issues: October 2000,
November 2000, December 2000
Category: Magazine of the
Year Finalist

273
Fast Company
Design Director: Patrick Mitchell
Designers: Patrick Mitchell, Emily
Crawford, Melanie deForest,
Kristin Fitzpatrick, Julia Moburg
Illustrators: Philip Burke,
Christoph Niemann, BrianCronin
Photo Editor: Alicia Jylkka
Photographers: Catherine Ledner,
Chris Buck, Michael McLaughlin,
Angela Wyant, Dan Winters,

Dennis Klieman, Sian Kennedy,
Brian Smale, Harry Borden, Anton
Corbijn, Sam Jones, Fredrik Broden
Publisher: Fast Company
Issues: April 2000, August 2000,
September 2000
Category: Magazine of the
Year Finalist

274
Nylon
Art Director: Lina Kutsovskaya
Designer: Kathleen McGowan
Illustrators: Rebecca Antoniou,
Istvan Banyai, Tanya Ling,
Julie Verhoeven
Photographers: Alex Antitch,
Guy Aroch, Mark Borthwick,
Clang, Wendelien Daan, James
Dimmock, Robert Erdmann,
Jenny Gage, Nick Haymes, Kayt
Jones, Georgia Kokolis, Marcelo
Krasilcic, Colin Lane, Serge
Leblon, Donald Milne, Jeremy
Murch, Andre Passos, Platon,
Kate Plumb, Chris Plytas, Vava
Ribeiro, Terry Richardson,
Peter Robathan, Ilan Rubin,
Derrick Santini, John Scarisbrick,
Jason Schmidt, David Slijper,
Jenny Von Sommers, Vanina
Sorrenti, Stephen Sprouse, Chris
Sturman, Takay, Toyin, Jan Welters,
Jonathan West, Christian Witkin
Publisher: Nylon LLC
Issues: April 2000, August 2000,
October 2000
Category: Magazine of the
Year Finalist

275
Suddeutsche Zeitung Magazin
Art Director: Michael Weies,
Friederike Gauss
Designer: Friederike Gauss
Publisher: Suddeutsche
Zeitung Magazin
Issue: December 29, 2000
Category Design: Entire Issue

276
Esquire
Design Director: John Korpics
Photo Editor: Fiona McDonagh
Photographer: Dan Winters
Publisher: The Hearst
Corporation-Magazine Division
Issue: January 2000
Category Design: Feature

277
Esquire
Design Director: John Korpics
Photo Editor: Fiona McDonagh
Photographer: Platon
Publisher: The Hearst
Corporation-Magazine Division
Issue: December 2000
Category Design: Cover

278
Rolling Stone
Art Director: Fred Woodward
Designers: Fred Woodward,
Siung Tjia
Photo Editor: Rachel Knepfer

Photographer: Mark Seliger
Publisher: Wenner Media
Issue: March 2, 2000
Category Design: Feature

279
Esquire
Design Director: John Korpics
Designers: John Korpics,
Hannah McCaughey,
Erin Whelan
Photo Editor: Fiona McDonagh
Photographers: Sam Jones,
Dan Winters
Publisher: The Hearst
Corporation-Magazine Division
Issue: September 2000
Category Design: Entire Issue

280
Rolling Stone
Art Director: Fred Woodward
Designers: Fred Woodward,
Siung Tjia
Photo Editor: Rachel Knepfer
Photographer: Mark Seliger
Publisher: Wenner Media
Issue: April 23, 2000
Category Design: Feature

281
Architecture
Art Director: Lisa Naftolin
Designers: Lisa Naftolin,
Claudia Brandenburg
Photo Editor: Alexandra Brez
Photographers: Steve Pyke,
Michael Moran
Publisher: VNU
Issue: June 2000
Category Design: Feature

282
Big
Creative Director:
Marcelo Jünemann
Art Directors: Fernando
Guiterrez, Marc Catala
Photo Editor: Inigo Asis
Photographer: Txema Salvans
Publisher: Big Magazine, Inc.
Issue: #29
Category Photography:
Reportage Story

283
Esquire
Design Director: John Korpics
Photo Editor: Fiona McDonagh
Photographer: Sam Jones
Publisher: The Hearst
Corporation—Magazines Division
Issue: March 2000
Category Photography:
Portrait Spread

284
The New York Times Magazine
Art Director: Janet Froelich
Designer: Andrea Fella
Photo Editor: Kathy Ryan
Photographer: Jodi Bieber
Publisher: The New York Times
Issue: December 24, 2000
Category Photography:
Reportage Spread

285
Details
Creative Director: Dennis Freedman
Design Director: Edward Leida
Art Director: Rockwell Harwood
Photo Editor: Alice Rose George
Photographer: Stephen Shore
Publisher: Fairchild Publications
Issue: November 2000
Category Photography: Portrait Story

400

286
Fast Company
Design Director: Patrick Mitchell
Designer: Emily Crawford
Photo Editor: Alicia Jylkka
Photographer: Sian Kennedy
Publisher: Fast Company
Issue: January/February 2000
Category Photography:
Reportage Story

287
The New Yorker
Visuals Editor: Elisabeth Biondi
Photographer: Martin Schoeller
Publisher: Condé Nast
Publications, Inc.
Issue: August 21, 2000
Category Photography: Portrait Story

288
Max
Creative Director: Diddo Ramm
Designers: Diddo Ramm,
Sandra Kaiser
Photo Editors: Sabine Dottling,
Andreas Wellnitz
Photographers: Geo Fuchs,
Daniel Fuchs
Publisher: Verlagsgruppe Milchstrasse
Issue: July 2000
Category Photography: Still Life
& Interiors Story

289
Vanity Fair
Design Director: David Harris
Art Director: Gregory Mastrianni
Photo Editors: Susan White,
Kathryn MacLeod
Photographer: Annie Leibovitz
Publisher: Condé Nast
Publications, Inc.
Issue: November 2000
Category Photography:
Portrait Spread

290
Rolling Stone
Art Director: Fred Woodward
Designer: Fred Woodward
Photo Editor: Rachel Knepfer
Photographer: Mark Seliger
Publisher: Wenner Media
Issue: November 23, 2000
Category Photography:
Portrait Story

291
Nylon
Art Director: Lina Kutsovskaya
Designer: Kathleen McGowan
Photographer:
Marcus Tomlinson
Publisher: Nylon LLC

Issue: December 2000
Category Photography:
Fashion & Beauty Story

292
The New York Times Magazine
Art Director: Janet Froelich
Designer: Claude Martel
Illustrator: Maira Kalman
Publisher: The New York Times
Issue: November 5, 2000
Category Illustration: Story

293
GQ
Design Director:
Arem Duplessis
Art Director: Paul Martinez
Designer: Matthew Lenning
Illustrator: Brian Cronin
Publisher: Condé Nast
Publications, Inc.
Issue: November 2000
Category Illustration: Story

2001

294
The New York Times Magazine
Art Director: Janet Froelich
Designer: Joele Cuyler
Photographers:
Julian LaVerdiere, Paul Myoda,
Fred R. Conrad
Photo Editor: Kathy Ryan
Publisher: The New York Times
Issue: September 23, 2001
Category Design: Cover

295
Time
Art Director: Arthur Hochstein
Designer: Arthur Hochstein
Photographers: Spencer Platt,
Suzanne Plunkett, David
Surowiecki, James Nachtwey,
Gulnara Samiolava,
Angel Franco, Justin Kane,
Harry Zernike, Ruth Fremson,
Timothy Fadek
Photo Editor: Maryanne Golon
Publisher: AOL Time Inc.
Issue: September 11, 2001
Category Photography:
Reportage Story

296
Esquire
Design Director: John Korpics
Designers: Hannah McCaughey,
Todd Albertson, Erin Whelan,
Kim Forsberg
Illustrator: John Craig
Photo Editors: Nancy Jo Iacoi,
Catriona NiAolain
Photographers: Martin Schoeller,
Chris Buck, Nigel Dickson,
Julian Broad, Jeffrey Braverman,
Norman Jean Roy
Publisher: The Hearst
Corporation-Magazines Division
Issues: April 2001, July 2001,
September 2001
Category: Magazine of the
Year Finalist

297
Global
Art Director: David Armario
Designers: David Armario,
Candela D, Ethan Fowler
Illustrators: Tavis Coburn,
Jason Holley, Alain Pilon
Photographers: Fredrik Broden,
Mark Hooper, Gary Tannhauser,
Dan Winters
Studio: David Armario Design
Publisher: Deloitte & Touche, LLP
Issues: January 2001, July/August
2001, November/December 2001
Category: Magazine of the
Year Finalist

298
Martha Stewart Baby
Creative Director: Gael Towey
Art Director: Debra Bishop
Designers: Debra Bishop, Jennifer
Wagner, Sara Hicks, Jennifer Dahl
Photo Editor: Jodi Nakatsuka
Photographers: Gentl + Hyers,
Lisa Hubbard, Anna Williams,
William Abranowicz, Christopher
Baker, Maria Robledo, Formula z/s,
Frank Heckers, Sang An,
Maura McEvoy
Stylists: Jodi Levine, Ayesha Patel,
Amy Gropp Forbes, Melanio
Gomez, Cyndi DiPrima,
Katie Hatch, Lynn Butler
Publisher: Martha Stewart Living
Omnimedia
Issues: Spring 2001, Fall 2001
Category: Magazine of the
Year Finalist

299
Martha Stewart Baby
Creative Director: Gael Towey
Art Director: Debra Bishop
Designers: Debra Bishop, Jennifer
Wagner, Sara Hicks, Jennifer Dahl
Illustrator: Raymond Booth
Photo Editor: Jodi Nakatsuka
Photographers: Frank Heckers,
Lisa Hubbard, Anna Williams,
William Abranowicz, Christopher
Baker, Maria Robledo, Sang An,
Formula z/s, John Dolan
Stylists: Jodi Levine, Ayesha Patel,
Amy Gropp Forbes, Melanio
Gomez, Cyndi DiPrima,
Katie Hatch, Lynn Butler
Publisher: Martha Stewart Living
Omnimedia
Issue: Spring 2001
Category Design: Entire Issue

300
Esquire
Design Director: John Korpics
Designer: Hannah McCaughey
Photo Editor: Nancy Jo Iacoi
Photographer: Jose Picayo
Publisher: The Hearst
Corporation-Magazines Division
Issue: August 2001
Category Design: Feature

301
LA Weekly
Art Director: Bill Smith

Illustrator: Bill Smith
Publisher: Village Voice Media
Issue: February 16, 2001
Category Design: Cover

302
The New York Times Magazine
Art Director: Janet Froelich
Designers: Claude Martel,
Nancy Harris, Chris Dixon,
Andrea Fella
Photo Editors: Kathy Ryan,
Jody Quon, Kira Pollack,
Evan Kriss, Cavan Farrell
Photographers:
Mary Ellen Mark,
Lauren Greenfield,
Jeff Mermelstein, Lisa Kereszi,
Rodney Smith, Davies + Starr,
Julian LaVerdiere, Paul Myoda,
Fred R. Conrad,
Justine Kurland, Sally Mann
Publisher: The New York Times
Issues: September 9, 2001,
September 23, 2001,
December 9, 2001
Category: Magazine of the
Year Finalist

303
Esquire
Design Director: John Korpics
Photo Editor: Nancy Jo Iacoi
Photographer: James Fee
Publisher: The Hearst
Corporation—Magazines Division
Issue: June 2001
Category Design: Spread/
Single Page

304
Magazine El Mundo
Design Director:
Carmelo Caderot
Art Director: Rodrigo Sanchez
Designers: Rodrigo Sanchez,
Maria Gonzalez
Photo Editor: Rodrigo Sanchez
Photographer: Gerard Rancinan
Publisher: Unidad Editorial S.A.
Issue: April 22, 2001
Category Design: Entire Issue

305
Big
Creative Director:
Marcelo Jünemann
Art Directors: Rafie Farah,
Eduardo Hirama
Publisher: Big Magazine, Inc.
Issue: November 2001
Category Design: Entire Issue

306
Utah Carol.com
Creative Director:
The Speared Peanut
Designer: The Speared Peanut
Photographer: Utah Carol
Photo Editor: The Speared Peanut
Illustrators: The Speared Peanut,
Eun-ha Paek
Online Address:
www.utahcarol.com
Category New Media:
Self Promotion

307
Condé Nast Traveler
Design Director: Robert Best
Art Director: Kerry Robertson
Designer: Robert Best
Photographer: Raymond Meier
Photo Editors: Kathleen Klech,
Esin Goknar
Publisher: Condé Nast
Publications, Inc.
Issue: March 2001
Category Photography:
Reportage Story

308
The New York Times Magazine
Art Director: Janet Froelich
Designer: Claude Martel
Photographer: Jeff Riedel
Producers: Robert Bryan,
Mimi Lombardo
Publisher: The New York Times
Issue: November 25, 2001
Category Photography: Fashion
& Beauty Story

309
Martha Stewart Living
Design Director:
Barbara de Wilde
Art Director: Helen Sanematsu
Photographer: Gentl + Hyers
Photo Editor: Mary Dail
Stylists: Ayesha Patel,
Jennifer Hitchcox
Publisher: Martha Stewart Living
Omnimedia
Issue: March 2001
Category Photography: Still Life
& Interiors Single Page/Spread

310
The New York Times Magazine
Art Director: Janet Froelich
Designer: Claude Martel
Photographer: Carlton Davis
Producer: Anne Christensen
Publisher: The New York Times
Issue: February 11, 2001
Category Photography: Fashion
& Beauty Story

311
The New York Times Magazine
Art Director: Janet Froelich
Designers: Andrea Fella,
Nancy Harris
Illustrator: Christoph Niemann
Publisher: The New York Times
Issue: April 8, 2001
Category Illustration:
Single Page/Spread

312
The New York Times Magazine
Art Director: Janet Froelich
Designers: Joele Cuyler
Illustrators: Moonrunner
Design: LTD, Natasha Tibbott
Photo Editors: Kathy Ryan,
Kira Pollack
Photographers: Rodney Smith,
Davies + Starr, Eika Aoshima
Publisher: The New York Times
Issue: December 9, 2001
Category Design: Entire Issue

313
Nylon
Art Director: Lina Kutsovskaya
Designers: Kathleen McGowan,
Jason Engdahl
Photographer: Marcelo Krasilcic
Publisher: Nylon LLC
Issue: April 2001
Category Photography: Fashion
& Beauty Story

314
Rolling Stone
Art Director: Fred Woodward
Designers: Fred Woodward,
Gail Anderson
Photographer: Mark Seliger
Photo Editor: Fiona McDonagh
Publisher: Wenner Media LLC
Issue: March 29, 2001
Category Photography:
Portraits Story

2002

315
Martha Stewart Kids
Creative Director: Gael Towey
Design Director: Deb Bishop
Art Directors: Jennifer Wagner,
Sara Hicks, Jennifer Dahl,
Ellen Burnie
Illustrators: Jessie Hartland,
J. Otto Seibold, Natasha
Tibbott, Greg Clarke
Photo Editors: Stacie
McCormick, Jamie Bass
Photographers: Anna Williams,
William Abranowicz, Sang An,
Stephen Lewis, Achim Lippoth,
Victoria Pearson, Davies + Starr,
Victor Schrager, Gentl + Hyers,
Amy Neunsinger, Christopher
Baker, Monica Buck
Stylists: Tara Bench, Melanie
Gomez, Anna Beckman, Jodi
Levine, Sarah Conroy, Ayesha
Patel, Silke Stoddard, Tanya Graff
Publisher: Martha Stewart Living
Omnimedia
Issues: June 2002, August
2002, October 2002
Category: Magazine of the
Year Finalist

316
Details
Design Director:
Rockwell Harwood
Associate Art Director:
Nathalie Kirsheh
Director of Photography:
Amy Steigbigel
Photographers: Matt Jones,
Jenny Gage, Tom Betterton,
Mark Heithoff, Tom Munro
Publisher: Condé Nast
Publications, Inc.
Issues: March 2002, September
2002, December 2002
Category: Magazine of the
Year Finalist

317
Real Simple
Creative Director: Robert Newman

Art Directors: Eva Spring,
Chalkley Calderwood-Pratt
Designers: Leslie Long,
Millie Kidd, Monica Ewing,
Ellene Standke
Photo Editors: Jean Herr,
Deborah Kozloff, Naomi Nista,
Annemarie Castro
Photographers: Dan Chavkin,
John Dolan, Bob Hiemstra,
William Meppem, Minh + Wass,
William Waldron
Publisher: AOL Time Inc.
Issues: April 2002, June 2002,
September 2002s
Category: Magazine of the
Year Finalist

318
Esquire
Design Director: John Korpics
Designers: Todd Albertson,
Erin Whelan, Kim Forsberg
Photo Editors: Nancy Jo
Iacoi, Catriona NiAolain,
David Carthas, Beth Johnson
Photographers: Sam Jones,
Richard Phibbs, Lorenzo
Agius, Roxanne Lowit, Nigel
Dickson, Norman Jean Roy,
Deborah Turbeville, Johathan Skow
Publisher: The Hearst
Corporation—Magazines Division
Issues: May 2002, August 2002,
September 2002
Category: Magazine of the
Year Finalist

319
Beople
Creative Director: Base Design
Photographer: Kenji Toma
Food Stylist: Victoria Granoff
Studio: Kenji Toma Studio
Publisher:
American Express Publishing
Issue: September/October/
November 2002
Category Photography:
Still Life Story

320
Copy
Creative Director: Stefan Sagmeister
Designers: Matthias Ernstberger,
Eva Hueckmann
Photographer: Matthias Ernstberger
Illustrator: Eva Hueckmann
Studio: Sagmeister, Inc.
Publisher: Falter
Category Design: Feature

321
GQ
Design Director: Fred Woodward
Designers: Fred Woodward,
Paul Martinez, Matthew Lenning,
Gillian Goodman
Photo Editors: Jennifer Crandall,
Catherine Talese, Kristen Schaefer,
Michael Norseng, Eve Ekman
Fashion Editor: Madeline Weeks
Publisher: Condé Nast
Publications, Inc.
Issue May 2002
Category Design: Entire Issue

322
GQ
Design Director: Fred Woodward
Designer: Paul Martinez
Photographer: Norman Jean Roy
Photo Editor: Jennifer Crandall
Publisher: Condé Nast
Publications, Inc.
Issue: March 2002
Category Design:
Single Page/Spread

323
GQ
Design Director: Fred Woodward
Designer: Paul Martinez
Photographer: Mark Seliger
Photo Editor: Jennifer Crandall
Creative Director, Fashion: Jim Moore
Publisher: Condé Nast
Publications, Inc.
Issue: July 2002
Category Design: Spread/Single

324
Interior Design
Art Director: Claudia Marulanda
Designer: Claudia Marulanda
Photographer: Justin Maconochie
Publisher: Reed Business Information
Issue: December 2002
Category Design: Cover

325
The New York Times
Design Director: Tom Bodkin
Art Director: Gigi Fava
Illustrator: Mirko Ilic
Publisher: The New York Times
Issue: September 8, 2002
Category Illustration:
Single Page/Spread

326
GQ
Design Director: Fred Woodward
Designers: Fred Woodward,
Paul Martinez, Matthew Lenning,
Ken DeLago, Gillian Goodman
Photo Editors: Jennifer Crandall,
Catherine Talese, Kristen Schaefer,
Michael Norseng, Eve Ekman
Fashion Editor: Madeline Weeks
Publisher: Condé Nast
Publications, Inc.
Issue: September 2002
Category Design: Spread/
Single Page

327
Martha Stewart Kids
Creative Director: Gael Towey
Design Director: Deb Bishop
Art Directors: Jennifer Wagner,
Jennifer Dahl, Sara Hicks, Ellen Burnie
Photographers: Anna Williams,
Annie Schlechter, Sang An,
Victor Schrager, Tosca Radigonda,
Gentl + Hyers, Amy Neusinger,
Raphael Buchler, Stefan Anderson,
Stephen Lewis
Photo Editors: Stacie McCormick,
Jamie Bass
Illustrator: Greg Clarke
Publisher: Martha Stewart Living
Omnimedia

Index

406

407

408

409

Editors' Note:

For many of SPD's early years, notably 1965 to 1972, there is very little documentation available. There are no records of when judged competitions actually began. Furthermore, we meticulously combed our archives and asked members and friends for volumes 18 and 19 (1983-1984) of our publication design annuals. Unfortunately they were simply not available to us.

410

Please accept our apologies in advance if you or a colleague has been omitted in error. We ask you to write us at mail@spd.org if you think you can help us improve the breadth of our archives, which we are eager to update.

—*Solid Gold* project coordinators

Special Thanks to:
Diana LaGuardia, without whom none of the work would have been preserved for this and future projects.

Steven Heller, for his guidance and advice throughout.

Thanks to:
Anthony Clarke
Hajime Yoshida
George Maier

Our Corporate Partner:
Adobe Systems, Inc.

Solid Gold: 40 Years of Award-Winning Design from the Society of Publication Designers

Project Coordinators:
Florian Bachleda,
Arem Duplessis,

Carla Frank
Managing Editor:
Marc Einsele

Archivist:
Diana LaGuardia

Designed and produced by the Office of Paul Sahre

Design Assistants:
Karsten Petrat, Scott Massey, Joon Moo Kang, Jamie Prokell and Loren Flaherty

Magazine of the Year Photography by Peter Hoang

SPD Board of Directors:

Fred Woodward, DD,
GQ, President
Diana LaGuardia,
Vice President
David Matt, AD,
Men's Journal, Vice President
Janet Froelich, CD,
The New York Times Magazines,
Secretary

Florian Bachleda, DD,
Vibe
Jennifer Crandall, DP,
O, The Oprah Magazine
Emily Crawford, DD,
Travel + Leisure
Arem Duplessis, AD,
The New York Times Magazine
Carla Frank, DD,
O, The Oprah Magazine
David Harris, DD,
Vanity Fair
Luke Hayman, DD,
New York
Melanie McLaughlin, CD,
Schematic
Francesca Messina, DD,
Guideposts
Bruce Ramsay, Director of Covers, *Newsweek*
Linda Root, Deputy AD,
Sports Illustrated
Ina Saltz, Principal,
Saltz Design
Paul Schrynemakers, CD,

Rodale Interactive
Mitch Shostak, Principal,
Shostak Studios

Robert Newman, DD,
Fortune, Ex Officio

SPY

KENNED
BASHING

CHAPPAQUIDDICK:
The Unsold Story

CHAPPAQUIDDICK GIRLS:
SPY Goes on an Update

THE KENNEDY MEDIA CONSPIRACY

Experts Decide:
WILL TEDDY GO TO HELL?

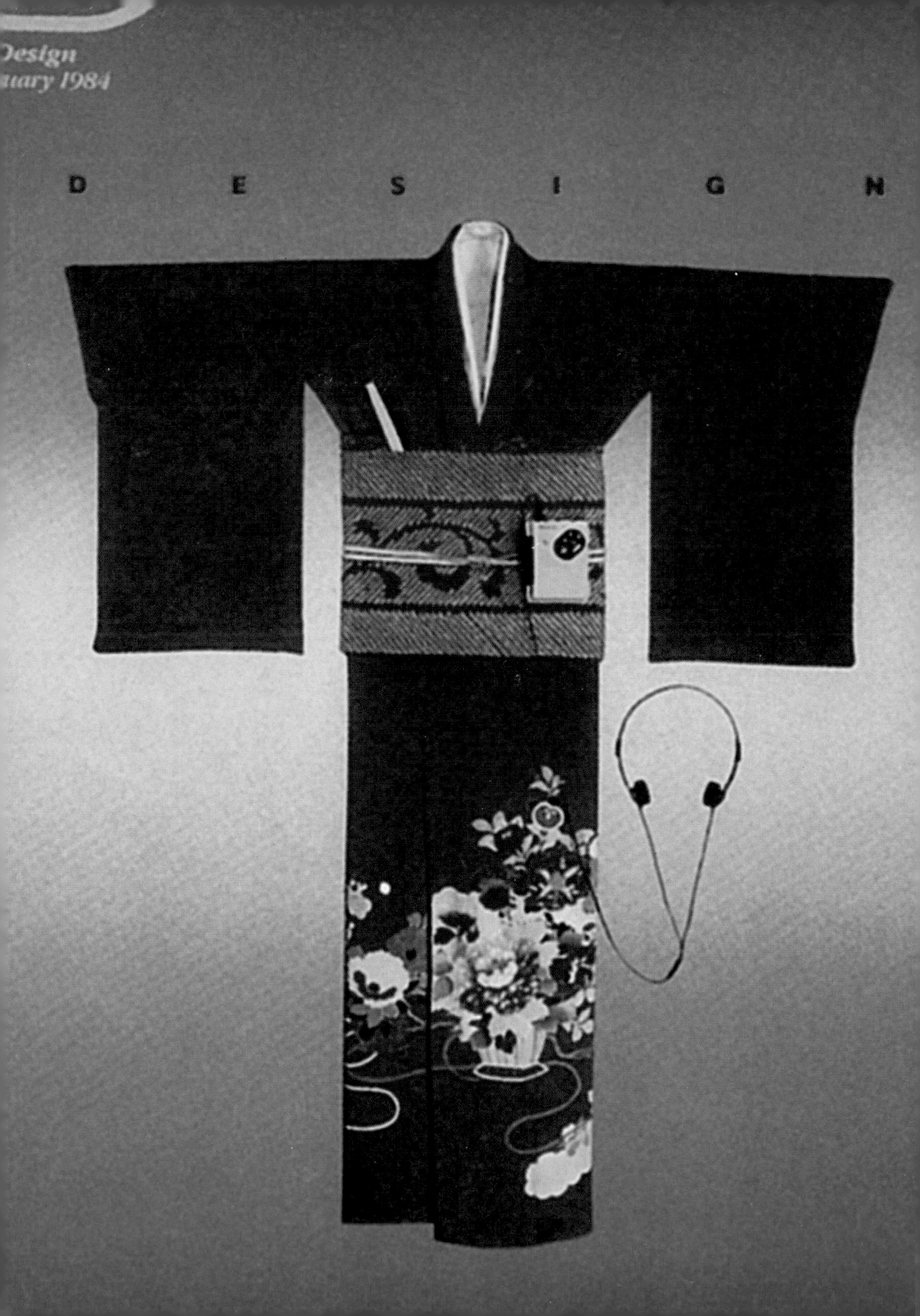
Design
uary 1984
D E S I G N

TIME

Does it exist — or
do bad things just happen?

February 1960